ACTA UNIVERSITATIS UPSALIENSIS

BOREAS. Uppsala Studies in Ancient Mediterranean and Near Eastern Civilizations

21

ECONOMICS OF CULT IN THE ANCIENT GREEK WORLD

Proceedings of the
Uppsala Symposium 1990

Edited by
Tullia Linders and Brita Alroth

UPPSALA 1992

ACTA UNIVERSITATIS UPSALIENSIS

BOREAS. Uppsala Studies in Ancient Mediterranean
and Near Eastern Civilizations. 21

Editors: Rostislav Holthoer
Pontus Hellström

Editors' address: Gustavianum, S-753 10 Uppsala, Sweden

The English text was revised by Mr. Neil Tomkinson and Dr. Jon van Leuven

Distributors: Almqvist & Wiksell International, Box 4627, 116 91 Stockholm

Published with the aid of a grant from the Swedish Council for Research in the Humanities and Social Sciences

Abstract
Linders, T. and Alroth, B. (eds.), *Economics of cult in the ancient Greek world. Proceedings of the Uppsala Symposium 1990.* Acta Univ. Ups. *Boreas. Uppsala Studies in Ancient Mediterranean and Near Eastern Civilizations* 21. Uppsala 1992. 99 pp., with ill. ISBN 91-554-3031-7

Ten papers read at an international symposium at Uppsala, followed by short transcripts of the discussions. The papers deal with the following subjects: a general picture of the sacred finances of the Classical and Hellenistic periods, the question whether the sanctuaries owned cattle, the unit/units of currency in Delos, the rent of temple land in southern Italy and Sicily, the metal production in sanctuaries in the Bronze Age and in the Geometric period, the iron spits, *obeloi*, of pre- or proto-monetary value, the metrology of gold and silver plate, offerings, esp. of sculpture, in Cypriote sanctuaries and the votive offerings and inscriptions from the Athenian Asklepieion.

Key words: sanctuaries, metal-working, workshops, metal; temple inventories, votive offerings, temple land, sacred cattle, coin standards, *obeloi*, metrology, *tabulae Heracleenses*, Delos, Athenian Asklepieion, Argive Heraion, Cyprus, temple-boys.

Tullia Linders and Brita Alroth, Department of Classical Archaeology and Ancient History, Uppsala University, Gustavianum, S-753 10 Uppsala, Sweden.

ISBN 91-554-3031-7
ISSN 0346-6442

Printed in Sweden 1992
Textgruppen i Uppsala AB

Contents

Preface

The Uppsala Symposium on *The Economics of Cult in the Ancient Greek World* is the third in a series of symposia arranged by the Department of Classical Archaeology and Ancient History. The subject was chosen since it has been treated by the head of the department, Tullia Linders, who was going to retire. The symposium took place on 20–23 September 1990 and brought together ten lectures with an audience of about 70 people. Among the scholars we had hoped to see, we regret especially the absence of Cristiano Grottanelli, who was unable to attend for reasons of health.

The economics of cult may seem a small and clearly defined subject. The papers published here show, however, that it can be treated from a great many different angles.

Tullia Linders, Uppsala University, who has particularly studied temple inventories, gives a general picture in her paper, 'Sacred finances', with the aid of epigraphical material of the Classical and Hellenistic periods. The expenses which had to be covered were mainly caused by the cult and the upkeep of the sacred buildings, and involved supply of commodities as well as wages for temple staff and temporary workers. The income was commonly rent from land owned by the sanctuary and, in the case of more important temples, taxes and dues assigned to them by the city. The larger sanctuaries served not only as consumers of commodities but also as employers, and thus contributed to the support of a considerable number of people.

Signe Isager, Odense University, who has, among other things, written about epigraphical sources on Greek agriculture, examines the question whether sanctuaries owned cattle. Although the evidence is somewhat ambiguous, she argues that animals were owned by a number of gods, Apollon of Delos and of Delphi among them.

In the temple accounts, especially those from Delos, the items of income and expenditure are rendered in terms of money. *Jacques Tréheux*, the great authority on Delian inscriptions, examines the unit, or units, of currency in Delos. He shows that both the Attic drachma, the drachma of Alexander of the same weight, and the lighter Delian drachma on the Rhodian standard circulated in Delos, reckoned at the same value. For the administrators evidently "a drachma was a drachma". When their books were balanced, however, the sums were converted to the Attic unit.

Carmine Ampolo, Pisa University, has written extensively about economy and society in the Greek world. Whereas in Greece money was the normal measure of values and means of exchange, he takes us to a region where the money economy was not exclusive, Southern Italy and Sicily in the 4th and 3rd centuries B.C. There the rent of temple land was paid in cereals; even loans and interest could be paid in kind. In Heraclea rent on temple land had to be paid in barley and brought to the public granary. The temple produce thus formed part of the food-supply of the city.

An activity with economic implications which is found in Greek sanctuaries in the early periods is metal production. *Robin Hägg*, director of the Swedish Institute in Athens, discusses such finds from the Bronze Age Mediterranean. Whereas in Cyprus metallurgical production in general seems to have been placed under divine protection in sanctuaries, the purpose of the workshops and storage rooms in the sanctuaries of Minoan and Mycenaean Greece, according to Professor Hägg, was to produce equipment of precious materials for sacred use.

Christina Risberg, Uppsala University, is currently studying the metal production of the late Geometric period in Greece, notably the remains of workshops in sanctuaries. She gives an outline of the research and traces some of the problems concerning the type of economy and the social organization in this early period.

The votive offerings played an important role in the prestige of a sanctuary. Four of the participants treated different aspects of this subject.

Ingrid Strøm, Copenhagen University, who has written about the Archaic Age, discusses here the well-known iron spits, the *obeloi*, from the Argive Heraion using comparative material from inscriptions and archaeological finds. Since "drachmai of spits" are found in temple inventories with other items of banquet services, like lebetes and cups, she concludes that the system of six *oboloi* to the drachma, as well as the assignment of monetary value to the spits, occurred in Greek sanctuaries, primarily in those of Apollon, Artemis, Athena and Hera, in the 7th century B.C.

Michael Vickers, Ashmolean Museum, Oxford, has studied gold and silver plate registered in temple inventories as well as actual finds of such vessels and their relation to pottery. In his paper on the metrology of gold and silver plate, he is able to demonstrate the surprising fact that not only silver vases found, for instance, in Thrace but also votives in Greek inventories were very often manufactured to a Persian standard. This is so even when they were obviously of Greek workmanship.

Cecilia Beer, Stockholm University, is currently working on the Cypriote sculptures called temple boys. Her subject here is votive offerings, especially sculptures from Cypriote sanctuaries. She uses them to try and elucidate the identity of the donors, their origin and social strata.

This is also the subject of *Sara Aleshire*, University of California, Berkeley, author of two recent books on the Athenian Asklepieion. With the help of statistical data she examines the votive offerings and the inscriptions of this sanctuary to throw light on two questions: who were the dedicants and what can be said of the dedicatory process. The paper is an addendum to her books on the Asklepieion.

Gratitude is extended to a number of people who helped in organizing the symposium, notably Christina Lundquist, Uppsala, who acted with zeal as secretary, Lena Johansson, Uppsala, who typed the discussions, the other members of the Department of Classical Archaeology and Ancient History at Uppsala, and the staff of the Gustavianum.

The symposium was financed with a generous grant from the Royal Academy of Letters, History and Antiquities (Kungl. Vitterhets Historie och Antikvitets Akademien). Other sponsors were Länsförsäkringar, Västmanland and Länsförsäkringar, Uppsala. The proceedings were printed with the aid of a grant from the Swedish Council of Research in the Humanities and Social Sciences. We express our thanks to all those who have assisted us, financially and otherwise, with the symposium and the publishing.

Tullia Linders *Brita Alroth*

Tullia Linders

Sacred Finances: Some Observations

It is a well known fact that in ancient Greece the cults of the gods were linked to a community, and a community could not exist without a cult as its centre. Since the *polis* and its cults were thus inseparable, it is natural that the financing of the cults was quaranteed by the *polis* and that it closely followed the economic models current in the community.

The sources of this information are almost wholly epigraphical. Since the Attic temple inventories deal only with the votive offerings, we know very little about the economy of the Athenian gods, except, for instance, that Athena owned land and that, in the fifth century, one-sixtieth of the tribute of the Allies went into her treasury.[1]

Other sources reveal that, in order to provide income for a sanctuary, the regular procedure was to allocate certain items of revenue to it. We have a fine example in an inscription concerning the sanctuary of Apollon Aktios. This is indeed the god who was celebrated by Augustus, but this inscription, which is a decree of the Akarnanian League, is dated to a time almost 200 years before the battle of Actium, probably to the year 216 B.C.,[2] and there is no trace of the Romans in it. The situation is as follows: There has been a war which has ravaged, among other parts, the town of Anaktorion and the sanctuary, which up to that time had belonged to Anaktorion. After the depredations of the war, however, the town no longer has the means to carry out its economic responsibilities towards Apollon and so the League of the Akarnanians decides to take over the obligation.

The immediate task is to restore the buildings and to see to it that the sacrifices and the festival with its contests can be conducted in a traditional manner. The revenue to cover this is to be half the amount of the customs duties and other tolls collected in the harbour of Anaktorion during the festival. Two items are emphasized, the tax of one-fiftieth (2 per cent) and the tax on the sale of slaves; the former was a tax raised in all Greek cities on imported and exported goods. Presumably the volume of trade in all commodities was increased considerably by the large number of visitors at the time of the festival. (The other half of the harbour dues during the festival goes to Anaktorion, which during the rest of the year has the sole control of them.) Thus the Akarnanian League acts in the same way as a city in allocating specified sources of revenue to cover the sanctuary's expenses. It is true that the city of Anaktorion is deprived of part of its income; on the other hand, it is relieved of the liability to maintain the temple. This is taken over by the League, which solemnly guarantees the maintenance and thus declares itself ready to find additional sources if necessary.[3]

The fact that other income is not mentioned in the inscription does not, I think, mean that no other sources existed. Apollon Aktios may well have owned land, like other gods, but since these possessions caused no controversy, they were not mentioned in the decree.

More details about temple revenue are known from the accounts of Delos, especially those of the third and the early second centuries B.C.[4] Apollon of Delos owned lands not only on Delos but also, for instance, on Rheneia and Mykonos and let them out on lease for periods of 10 years to the highest bidder. In the same manner, buildings, dwelling houses, workshops, etc. were let out for periods of five years.[5]

---

[1] Athena's *temene*, D.M. Lewis, *Hesperia* 28, 1959, 239–247 (a new fragment belonging to *IG* II^2 334 (a. 335/4), also L. Robert, *Hellenica* 11–12, 1960, 189–203 (*SEG* 18, 13; 21, 269); F. Sokolowski, *Lois sacrées des cités greques*, Paris 1969, 33; *IG* II^2 1590, 1591 + M. Crosby, *Hesperia* 6, 1937, 454–456, no. 5; and *IG* II^2 2495. For these inscriptions, see also D. Behrend, *Attische Pachturkunden* (Vestigia, 12), 1970, 62–68, nos. 10–11, 13–14.

[2] *IG* IX 1:2, 583; the *editio princeps* is Chr. Habicht, *Hermes* 85, 1957, 86–122 (text, translation and fundamental commentary).

[3] See lines 24–34 and 43–52 of the inscription.

[4] *Inscriptions de Délos* (nos. 89–104–33), Paris 1972; *IG* XI 2 (nos. 105–289), Berlin 1912; *Inscriptions de Délos* 1–2 (nos. 290–498), Paris 1926–1929; the inscriptions are referred to by number only.

[5] J.H. Kent, 'The temple estates of Delos, Rheneia and Mykonos', *Hesperia* 17, 1948, 245–338; D. Hennig, 'Die "heiligen Häuser" von Delos', *Chiron* 13, 1983, 411–495. See also C. Vial, *Délos indépendante (314–167 av. J.-C.). Etude d'une communauté civique et des ses institutions* (*BCH* Suppl. 10), Paris 1984, 229f.

Furthermore, in Delos, which already in the third century had a busy port, the sanctuary shared this revenue with the city. Thus the tax of one-fiftieth, i.e. 2 per cent on imports and exports, and a few other taxes were levied by the city.[6] The sanctuary, on its own behalf, collected charges for the use of the port, of the windlass and other dues, also for activities connected with the sea around Delos, like the fishing for *Murex* and the ferry traffic to Rheneia and Mykonos. From the point of view of the administration, we may regard these revenues as allocated by the city. On the other hand, were it not for the sanctuary the city would never have existed. Since the whole island belonged to Apollon, it was therefore natural that the god should have income from it and the adjoining sea, as well as from land which belonged to him on other islands, such as dues paid for pasturage on Rheneia and for the right to haul boats across the isthmuses of Rheneia and Mykonos.[7] In the case of Delos, it may be as correct to regard the city as dependent on the sanctuary as vice versa. Anyhow, the main revenues of the temple of Apollon (leases and dues), were of the same kind as those of a typical Greek *polis* and the dues were collected in the manner used by most cities, by contractors.

In the inscription concerning Apollon Aktios the expenditures which the Akarnanian League had to cover concerned the sacred buildings and, furthermore, the contests, sacrifices and the festival. As I have tried to show, Apollon of Delos, in contrast to Apollon Aktios, had financial resources of his own with which to defray such expenses. Nevertheless, the city of Delos contributed quite substantially to the contests of the Dionysia and Apollonia and the hiring of performers for these events.[8]

The Delian temple accounts thus show us a very detailed picture of the expenditure caused by the building activity and the cult, information which is rarely found elsewhere: to take a few examples, the annual consumption of firewood for the altars, the prices of sacrificial pigs, of natron and sponges for the cleaning of temples, the outlay for garlands to adorn the buildings during the festivals, etc.[9]

Another striking fact is the multitude of people involved, often mentioned by name in the inscriptions. Thus the commodities needed by the sanctuary were bought from a large number of private persons. Some of them have been identified by Claude Vial as well-to-do Delians, who may even have raised the products on land leased from the temple. Others were probably of smaller means.[10]

In the same way, besides the permanent staff of priests, neokoroi and slaves, the sanctuary had a constant need of labour. For the perfect functioning of the sacrifices and festivals, flute-players for instance, were required, as well as braiders of garlands etc. and also a considerable number of workmen. These were to a large extent required by the building activity which was especially lively in the Delian sanctuary in the third century. But they were also needed for other tasks. It is, however, to be noted that only those activities are mentioned in the temple accounts which cause outlay or produce income for the administrators. To give one example, the festival of Dionysos was celebrated on Delos, as in other places, with a procession in which a phallos made of wood was drawn on a cart. For its construction, which was undertaken anew every year, carpenters, smiths and painters were employed, as well as roadmenders and sweepers to clear the road.[11]

This not very extensive task thus engaged a number of workmen, each doing only a small part. The same thing is especially conspicuous in the sections of the temple accounts which record the expenditures for the building activity. Moses Finley referred to them as some of the best evidence of how such work was organized in the ancient world: the work was broken down, as it were, into small jobs, each given out on a separate contract.[12]

In the same way, the cults created job opportunities and thereby provided a not inconsiderable number of people with a living or at least an additional living. While some of them were slaves, others were undoubtedly free persons, citizens and resident foreigners. One

---

[6] Vial (supra n. 5), 214, n. 100, 339f.

[7] Vial (supra n. 5), 231.

[8] Ph. Bruneau, *Recherches sur les cultes de Délos à l'époque hellénistique et à l'époque impériale*, Paris 1970, 66f., 72f.; Vial (supra n. 5), 276.

[9] For the cults, see Bruneau (supra n. 8), *passim*; for firewood, *idem*, 118–121; pigs, 93, 286–290, garlands, 119f.; for the cleaning of statues with natron and sponges, J. Marcadé, *Au Musée de Délos*, Paris 1969, 98f.; some relevant paragraphs, 287 (a. 250) A 42, 50, 51 etc. (firewood), 41, 47, 50 etc. (pigs), 54, 84 (natron and sponges), 47, 65 (garlands); 442 (a. 179) A 180–184 etc. See also T. Linders, in *Early Greek cult practice. Proceedings of the Fifth International Symposium at the Swedish Institute at Athens 1986* (ActaAth-4°, 38), Stockholm 1988, 268.

[10] Vial (supra n. 5), 348–356, Linders (supra n. 9), 269.

[11] Bruneau (supra n. 8), 312–319; Linders (supra n. 9), 267f.

[12] See, for example, 161 (a. 279) A 44–82, construction work on the new temple of Apollon and other buildings. For the organisation, see Vial (supra n. 5), 228f., 246–250. Cf. also A. Burford, *The Greek temple builders at Epidauros*, Liverpool 1969, 119–158; M.I. Finley, *The ancient economy*, 1973, 74f.

might therefore say that a sanctuary like that of Delos was a large-scale employer.[13]

It is a common opinion that the banking activities of the temples, for instance, of the Delian temple, played an important part in the economic life of antiquity. It is true that in the fourth century Apollon lent large sums to cities in the Aegean and that in the third century he gave loans, at the regular interest of 10 per cent, to the city of Delos and to private persons there. On the whole, however, these transactions seem not to have been advantageous to the temple. Thus, the fourth-century loans to the Aegean cities could not be recovered in the end, no doubt because of the political situation. This was probably the reason why after that the temple lent its money only to the town of Delos and to private persons. The loans to the city were free of interest during the year the loan was contracted and were repaid within two years at the most. Their function was probably, as Raymond Bogaert suggests, to tide the city over a temporary shortage of liquid funds, for instance, when a large outlay was necessary, as for the purchase of grain.[14]

As for the loans to private persons, it is obvious that the sanctuary showed great leniency in collecting the debts. The delinquent debtors, who are listed in some numbers in the accounts, seem rarely to have been requested to pay. There are in fact debts which had been outstanding for several decades. This may have been due to widespread financial difficulties but may also have been caused by other circumstances. The sanctuary was administered by the Delians and, as Claude Vial stresses, they seem to have regarded the god's funds as specially intended to help them. On the other hand, they were supposed to be his own servants and were therefore entitled to some recompense. In any case, neither the loans conceded to the city nor those given to private persons were particularly profitable to the sanctuary.[15]

Thus, the sanctuary of Delos, on the one hand, provided a market for a large number of goods and, on the other, served as an employer of labour. From Max Weber we all know that the ancient city was a consumer which lived on the production of its countryside, in contrast to the medieval town, which lived on trade and thereby created a surplus.[16] The sanctuary resembled Weber's city in that—on the whole—it lived on contributions and did not produce any material goods. I suggest, however, that what we may call its spiritual wares, the cult, created a demand for certain material commodities, which stimulated production and provided the producers with a market they might not otherwise have had.

Evidently the sanctuary of Delos was a special case: it was the religious centre of the Cyclades and celebrated sacrifices and festivals all the year round. Further, through its geographical location, it had good communications for visitors and traders. I would, however, suggest that, taken together, the cults of any one *polis* had the same effect. Not that they created economic growth in the modern sense, but that in the static economy of antiquity they served as an incentive. On the one hand, they were supported by revenues allocated by the city, while, on the other, they stimulated the production of the citizens and metics and provided employment.

It is characteristic of the temple accounts that all the items of income and expenditure are in terms of money. Thus, for instance, all the wages and other renumerations paid to the employees are in coin, even items labelled "for clothing".[17] As regards the income, revenues like land rent and harbour dues clearly presuppose the invention of coinage. Although it is possible to collect such dues in kind, as is demonstrated in Carmine Ampolo's paper in this volume, it is so much simpler in money and the same is true of the lending operations. One of the most important functions of coinage was probably to provide rulers with easy means of collecting taxes and, perhaps even more important, for storing the revenue in a convenient manner.

In the temple accounts of Delos, we thus gain an insight into the activities of the sanctuary as well as its finances, as they were in the Hellenistic age. It is also possible to draw inferences from this material about the finances and economic life of the contemporary city. Many details of this picture are in my opinion also relevant to other sanctuaries and for the preceding period as far back as the adoption of coinage. It may, however, be legitimate to ask what a sanctuary's finances were be-

[13] Cf. Linders (supra n. 9), 269.

[14] R. Bogaert, *Banques et banquiers dans les cités grecques*, Leyden 1968, 126–138.

[15] Bogaert (supra n. 14), 138–153; Vial (supra n. 5), 357–380; notice her remark, p. 144, that "il est évident que ... [the Ekklesia] faisait passer l'interêt du dieu après celui de la cité".

[16] M. Weber, 'Agrarverhältnisse im Altertum', in Weber, *Gesammelte Aufsätze zur Social- und Wirtschaftsgeschichte*, Tübingen 1924, 1–288, esp. 13; Finley (supra n. 12), 124f. See now *Opus* 6–8, 1987–1989 (1991), esp. the article by H. Bruhns & W. Nippel, 'Max Weber, M.I. Finley et le concept de cité antique', 27–50.

[17] See, for instance, 161 (a. 279) A 83f., "To the woman for provisions 120 dr. ... To the masons Leptines and Bakchos for provisions 480 dr. and clothing 34 dr." 287 (a. 250), A 86f., "To the servant Apollonios 120 dr., for an epomis 15 dr. 4 ob. and a chiton 10 dr."

fore that event. I shall conclude this paper with a few tentative suggestions.

It is now commonly assumed that money was adopted in Greece only in the course of the sixth century, that is, in the age of the early *polis*. It is to be assumed that the community decreed in the *ekklesia* the building of new temples and the repair of old ones. The necessary contributions were probably made in kind, either by the whole city or by its constituent parts, for instance, the tribes. Thus, in an inscription from Eretria, of the fourth century, it is true, the animals for sacrifice are to be supplied by the different villages.[18] Labour might also be provided voluntarily by the people. A parallel, though later, and so to speak, in an emergency, is the building of the Themistoklean wall, which, according to Thucydides (1.90.3), was carried out by "the whole population of the city, men, women and children". Since the early city was dominated by the aristocracy, it is probable that the noblemen provided resources with which to build and maintain temples. When the Alcmaeonids, according to Herodotus (5.62), contracted for the building of the temple in Delphi and built it finer than had been planned, they obviously followed an old tradition. So did also the wise tyrants of that age, like Peisistratos, who, as Aristotle (*Pol.* 1314b) mentions, supported the temples. Before the adoption of coinage, they must have done this by making contributions in kind and by inducing the people to work for them. In simple societies, leading persons may command the labour of others to a greater extent by being able to give feasts for the people, who are thereby obliged to do a service in return.[19]

Perhaps Greek noblemen could in addition call on their dependents for work, such as the building of a temple.

In the Classical and Hellenistic age small shrines especially were maintained by owning a piece of land, as we have seen, which was leased in order to provide an annual sum of money. Thus, around 300 B.C., Diomedon of Kos founded a cult and bequeathed to it a garden. He also freed one of his slaves on the condition that he and his descendants leased the land and looked after the sanctuary, providing the annual rent with which to buy not only sacrificial animals but also, for instance, firewood.[20] Similar leases, supplying the necessary commodities for the ritual, may have been given to shrines in the Archaic age. Liturgies, which played such a large part in classical and later times, evidently were also important in the Archaic city-state, since they must have been rooted in an early age, long before the *polis*.[21]

Tullia Linders
Drömstigen 30
S-161 38 BROMMA
Sweden

[18] *IG* XII 9, 189; L. Ziehen, *LGS* II, 88; F. Sokolowski, *LSCG*, 92, lines 26–32.

[19] See, for instance, M. Mauss, *The gift. Forms and functions of exchange in archaic societies*, 1969, paperback 1974, 27f. (from B. Malinowski, *Argonauts of the Western Pacific*), distributions of food "to groups that have given their services to the chief or to his clan", for example, to build a house for him. Cf. also M. Sahlins, *Stone age economics*, Chicago 1972, 136f., the big man "sponsors or contributes heavily to great public feasts and distributions that reach outside his own circle to establish his dignity, to 'build his name', Melanesians say, in society at large". For attempts to identify a big-man society in early Iron Age Greece, see now M. Pettersson, *Cults of Apollo at Sparta. The Hyakinthia, the Gymnopaidiai and the Karneia* (ActaAth-8°, 12), Stockholm 1992, 102–104.

[20] *Syll.*[2] 734, [3]1106; L. Ziehen, *LGS* II, 144; F. Sokolowski, *LSCG*, 177, esp. lines 1–39.

[21] Finley (supra n. 12), 150f.

Discussion

Ingrid STRÖM: Concerning the Archaic age, I wondered whether one shouldn't distinguish more between *before* and *after* the city-states. The problem is: when do the city-states arise?

TL: Yes, you're right. The city-state is a very peculiar organization and it must have meant a great change.

Carmine AMPOLO: An observation on the Archaic age: one of the few documents that we have on temple finance in the Archaic age is the famous inscription of the Artemision at Ephesos. In this inscription there is a relatively wide range of income, of revenues from taxes etc. We may therefore apply models of the Classical-Hellenistic period to the Archaic age. If we accept some of Max Weber's theories, there is a difference between different kinds of rationality, and for antiquity and pre-capitalistic societies we have to do with a *Zweckrationalität*, rationality for a single or a few purposes. I think that the majority of our texts are dealing with this kind of rationality, for instance the financing of temples, of ceremonies of the temple, of festivals, of buildings and other activities, but there is not a general calculation of all the revenues.

Ingrid STRÖM: You were referring to the Alcmaeonids at Delphi, and you saw their contribution to the erection of the Apollo temple as a continuation of tradition. Don't you think it might be a quite new demonstration, politically determined?

TL: Yes, but would you then say that those contributions in the earlier age were not politically determined?

IS: I don't think that the temples were dedicated by private persons in the earlier age. Do we have any sign of that?

TL: No, that is something I postulated.

Signe ISAGER: I first want to thank you very much for this lecture and I don't have anything to add. One might stress that it's not the temple which is the employer, but the cult is considered necessary, and the authority responsible for the functioning of cult varies from time to time. We know how Polykrates conquered Rheneia and gave it to Apollo so that the cult could function. The cult has to be maintained and those in power consider it as part of their responsibility, or else they wouldn't be in power any more.

Signe Isager

Sacred Animals in Classical and Hellenistic Greece

In discussing the economics of the Greek temples, it is relevant to ask about the role played by sacred animals,[1] whether they are cattle in the strict sense of the word or other, four-footed, domesticated animals.[2]

The evidence on the subject is mostly epigraphical and has been treated by scholars in connection with a single inscription and/or location at a time. The following is an attempt to treat the subject in a more general way.

Another characteristic of the evidence is its scarcity. As we shall see, this does not necessarily reflect the importance of the phenomenon.

There is no doubt that, just as the Greek gods could be land-owners, they could also own animals, which were then called sacred. What we want to know is how, to what extent and for what purpose they came into the possession of a particular god, and how this sort of property of the god was administered. In trying to answer these questions, we shall do well to remember that sacred animals belonged to quite another category than did both the belongings of the gods made of precious metal[3] and—to remain in an agricultural context—the sacred land.[4] First and foremost, the sacred animals were mortal. No maintenance of the *status quo* for each particular animal would be possible. It is only in myth that god-owned animals may neither give birth nor die.[5]

In the classical period, we meet sacred animals in an often-quoted inscription concerning the sanctuary of Zeus in Arkesine on Amorgos.[6] It lays down the rules for the leasing of land belonging to Zeus. The area is to be cultivated carefully, but one rule says that the tenant is not allowed to have animals grazing in the area. A transgression of this rule will mean that the animals in question will hereafter be regarded as sacred, that is, as the property of Zeus. What will happen to them then is not to be read from the inscription.

Sacred animals are also mentioned in a Tegean inscription from the first half of the fourth century B.C.[7] The stone in question is well preserved at the top, but its inscription starts very abruptly without any explanatory formulas. If the text did not start on another stone lost to us,[8] this stone must originally have been placed where nobody would be in doubt as to the status of the land concerned. But today it is a matter of discussion whether it is sacred land belonging to Alea Athena or rather public land belonging to the citizens of Tegea.[9] We believe the former, which is also the traditional view.[10]

The sanctuary of Alea Athena was located on a plateau, and the land was well suited for grazing. Access to this privilege was regulated by the citizens of Tegea.

---

[1] I am happy to have had the opportunity to present for discussion at Uppsala some results from a forthcoming book by S. Isager & J.E. Skydsgaard, *Ancient Greek agriculture: an introduction*, in which Skydsgaard treats the subject of animal husbandry as such, whereas I myself have worked especially on sacred animals.

[2] In the following pages, I shall normally prefer the neutral term 'animal' to the ambiguous 'cattle'.

[3] For which see, recently, T. Linders, 'Gods, gifts and society', in *Gifts to the Gods. Proceedings of the Uppsala Symposium 1985*, T. Linders & G. Nordquist, eds. (Acta Universitatis Upsaliensis, Boreas 15), Uppsala 1987, 115–122.

[4] Cf. S. Isager, 'Som guderne vil: De græske guder som jordejere', *Den Jyske Historiker* 51–52, 1990, 33–44; *eadem*, 'Sacred and profane ownership of land', in *Agriculture in Ancient Greece. Proceedings of the Seventh International Symposium at the Swedish Institute at Athens 16–17 May 1990*, B. Wells, ed. (ActaAth-4°, 42), 1992, 119–122; Isager & Skydsgaard (supra n. 1).

[5] The cows and sheep of Helios, Hom., *Od.* 12.127–131. Cf. also *The Homeric Hymn to Apollo* 411–413.

[6] Dittenberger, *Syll.* 963.

[7] V. Bérard, 'Inscription archaïque de Tégée', *BCH* 13, 1889, 281–293; *IG* V.2.3; Sokolowski, *LSCG* 67. For recent discussions, see M. Guarducci, 'La legge dei tegeati intorno ai pascoli di Alea', *RivFil* 80, 1952, 49–68; S. Georgoudi, 'Quelques problèmes de la transhumance dans la Grèce ancienne', *REG* 87, 1974, 155–185; M. Jost, *Sanctuaires et cultes d'Arcadie* (Études Péloponnésiennes, 9), Paris 1985, 382–385.

[8] Suggested by Guarducci (supra n. 7), 51f.

[9] For the latter view, see Jost (supra n. 7), 382 and cf. Guarducci (supra n. 7), 51. More details about the administration of the money mentioned in the inscription would be needed to decide the matter.

[10] For example, Bérard (supra n. 7), 286; Sokolowski, *LSCG* 135.

Sacred animals on their way to a different place, perhaps in connection with transhumance, had a right to graze and rest for a day and a night on the sacred land.[11] If the period turned out to be protracted, it cost one drachma per day for a cow or a pig and one obol per day for a goat or a sheep. The *hierothytes* of Alea was allowed to have animals suitable for offering grazing in the area; perhaps these were animals belonging to the goddess, but we cannot read that from the inscription. Her priest might graze 25 sheep, a couple of draught-animals, and a goat in the sacred area. They were his private animals and if he allowed more animals to graze there, he was fined for each large animal whereas smaller animals were subjected to *inphorbismos*. The meaning of this otherwise unknown word has been discussed ever since the inscription was first published in 1889 and no definite solution has, as yet, been found. Confiscation is one plausible suggestion.[12] Animals owned by private persons were otherwise allowed to graze in the area only when they were on an errand to the sanctuary, either because they were to be sacrificed or because they pulled the cart for a worshipper. Finally, private persons in transit could be allowed to graze their own team, but no other animals, there in connection with a single overnight stay. As we have seen, the Tegean inscription gives no unambiguous information on local, sacred animals, but it contains provisions for the special treatment of sacred animals passing through.

South of Delphi lay the land which once belonged to the Kirrhaians. It was forbidden to inhabit the area, just as it was forbidden to cultivate it. The general assumption is that the area could be used for pasture.[13] But there is in fact no indication to this effect in the written sources from the classical period. In an important inscription from the middle of the 4th century, inspection of the area was ordered with a view to putting a stop to the illegal agricultural exploitation of the land by private people, and it is emphasized that the area is not to be fertilized or inhabited.[14] This does not in itself exclude the possibility that animals may have been allowed to pasture there.[15]

No accounts of ordinary income from land or animals have been preserved from Delphi.[16] It is the exceptions that we hear about. We do know, for example, that in 275 B.C. Apollo in Delphi received 50 oxen from a Lakedaimonian village as a present. The oxen were purchased in Lokris, probably to save transport. At that time, at least, Apollo probably had sacred cattle to which the 50 new ones were then to be added.[17] It is, however, only in an inscription from 178 B.C. that we have certain evidence showing that Apollo owned cows as well as horses. At that time, they were to graze within a defined part of the sacred area. Private persons were not permitted to graze their flocks (*thremmata*) there.[18] We cannot determine whether this means that privately owned animals were allowed on the other part of the ground.

One might think that the idea of sacred animals was a safeguard to ensure a supply of sacrificial animals there and then. This explanation may apply to the holy cows, but not to the horses. Horses were not eaten in the classical period and were not normally to be found among the sacrificial animals.[19] We know that the ordinary Greek *bought* his horse when it had come of age, if he had the need and the means to keep a horse at all.[20] Perhaps the sanctuary of Delphi was, or in the Hellenistic period, became simply one of the places where the breeding of horses (and undoubtedly also cows) took place. If by sale the animals became privately owned, they would lose their sacred status. I do not think that this would be against what was considered proper behaviour towards the gods. But, if it was, the other available solution is that the sacred horses were used in processions.

Apparently, by 117/16, complaints about the abuse and neglect of Apollo's possessions at Delphi had been brought before the Roman Senate. The Romans asked the Amphictyonians to conduct a general revision—*inter alia*, the boundaries of Apollo's land were readjusted—and then there was to be an investigation of Apollo's income from his flocks (*agelai* and *thremmata*)

[11] Cf. Georgoudi (supra n. 7), 179f.

[12] Bérard (supra n. 7), 289. W. Vollgraff, 'Remarques sur une inscription de Tégée', *BCH* 70, 1946, 617–627, esp. p. 619. Guarducci argues for a temporary retention within a fence, the point being that the owner, on retrieving his animals, would be obliged to pay for the food they had consumed (supra n. 7), 54–58.

[13] É. Bourguet, *L'administration financière du sanctuaire pythique au IVᵉ siècle avant J.C.*, Paris 1905, 26; U. Kahrstedt, 'Delphoi und das heilige Land des Apollon', in *Studies presented to D.M. Robinson* II, G.E. Mylonas & D. Raymond, eds., Saint Louis (Missouri) 1953, 749.

[14] *GD* II,2501; IV,15–26. Cf. Aischines 3.107–113.

[15] But cf. Dittenberger, *Syll.* 986; Sokolowski, *LSCG* 116.

[16] Although we have in Dittenberger, *Syll.* 178, part of the lists of lands and houses belonging to men exiled by Onomachos in 353 B.C. and leased by the temple authorities in the period 346–324 B.C., cf. Dittenberger, *Syll.* 175, and H. Pomtow, 'Eine delphische *stasis* im Jahre 363 v.Chr.', *Klio* 6, 1906, 89–126.

[17] Dittenberger, *Syll.* 407, with commentary.

[18] Dittenberger, *Syll.* 636.

[19] M. Jameson, 'Sacrifice and animal husbandry in Classical Greece', in *Pastoral economies in classical Antiquity*, C.R. Wittaker, ed. (Cambridge Philological Society, Suppl. 14), Cambridge 1988, 88.

[20] Skydsgaard in Isager & Skydsgaard (supra n. 1).

to establish how much money was lacking. But the Amphictyonians had to give up the investigation. All those questioned answered that they did not know how many animals they had taken over, how many they had passed on or what had been the income from them. And there was nothing written in the public accounts about it.[21]

What we can conclude is that Apollo should have had an income from his animals. We can also see that every mention of sacred animals at Delphi points to animal-breeding, independently of agriculture.

The situation at Delphi was quite opposite that at Delos.[22] At Delos, the sacred land was leased out and meant to be cultivated intensively. Large parts of the accounts showing Apollo's ordinary income and expenses have been preserved, but one searches almost in vain for mentions of sacred animals in the accounts.

We know that on Delos Apollo had his own animals and that they grazed on his land. Yet, in the accounts, tenants are listed only as tenants of land, and in the lists of what came with a piece of land when taken over by the tenant, buildings, vines and other fruit-trees are mentioned but not the number of sacred animals nor indeed a word to suggest that animals may have been included. Nor are they mentioned as a separate category in connection with the official accounts.

In the 4th century B.C. there are a few references to income for Apollo from the sale of wool of the sacred sheep.[23] Apart from that, incontestible evidence to show that sacred animals were a permanent phenomenon may be derived from a revision of the rules guiding the leasing out of the god's land dating from about the year 300 B.C., the so-called *hiera syggraphe*.[24] There are different rules for the animal-breeders and those who did not breed animals. Whereas the latter paid their rent only once a year, in Metageitnion, corresponding to August–September, the animal-breeders had to pay their rent in two instalments. In Artemision, our April–May, the first instalment fell due. In the inscription, which is badly damaged, we read that at that time the animal-breeders had to pay a certain amount per animal.[25] Apparently the animals referred to here were not sacred but belonged to the tenant himself or to some other mortal.

In Lokris, Artemision was called Pokios, the wool-month; that was the month when sheep were sheared or plucked, and the month when lambs were old enough to be sold. It was also the time to transport the animals from the island, if there was not sufficient grass for them in the summer. This must have been an additional motive for selling some of them.

Naturally, the animal-breeders received a great part of their income at that time. The remainder of the rent was paid in Lenaion of the following year, our January–February; this was the month when the herds of sheep and goats from the previous year were fully grown, and it was a suitable time to reduce the numbers of males among them. The females, on the other hand, had their sucking lambs and kids to tend.[26]

The distribution of the rent into two instalments was probably a measure of assistance or insurance: it fell due when income was available. The demand for sacrificial animals might also be especially high at these seasons. Unfortunately, we know too little about the Delian festival calendar to tell.[27]

The tenant's animals grazed together with those of Apollo. In the month before Artemision,[28] the *hieropoioi*, according to the *hiera syggraphe*, were to inspect "the branded cows"[29] and perhaps the inspection was repeated in Metageitnion.[30] It was probably in connection with the inspection by the *hieropoioi* of the animals already branded that animals of the new brood were branded.[31] The *hieropoioi* had to swear that the sacred animals which the tenant might now raise would have no influence on or be included in the payment of the rent. This must mean that no fixed amount was to be paid for them, but only for the animals in private ownership.

As a rule, the branded animals were not for sale. If the particular tenant nevertheless wanted to sell one of Apollo's animals, he had to report it to the *hieropoioi* and provide a guarantor for the price of the animal.[32] In other words, the tenant was called upon to replace the

---

[21] Dittenberger, *Syll.* 826 G.

[22] All studies of the property of Apollo at Delos should and as a rule, do start with J.K. Kent, 'The temple estates of Delos, Rheneia and Mykonos', *Hesperia* 17, 1948, 243–338. On the religious life, see Ph. Bruneau, *Recherches sur les cultes de Délos à l'époque hellénistique et à l'époque impériale*, Paris 1970.

[23] A wine-cooler (*psykter*) was bought from the money, *IG* II^2 1639, 15–16, 17; cf. 1638 B, 66; 1640, 28.

[24] *ID* 503, thoroughly commented on by Kent (supra n. 22), 267–285.

[25] *ID* 503, 20–21.

[26] Cf., on the Attic calendars, Jameson (supra n. 19), 102f.

[27] Apollonia was celebrated in Hieros, the month following the Artemision; cf. Bruneau (supra n. 22), 65.

[28] Galaxion, the Elaphebolion in Athens, i.e. March–April.

[29] Kent interprets the text as saying that Apollo only owned cows (Kent, supra n. 22, 293). One might be tempted to think that he is right, and that Apollo in Delphi only had cows and horses, i.e. the more expensive animals. But, concerning sacred sheep, see n. 25 and B. Cavagnola, 'Aspetti economici dell'allevamento a Delo e Reneia in eta ellenistica', *Istituto Lombardo, RendLett* 107, 1973, 511–545, esp. 518.

[30] *ID* 503, 22.

[31] *IG* XI,2, 287 A, 44 and 58.

[32] *ID* 503, 25–27.

animal sold with a new one, which was then to be branded when the time came.

The tenant took care of the branded sacred animals along with his own. In return, he probably had a right to the milk of the animal and perhaps to part of the wool, as long as he took care of them. When a sacrificial animal was needed, the *hieropoioi* could have the animals fetched and, as there was no question of purchase or sale, it did not appear in their accounts. This is at least a plausible explanation of the fact that we know of only one instance in which the *hieropoioi* had to pay for sacrificial animals for the *Apollonia*.[33] In the accounts of the *hieropoioi* for 250, which are the best preserved of all, only the hide of the ox and the goat which had been sacrificed at the Poseidon Festival in Posideon are listed as income. Under expenses, one looks in vain for a corresponding expense connected with the purchase of animals; the reason for this may have been that Apollo himself delivered the sacrificial animals that year. But there are several other possibilities. Perhaps the sacrificed animals were financed by Delian citizens by means of a liturgy or from the amount of 600 drachmas which, during the period of independence, the Delian state seems to have paid as an annual contribution to the Posideon Festival.[34]

Each month, an offering of purification of the sanctuary of Apollo was performed, and for this purpose each time a pig was purchased, as it appears from the accounts.[35] In other words, Apollo himself probably did not own pigs, and this is understandable if the only advantage for the tenant in looking after Apollo's animals was the benefit which he could derive from them while they were alive. In that case, he had no interest in tending pigs for Apollo. This he would have had if he had a right to the young of the sacred animals. The question is what benefit the tenant could derive from the cows. They were good plough- and draught-animals, but hard-worked draught-animals were not considered suitable for sacrifice.[36] Cow's milk was not highly valued by the Greeks.

Since the sacred animals were kept by the tenants of Apollo together with the privately owned animals, it would be of interest to know what part the latter played in the farming on Delos and Rheneia.

The technical word for the rent of Apollo's land in the accounts is *enerosion*, i.e. tax on grain.[37] When a lessee is unable to pay his *enerosion*, he risks a confiscation of his property and the first thing to be confiscated is his harvest (*karpoi*); secondly, cows, sheep, goats and slaves can be confiscated.[38] This should be kept in mind when attention is focussed on the animals.

As animals hardly ever appear in the accounts, I shall attempt to make deductions about their presence or absence by other means. The seemingly firm point of departure is the occurrence of stables or shelters on several of Apollo's properties, as mentioned in the accounts. *Boustasis* and *probation* are terms used to denote stables or rather shelters designed for cows, oxen and smaller animals, respectively. In the accounts, cowsheds appear in thirteen of Apollo's properties, Charoneia had two cowsheds, so that altogether 14 cowsheds are attested in inscriptions, and twelve "stables" for smaller animals, two of which belong to Charoneia.[39] On the basis of these inventories of the estates, combined with what the accounts of the *hieropoioi* can tell us about the rise and fall of rents and the possible difficulties of the lessees, J.H. Kent has made a description of each estate. He does not try to hide the difficulties of the task clearly illustrated in his characterization of the so called Hippodromos: 'The absence of vineyards, orchards, storehouse for chaff, and mill-house shows that the estate was almost entirely devoted to livestock. In 189 B.C. there was no cattle shelter; therefore, the estate was primarily a sheep ranch.'[40]

Nevertheless it appears that upon one occasion at the end of the 4th century the *hieropoioi* of Apollo recovered part of the areas of the Hippodromos tenant by 'selling the barley'. In addition two cows or oxen belonging to the tenant were sold and the man was still in

---

[33] *ID* 354, 63; Bruneau (supra n. 22), 65. Since these animals cost only 7 drachmas apiece, they cannot have been cows. For a purchase outside Delos of 109 cows by the Athenian amphictyonians in 377/6–375/4 B.C. see Dittenberger, *Syll.* 153; cf. H. Grassl, 'Zur Geschichte des Viehhandels im klassischen Griechenland', *Münchener Beiträge zur Antiken Handelsgeschichte* 4,2, 1985, 77–87, esp. 84f.

[34] Bruneau (supra n. 22), 360f. Claude Vial reckons among the tasks of the *hieropoioi* the administration of the income from the sacred animals of Apollo, and he adds "Ils vendaient également tous les animaux sacrés qui mouraient". The example given is the sale of a goat which had been dedicated by a certain Philokleides, IG XI,2, 158 A, 31; C. Vial, *Délos indépendante (314–167 av. J.-C.)* (*BCH* Suppl. 10), Paris 1984, 231. Osborne makes no mention of the sacred animals in R. Osborne, 'Social and economic implications of the leasing of land and property in classical and Hellenistic Greece', *Chiron* 18, 1988, 279–323.

[35] Listed in Vial (supra n. 34), 321.

[36] For example Cavagnola (supra n. 29), 515 with n. 18, against Kent (supra n. 22), 293; Jameson (supra n. 19), 87 with n. 3.

[37] For example, *IG* XI,2, 162.

[38] *ID* 503, 33–36.

[39] Kent (supra n. 22), 299f.

[40] Kent (supra n. 22), 301, based on *IG* XI,2, 287 A, 143–145; *ID* 403, 51–53.

debt, so his guarantor had to step in.[41] No sheep are mentioned as possible objects of sale.

Because of its name, the Hippodromos has been looked upon as something special: it has been thought that it was perhaps identical with the area which in the 5th century B.C. the Athenian general Nikias presented to Apollo, with the stipulation that a regular festival should be held, during which, among other things, Nikias should be commemorated.[42] At the same time, however, this example may also serve as a warning against deducing too much from the inventory of the accounts whenever we are not exactly dealing with well-rooted plants like vines and figs.

The example of the estate (*temenos*) called Hippodromos and its defaulting tenant may support the theory that there was a tendency towards more animal-breeding and less agriculture. The account of the debtor is namely earlier than the oldest inventory preserved. It may also render possible an interpretation that the cowsheds were filled with Apollo's own cows, whereas the tenants had only a few. It may be taken to confirm the theory that the cowsheds mentioned in the accounts were only built for a team of draught-animals each.[43] Finally, it may be viewed as a support for the explanation of why animal-breeders were to pay twice a year. Individually, at odd times of the year, they could reduce their ability to pay by selling some of their animals.

An argument against the assumption that Apollo's animals exceeded the others in number is the fact that the sacred estates identified by Kent as being dependent not on viticulture but rather on animals managed better when rents decreased at the beginning of the third century.

To sum up, in classical and Hellenistic Greece, a sacred animal is an animal owned by a god (its opposite is a privately owned animal).[44] An animal could become sacred (1) by the mere fact that it had grazed on land belonging to a god, if that was forbidden, (2) by gift or, probably, (3) by being born so. Sacred land seems to be a prerequisite for sacred animals but not, of course, *vice versa*.

The sacred animals could be kept in flocks and apart, as we saw at Delphi, or they could be part of a mixed flock and possibly of mixed agriculture. They could, as in Delphi, be expected to be a source of income for the god, although we do not know exactly in which way or they could, as we perhaps see at Delos, present a way in which the temples could make sure that sacrificial animals of the more costly type would be available. It is not possible to assess in general terms the importance of sacred animals in the economy of the Greek temples.

Signe Isager
Institut for Historie, Kultur
og Samfundsbeskrivelse
Odense Universitet
DK-5230 ODENSE M

---

41 *IG* XI,2, 242,5–12. The number of cows sold is in fact unreadable in the text, but the sum total of 150 drachmas speaks for the restoration 'two'.

42 Kent (supra n. 22), 255f.

43 Skydsgaard's suggestion. As applied only to the Hippodromos Cavagnola (supra n. 29), 536.

44 Any comparison with the animal gods of Egypt would be out of place. As for impure animals, no such category is to be found in Greece; cf. R.C.T. Parker, *Miasma*, Oxford 1983, 356. On the other hand, certain animals were considered to cause pollution if found in certain places, for example pack-animals at the sanctuary of Alektrone in Ialysos (*IG* XII,2, 677; Dittenberger, *Syll.* 338; Sokolowski, *LSCG* 136, 20–23) and dogs at Delos and at the Akropolis of Athens (Strabo 10.486; Plutarch, *Quaest. Rom.* 111).

Discussion

Tullia LINDERS: I was glad to hear you discuss the sacred cows of Apollo at Delos because I, like other people, have been struck by their absence in the accounts. There are traces of them in the 5th and 4th centuries, but in the Hellenistic accounts one looks in vain for, for instance, outlay for cows or oxen to sacrifice. You told us about the outlay for pigs. But at the great festival of the Apollonia in the month *Hieros*, I suppose they must have sacrificed quite a number of big cattle and there is no trace of them in the accounts. So where did they come from? Perhaps, as you suggest, from cattle that Apollo owned, but it's difficult to trace.

SI: Yes, it certainly is. One could think of liturgies just like those in Attica; that was one possibility.

Jacques TRÉHEUX: Je crois que le sanctuaire ne possédait pas d'animaux à Délos et que tous les animaux qui sont sacrifiés sont achetés. Par exemple, au début de chaque mois, on sacrifiait un porc et à chaque fois on nous dit le prix du porc, « il vaut cinq drachmes », par example. Par conséquent, les hiéropes l'ont acheté probablement à des paysans de l'île ou de l'île voisine. Mais je ne crois pas qu'ils aient tué des animaux qu'ils possédaient en propre.

SI: But what would be the function of the sacred cows then? Why would they appear in the *hiera syggraphe* as something to legislate about?

JT: La *hiéra syngraph*è formule les règles que les tenanciers des fermes sacrées devront suivre et alors les tenanciers des fermes sacrées ont dit à quelle période ils verseront les loyers, que ces obligations varient selon que la ferme a ou non des animaux, mais ces animaux appartiennent, je crois, aux fermiers.

SI: Why should some of them be called sacred animals?

JT: Mais, évidemment, vous avez l'argument que lorsqu'un animal disparait il doit être remplacé par un autre. C'est un peu comme pour les arbres — si un arbre disparait, le fermier doit une indemnité au sanctuaire.

TL: But it is strange that if the *hieropoioi* bought animals from the farmers of Delos or Rheneia or other islands, they don't account for it in the inscriptions.

JT: Non. Ils paient cinq drachmes pour, par exemple, un porc, et puis ils notent *Lenaionos*, « au mois de Lènaion », *Xoiros to hieron katharasthai*, « un porc pour purifier le sanctuaire — cinq drachmes ».

TL: But never for a cow, or a "boeuf", and that is what I find strange.

JT: Ce serait étrange si les hiéropes sacrifiaient de gros animaux, des boeufs ou des vaches?

JT: N'oubliez pas que les hiéropes font les comptes du sanctuaire. Si effectivement des animaux de grande taille sont sacrifiés à l'occasion des Apollonia est-ce que c'est le sanctuaire ou la ville qui les fournit? Nous avons à l'époque athénienne des sacrifices qui sont faits par des bienfaiteurs, et il y a des processions, des processions de boeufs. Mais naturellement l'achat des animaux de la procession n'entre pas dans le compte des administrateurs sacrés car ce ne sont pas eux qui en font les frais. Par conséquent, il est vrai que jamais les hiéropes n'achètent une vache ou un boeuf. N'oublions pas que les hiéropes n'écrivent pas leurs comptes pour nous, ils les font pour eux, et ils les font pour leurs successeurs. Les inventaires, madame Linders, je sais que vous n'êtes pas d'accord avec moi là-dessus spécialement, c'est une espèce de parapluie que les hiéropes ont ouvert pour se justifier. C'est un contrôle.

TL: Je suis d'accord.

Carmine AMPOLO: What do you think about the passage in the fifth book of the *Anabasis* (5.3.7-13) where Xenophon describes the Artemision in Skillous, and the herd of cattle belonging to the sanctuary?

SI: Yes, there are cattle belonging to Artemis. And every year a big feast takes place where Artemis provides her cattle and produce from the land. It's her expense.

Jacques Tréheux

L'unité de pesée et l'unité de compte des hiéropes à Délos

Il est évident que l'unité de pesée et l'unité de compte utilisées par les administrateurs sacrés constituent un élément essentiel de l'économie d'un sanctuaire. Notre communication se limitera au sanctuaire sur lequel nous sommes le mieux renseignés, le sanctuaire de Délos.

I. L'unité de pesée

Au cours de la période amphictyonique (entre 478 environ et 314 avant J.-C.), pendant laquelle le sanctuaire est administré par les magistrats Athéniens et, certaines années, Andriens, les Amphictyons, l'unité pondérale, comme l'unité monétaire, est la drachme attique (4 gr., 25).

Sous l'Indépendance (314–166 avant J.-C.), où le sanctuaire est administré par des magistrats Déliens, les hiéropes, on aurait pu penser, Délos frappant des monnaies sur l'étalon rhodien (3 gr., 25 environ)[1], que l'unité pondérale et l'unité monétaire étaient la drachme délienne. En fait, il n'en est rien. L'unité pondérale, pour ne parler que d'elle en un premier temps, n'a pas changé avec le changement de régime politique : c'est toujours la drachme attique ou, ce qui revient au même, la drachme d'Alexandre. On peut le prouver de diverses facons : voici les deux qui nous semblent le plus démonstratives.

1° Sous l'Amphictyonie, les théores d'Athènes avaient consacré dans le temple des Athéniens, lors des *Délia* pentétériques, une vingtaine de couronnes d'or qui furent appendues aux murs du temple[2]. Le poids de chacune d'elles était inscrit sur une étiquette attachée à la couronne ou à son support. Mais le poids indiqué par les inventaires amphictyoniques[3] n'est jamais le poids noté sur l'étiquette : c'est toujours le poids réel, légèrement supérieur au précédent. Sous l'Indépendance, le temple des Athéniens a changé de nom; il est devenu le temple aux sept statues (οὗ τὰ ἑπτὰ, *scil.* ἀγάλματα)[4]. Mais les couronnes n'ont pas changé de place. Elles sont recensées par les hiéropes qui, dans l'inventaire de l'année 279 avant J.-C. (*IG*, XI 2, 161, *B*,1. 107–115), indiquent, pour huit d'entre elles, à la fois le poids inscrit sur l'étiquette et celui qui résulte de la pesée.

Numéro de la couronne	Poids inscrit	Poids réel
5eme	113 dr. 3 ob.	(118 dr. 3 ob.)[5]
6eme	63 dr.	65 dr.
10eme	92 dr. 3 ob.	96 dr.
11eme	66 dr. 4 ob.	68 dr.
13eme	82 dr. 5 ob.	83 dr. 3 ob.
15eme	82 dr. 3 ob.	84 dr. 3 ob.
19eme	82 dr. 2 ob.	82 dr. 3 ob.
20eme	100 dr.	101 dr. 3 ob.

On observe d'abord que dans tous les cas le poids réel est légèrement supérieur au poids inscrit. Mais le fait s'observe déjà à l'époque amphictyonique. Pour rendre compte de cette différence, je n'ai pas d'explication assurée. On peut seulement supposer que l'étiquette indiquait le poids de l'or des couronnes et que les hiéropes, comme les Amphictyons, les ont pesées avec leur étiquette et leur attache. Il n'importe : la leçon à tirer de cette confrontation est que les différences entre les poids inscrits et les poids réels sont trop faibles pour qu'on postule un changement d'unité de pesée, donc que les hiéropes ont pesé les couronnes avec la même unité que les Amphictyons, la drachme attique.

2° On trouve à plusiers reprises dans les comptes des hiéropes un article ainsi libellé :

[1] Cf. T. Hackens, *Guide de Délos*[3], 107–111 et fig. 16, 4 à 8.

[2] Vingt et une ou vingt-trois? Cf. le tableau dressé par J. Coupry, comm. à *ID*, 104, p. 49.

[3] P. ex. *Timocratès* (*ID*, 104), 50–56.

[4] Sur l'identité des sept statues, Ph. Bruneau, *Recherches sur les cultes de Délos à l'époque hellénistique et à l'époque romaine*, Paris 1970, 62.

[5] La pierre porte, en 161, *B*, 109, 122 dr., ce qui implique une différence assez forte (8 dr. 3 ob.) entre le poids inscrit et le poids réel. Mais c'est certainement une erreur de transcription des hiéropes : le n. 199, *B*, 29 donne le chiffre exact, 118 dr. 3 ob.

καὶ παντοδαποῦ ἀργυρίου εἰς ἀλεξανδρείου λόγ[ον] δραχμὰς· Γ⊢⊢⊢[6], « et des pièces d'argent[7] de toute espèce (pesant) selon l'étalon d'Alexandre 8 drachmes ».

Ce texte et ses parallèles confirment que les poids indiqués par les hiéropes doivent s'entendre « selon l'étalon d'Alexandre », qui ne diffère pas de l'étalon attique.

II. L'unité monétaire

De ces pesées « selon l'étalon d'Alexandre » on pourrait passer sans peine à l'induction que, sous l'Indépendance, le système monétaire délien était, lui aussi, d'étalon d'Alexandre[8] ou d'étalon attique. L'équation doit se vérifier dans toutes les cités et dans tous les États où la documentation en permet le contrôle. Mais, à Délos, sous l'Indépendance, les choses sont loin d'être aussi simples et il convient d'aligner les faits avant d'en proposer une interprétation.

Rappelons d'abord en quoi consistent les fonds gérés ou conservés par les hiéropes.

Ce sont en premier lieu des fonds de réserve, la caisse sacrée (ἱερὰ κιβωτός) que les hiéropes administrent sous le contrôle du Conseil et du peuple et la caisse publique (δημοσία κιβωτός), gérée par les Trésoriers et dont les hiéropes ont seulement la garde. Ces fonds sont contenus dans des jarres auxquelles est attachée une étiquette[9] portant une inscription ainsi rédigée : p.ex., *ID*, 442 (*a.* 179), *A*, 3 sqq. : Τόδε παρελάβομεν ἀργύριον ἐν τῶι ναῶι τοῦ Ἀπόλλωνος ἐν τεῖ κιβωτῶι τεῖ ἱερᾶι ---· στάμνον ἐπιγραφὴν ἔχοντα· τὸ ἀπελθὸν ἐκ Τήνου· ΓX : « une jarre portant l'inscription : argent en provenance de Tènos : 6000 dr. ». J'ai expliqué *MusHelv* 42, 1985, p. 20 sqq. le sens de τὸ ἀπελθὸν ἐκ Τήνου : il s'agit de fonds appartenant au sanctuaire qui les avait mis en dépôt dans une banque de Tènos et qui lui ont été renvoyés par la banque. Mais l'étiquette — ou l'inscription faite à l'encre — ne précise pas quelles drachmes, drachmes déliennes ou drachmes attiques (= d'Alexandre), sont contenues dans la jarre. A compter de l'année 192 avant J.-C.[10], les hiéropes inventorient, en tête de leur compte rendu annuel de gestion, l'ensemble des jarres de la caisse sacrée et de la caisse publique[11].

C'est ensuite un fonds de roulement, l'encaisse métallique des hiéropes. Au début de chaque exercice, les hiéropes recoivent du collège qui les a précédés une certaine somme dont ils disposent, toujours naturellement sous le contrôle du Conseil et du peuple, pour leur gestion financière. Cette somme s'accroît des revenus encaissés au cours de l'exercice (location des fermes et des maisons sacrées, produit des impôts du sanctuaire etc. ...). Inversement, les hiéropes prélèvent sur cette somme le montant de leurs dépenses pour la construction et l'entretien des édifices du sanctuaire, pour la rétribution des fonctionnaires etc. ...

Au terme de leur mandat, les hiéropes dressent un bilan de leur gestion financière. Ce bilan englobe la totalité des sommes reçues par les hiéropes de l'année dans les fonds de réserve et le fonds de roulement et le montant de ces mêmes fonds à leur sortie de charge. Il est formulé dans la balance du compte inscrite en grands caractères au bas de la face principale de la stèle. Exemple : *ID*, 444 (*a.* 177) *A*, 1.56 : [Κεφαλὴ πάσης εἰσόδου· MMMMM]MXXXΓHHHHΔΔΔ⊢⊢⊢I. Κεφαλὴ πάσης ἐξόδου· MMMMMMXXXΓHHHHΔΔΔ⊢⊢⊢I· « Total des entrées : 63.933 dr. 1 ob.; total des sorties : 63.933 dr. 1 ob. ». Pas plus que pour les jarres des caisses sacrée ou publique ou que pour l'encaisse métallique, les hiéropes ne précisent de quelles drachmes il s'agit.

On se gardera de conclure qu'à la fin de l'exercice de l'année 177 la fortune d'Apollon était d'environ 65.000 drachmes. Elle était, en fait, très supérieure. Car le dieu détenait des avoirs dans les banques installées dans l'île voisine de Tènos. Nous connaissons le nom de plusieurs de ces banques. Mais nous ignorons le montant des avoirs.

Deuxième fait à considérer : sous l'Indépendance, les Déliens frappent des monnaies d'argent — drachmes, hémidrachmes, trihémioboles — et des monnaies de bronze suivant l'étalon rhodien[12]. Ces monnaies ne sont pas émises par la cité de Délos pour affirmer sa souveraineté[13]; elles sont destinées au commerce local. L'existence d'une monnaie épichorique, frappée sur l'étalon rhodien, soulève un problème qui crée la difficulté majeure de la présente enquête. Les hiéropes disposaient dans la caisse sacrée et dans leur encaisse métallique de deux monnaies distinctes, frappées sur des étalons différents : des drachmes attiques ou d'Alexandre, frap-

---

6 *IG*, XI 2, 161 (*a.* 179), *A*, 4.

7 Le mot ἀργύριον ne désigne que du métal monnayé : O. Picard, *CRAI* 1989, 674, n. 4.

8 Même article en 199, *A*, 3; *ID*, 460, *k*, 6; 461, *Aa*, 49, 77. Cf. R. Bogaert, *Banques et banquiers dans les cités grecques*, Leyde 1968, 174, n. 231.

9 A moins que l'inscription n'ait été faite directement à l'encre sur la jarre, comme on voit p.ex. à Aï Khanoum : l'éventualité justifierait au mieux l'expression στάμνος ἐπιγραφὴν ἔχων.

10 *ID*, 399, *A*, 1–35; cf. J. Tréheux, *MusHelv* 42, 1985, 20, n. 1.

11 L'étude des mouvements de ces caisses est difficile; elle a été entreprise par Mlle C. Vial.

12 Cf. supra n. 1.

13 La monnaie n'est jamais en Grèce symbole de souveraineté : cf. T. Martin, *Sovereignty and coinage in Classical Greece*, London 1985, suivi par O. Picard, *CRAI* 1989, p. 682.

pées sur l'étalon attique, et des drachmes déliennes, frappées sur l'étalon rhodien. Sans compter des monnaies étrangères d'origine variée[14]. Or il est évident que les hiéropes ont manié pour leur gestion financière ces diverses monnaies. On peut admettre que les locataires des fermes et des maisons sacrées acquittaient leur loyer en monnaie délienne; c'est en monnaie délienne aussi que les hiéropes versaient les salaires des fonctionnaires du sanctuaire et rétribuaient les travaux des petits artisans qui travaillaient pour eux. Mais les entrepreneurs des travaux, qui sont en grande majorité des étrangers[15], ou les fournisseurs étrangers, comme les Macédoniens qui livraient de la poix[16], n'auraient jamais accepté d'être payés en monnaie délienne dont ils n'auraient su que faire une fois rentrés chez eux. Les hiéropes s'acquittaient donc envers eux avec une monnaie de valeur internationale, la drachme attique ou la drachme d'Alexandre.

Il résulte de là que, dans un compte annuel des hiéropes, certaines rentrées et certaines dépenses doivent s'entendre en monnaie délienne et certaines en monnaie attique ou d'Alexandre. Et pourtant, l'addition finale ou, plus exactement, le solde de l'exercice, τὸ περιὸν ἐκ τῆς στήλης, montre que le compte est juste. Les hiéropes n'y ont pas distingué la monnaie épichorique de la monnaie internationale. Pour eux, une drachme est une drachme, quels que soient son origine et son étalon. Cette pratique d'administration financière simple, ou plutôt simpliste, ne laisse pas au premier regard de surprendre. Elle ne peut s'expliquer que si la drachme délienne bénéficie sur le territoire de l'île d'un cours forcé, en sorte que, bien qu'inférieure d'environ un tiers en poids d'argent, elle est réputée avoir même valeur que la drachme attique ou d'Alexandre.

Faut-il alors conclure que les hiéropes utilisaient différemment deux unités de compte, la drachme attique ou d'Alexandre et la drachme délienne? A notre avis, pareille conclusion donnerait de la situation une image inexacte. Prenons l'exemple de la première jarre de la caisse sacrée dont nous avons ci-dessus reproduit l'inscription. La jarre contenait 6000 drachmes attiques ou d'Alexandre. Cela ne veut pas dire que toutes les monnaies contenues dans la jarre étaient des drachmes attiques ou d'Alexandre. Il pouvait y avoir toutes sortes de monnaie. Mais cela veut dire que la valeur de ces monnaies, appréciée εἰς ἀττικοῦ *vel* ἀλεξανδρείου λόγον, était de 6000 drachmes. La jarre venait de Tènos, où elle avait été remplie par une banque et c'est la banque qui, évaluant son contenu au cours du change, avait calculé qu'il valait 6000 drachmes attiques ou d'Alexandre. On comprend alors pourquoi les hiéropes ne font jamais d'opérations de change : c'est la banque qui les fait pour eux. Et l'on peut, si nous avons vu juste, conclure que les hiéropes n'utilisaient qu'une unité de compte, la drachme attique ou d'Alexandre.

Jacques Tréheux
1, Impasse Jules-Larcher
F-54000 NANCY

[14] La présence de ces monnaies dans le trésor du dieu apparait rétrospectivement après 167/6 dans les comptes des fonctionnaires athéniens préposés à l'administration du sanctuaire, les ἐπὶ τὰ ἱερά. Il s'agit de monnaies histiéiennes, érétriéiennes, rhodiennes et eubéennes. J'en traiterai dans un article à paraître dans le *BCH* 115, 1991, I : 'L'administration financière des ἐπὶ τὰ ἱερά à Délos : une théorie nouvelle'.
[15] Cf. M. Lacroix, 'Les architectes et entrepreneurs à Délos de 314 à 240', *RPh* 38, 1914, 303–330.
[16] Cf. G. Glotz, *REG* 29, 1916, 281–325.

Discussion

Tullia LINDERS: You have given a very interesting explication of why the Athenian administrators enumerate these jars of foreign money. I would like to add one reason, or one interpretation. After all, they enumerate those jars in the inventory of sacred offerings, and therefore it seems to me that they equate them with offerings, i.e. they made offerings of them. So in that manner I would prefer to say that they are "sacrés et intangibles".

JT: Que ces jarres soient intangibles, les textes le prouvent aussi longtemps que nous pouvons suivre leur histoire, c'est-à-dire sur une vingtaine d'années. Nous n'avons pas d'archives après 140 et même les comptes disparaissent avant 140, mais tant que nous pouvons suivre cette histoire, sur une vingtaine d'années, il est évident que ces sommes sont sacrées. Elles appartiennent à Apollon, on ne peut donc pas les détruire. Ce qu'on aurait pu en faire, et on l'a peut-être fait, je l'ignore, c'est de les fondre pour faire de la monnaie attique. Mais si on avait fait cette opération, vous connaissez mieux que moi les usages sacrés, il aurait d'abord fallu demander à Apollon par un sacrifice d'*aresterion* si cette transformation lui convenait. Il n'y a pas de degrés dans le sacré, pas plus qu'il n'y a de degrés du médiocre au pire.

TL: Yes, I think there are degrees in sacredness. I would maintain that votive offerings cannot, in principle at least, be changed into money—they remain votive offerings until someone steals them or something like that. The money in the sacred chest can be used for paying artisans, giving loans etc., in spite of its being sacred.

JT: Les sommes qui se trouvaient dans la caisse publique n'étaient pas sacrées, elles appartenaient à l'état délien et elles n'étaient pas administrées par les hiéropes; elles étaient tout simplement conservées par les hiéropes, c'est-à-dire qu'on avait appelé sur elles la protection du dieu en les plaçant dans le temple d'Apollon. Par conséquent, on pouvait détourner ces sommes vers n'importe quel achat sans priver le dieu. Mais avec les sommes conservées dans la caisse sacrée on ne pouvait faire que des achats destinés au sanctuaire, et même la caisse sacrée on n'y touchait pas régulièrement.

TL: On the other hand one did not take, for instance, silver vessels among the votive offerings and make money out of them to pay something for the sanctuary. They were untouchable in another way. What I mean is that the jars with foreign money, which the Attic administrators list in the inventories, had been equated with these untouchable votive offerings.

JT: Au cours du symposion que vous avez organisé et du symposion de Neuchâtel auquel vous nous avez fait le grand honneur de venir, nous avons déjà marqué nos différentes opinions sur un certain point. Madame Aleshire nous serait témoin que dans les inventaires de l'Asclépieion, on fond des petites monnaies et des petits *typoi*, pour en faire des offrandes plus grandes. C'est une opération très fréquente et c'est ce que madame Aleshire, et les textes aussi d'ailleurs, appellent la *kathairesis*. Mais avec ces petites monnaies et offrandes, ces *typoi* qui pèsent un gramme ou moins, on ne fait jamais de monnaies. Parce que le rôle du sanctuaire n'est pas de frapper de la monnaie.

TL: I don't think it is the only reason. To me a very important reason is that the sanctuary wants these small, insignificant offerings to remain offerings. If they were struck into money they would leave the sanctuary and be used as money. Simple Athenians had dedicated small coins to Asclepios and Asclepios should retain the offerings he had got, even if in another form. The circumstance that the duty of the sanctuary was not to strike money, I think, is secondary.

JT: Madame, nous sommes d'accord. Toutes ces offrandes, quand elles sont fondues, restent la propriété du dieu, n'est-ce pas? Cette *kathairesis* n'a rien à enlever à la propriété du dieu. Mais même pour cette transformation, il faut demander l'avis du dieu. Il peut vouloir conserver ses *typoi*. On demande au Héros Médecin par exemple, par un sacrifice dit *aresterion*, l'autorisation de faire avec des petites offrandes de grandes offrandes, qui serviront à son culte.

Carmine Ampolo

The Economics of the Sanctuaries in Southern Italy and Sicily

In this paper I shall attempt to explain some aspects of the sanctuaries of southern Italy and Sicily regarded from the point of view of a historian of economics. It is not my intention, however, to give a detailed account and to deal with the many epigraphical, institutional and religious problems, even though all these aspects are strictly related to each other. The whole matter is limited by the available evidence, and the obvious, preliminary question is: do the sources give us the rule or the exception, that is, does the evidence bear witness to the general situation or to unusual, exceptional circumstances? A general answer to this question cannot be given, as each case is different.

The two most important groups of epigraphical documents of the western Greeks prove that at least some western sanctuaries had considerable estates. These two groups are the two *tabulae Heracleenses* (beginning of the 3rd century B.C.), well-known since the 18th century, and the 39 texts from the Locrian archives (4th–3rd centuries B.C.), published all together in 1973 by De Franciscis, after some of them had been published in previous years.[1]

This feature is confirmed by some passages from literary sources, not always considered by scholars; this is well-known as regards Greece and other regions.[2] Estates belonging to sanctuaries were common and may have been the rule in the cases of relevant public cults, especially in the western colonies.

In Magna Graecia, we know of estates belonging to the following temples: Dionysos and Athena in Heraclea; Olympian Zeus in Locri; Boreas in Thurii; Parthenope in Neapolis; Hera Lakinia near Croton. In a country such as Campania, with a mixture of ethnic groups and cultures (Oscan, Etruscan, Greek and other) in a more recent period, there is evidence of a sanctuary of Hercules common to Abella and Nola and of the important temple of Diana Tifatina near Capua.[3] For Sicily, there is good evidence of temple estates in Engyon, a sanctuary of Hellenized communities.[4] But it may be supposed that temple estates were a much more common feature than the evidence shows.

We have information about the extent of the properties only for Heraclea. The estate of Dionysos was 368 ha in area, following Hultsch's metrological theory, or 356 ha, following Segré.[5] But the land was divided into four parcels (approximately 90 ha each). The estate of Athena, more fruitful and productive, had an area of 298 ha, following Hultsch, or of 288 ha, following Segré, and was divided into small parcels of 6–8 ha.

The two temple estates were different, both legally and in quality. In the first case, the parcels were partly wooded and partly cultivated with cereals, olive-trees and vineyards. Athenas property included only olive-trees, vineyards and orchards.

I would like to emphasize the two most important facts:

The abbreviations are those listed in *L'année philologique*.

[1] *Tabulae Heracleenses*: *IG* XIV 645 = *DGE* 62–63; V. Arangio-Ruiz & A. Olivieri, *Inscriptiones Graecae Siciliae et infimae Italiae ad ius pertinentes*, Milan 1925, 1; A. Uguzzoni & F. Ghinatti, *Le tavole greche di Eraclea*, Rome 1968 (with bibliography, 11f.). Locrian texts: A. De Franciscis, *Stato e società in Locri Epizefiri (L'archivio dell'Olympieion locrese)*, Naples 1972 (preliminary reports in *Klearchos* from 3, 1961, to 10, 1968, by De Franciscis and G. Foti). F. Costabile is preparing an *editio altera* in a publication of the 'Università di Reggio Calabria'. For further references, see n. 11.

[2] See recently M.B. Walbank, 'Leases of sacred properties in Attica', I–IV, *Hesperia* 52, 1983, 100–135, 177–199, 200–206 and 207–231, and V, *Hesperia* 53, 1984, 361–368, and R. Osborne, 'Social and economic implications of the leasing of land and property in Classical and Hellenistic Greece', *Chiron* 18, 1988, 279–323 (who do not consider the Greek colonies).

[3] For Heraclea and Locri, see n. 1. Thurii: Aelian 12.61; Neapolis: *Grom.vet.* 1,235, Lachmann; Croton: Liv. 24.3; Abella: E. Vetter, *Handbuch der italischen Dialekte*, Heidelberg 1953, 1; A. Franchi De Bellis, *Il cippo abellano*, Urbino 1988 (with bibliography); Capua: *CIL* X 3828 = *ILS* 251; *ILS* 3240; see A. De Franciscis, *Templum Dianae Tifatinae*, Naples 1957. In general, see F. Ghinatti, 'Per uno studio sociologico dei santuari della Magna Grecia', *StudPat* 23, 1976, 601–630.

[4] Diod. 4.80.3–6.

[5] Uguzzoni & Ghinatti (supra n. 1), 172ff. with references.

(1) The two sanctuaries had two different kinds of leases. The first was a perpetual one, and the second was a 5-year contract, following the usual practices in the Greek world.[6]

(2) The rent was not paid in money but in barley, even if the parcels did not produce any cereals!

The rent for Dionysos' estate was more than 410 medimnoi, i.e. 140 tons, and for Athena's 3,500 medimnoi, i.e. 1,200 tons. In his monograph about the *tabulae Heracleenses*, Ghinatti speculated on the values of these rents. If we accept for the value of the barley the price well attested in Athens (i.e. 3/4 drachmas a medimnos), we obtain a rent of 1230/1640 for Dionysos and of 10,500/14,000 for Athena. We may compare these totals with the revenues of the temple estates of Delos in 250 B.C. According to Kent, followed by Osborne and other scholars, "rent for estates totalled 11,091 dr. and although the temple authorities had a much larger sum in their hands, the rents of the larger estates constituted some of the largest individual items of income with which they dealt".[7]

Both these facts reveal a wide range of legal and economic statuses, even in sanctuaries in the same city–state and in the same years, not to speak of other colonies or Greece itself. Recently, Robin Osborne pointed out that "different types of property offer rather different economic and social opportunities".[8] But in Heraclea—I repeat—we can observe a difference between two sanctuaries in the same city, at the same time! These remarks undoubtedly invite us to be cautious about making wide generalisations, even if these are a necessity.

We may also remark that there is no exclusively monetary economy (as in Greece, following Osborne); the city–state of Heraclea wanted rents to be paid in cereals (barley). From the first *tabula* (I, 100–105), we learn the cause of this attitude: the inscription prescribes to tenants who thresh early that they are to bring barley to the public granary, while the *sitagertai* will measure barley quantities. The city wants to have not only soil improvements, payments and guarantors, but especially to have barley constantly available. Barley was a typical, traditional cereal in the Greek world, as we know very well, for instance, from Attica and Southern Italy (in Metapontum, the nearest Greek colony to Heraclea).[9] It is, of course, possible that Heraclea sold this barley for money; in any case, this demonstrates that here public sanctuaries were ruled by thinking about food-supply problems.

The community cares for the sanctuary; the *alia* i.e. the citizens' assembly, decides about the properties. Sanctuary estates are differently considered in comparison with other public lands, but decisions are taken by the city. The strong presence of the city, in this case, depends on the nature of the document (which is different from the Locrian texts, for example), but also on the fact that there is in Heraclea a sort of re-organisation of temple estates; the city wants to restore the original extent of the property, which had been partly occupied and usurped. The particular purpose of such a document explains why it does not say anything about other goods of the two sanctuaries, other revenues, income administration, votive offerings and so on. However, in Heraclea the relationship of sanctuary, land and city is very strong and may well go back to the foundation of the city in 433/2.

Before examining the Locrian texts, let us consider an example of the introduction of a new cult, geographically and chronologically quite near to the quoted inscriptions. Aelianus of Praeneste (12.61) tells us that the fleet of Dionysios of Syracuse was destroyed by a storm; the Thurians therefore created the cult of Boreas, in order to thank the god for their having avoided danger (this happened after 379 B.C.). They declared the god *polites*, and gave him a house, a parcel of land and citizenship.[10]

This passage is of much interest and reveals an im-

---

[6] In general, P. Guiraud, *La propriété foncière en Grèce*, Paris 1893, 425ff. In Athens, the *temene* were let for 10 years (Arist., *Ath.pol.* 47.4), but there is evidence of a 20-year lease (*IG* I[3] 84). See D. Behrend, *Attische Pachturkunden*, Munich 1970, 116, with references.

[7] J.H. Kent, 'The temple estates of Delos, Rheneia and Mykonos', *Hesperia* 17, 1948, 243–338; Cl. Vial, *Délos indépendante (314–167 av. J.-C.)*, Paris 1984, 317ff. The quotation is from Osborne (supra n. 2), 299, with reference to *IG* XI 2, 287 A, 199.

[8] Osborne (supra n. 2), 280.

[9] L. Gallo, 'Alimentazione e classi sociali: una nota su orzo e frumento in Grecia', *Opus* 2, 1983, 449–472. For Metapontum, see the well-known coins with ears of barley and the pollen and seeds analyzed by L. Costantini (from excavations at Pizzica-Pantanello): J. Carter *et alii*, *The territory of Metaponto 1981–1982*, Austin 1983; *idem*, 'Agricoltura e pastorizia in Magna Grecia (tra Bradano e Basento)', in G. Pugliese Carratelli (ed.), *Magna Grecia*, 2, Milan 1987, 173–212, with further references. For barley and food shortages, P. Garnsey, *Famine and food supply in the Graeco-Roman world*, Cambridge 1988. For another ground rent to be paid in barley, see *DGE* 419.

[10] Aelian. 12.61: Θουρίοις ἐπέπλει Διονύσιος, καὶ τριακοσίας ἦγεν ἐπ' αὐτοὺς ναῦς ὁπλιτῶν πεπληρωμένας· βορρᾶς δὲ ἀντιπνεύσας τὰ σκάφη συνέτριψε, καὶ τὴν δύναμιν αὐτοῦ τὴν ναυτικὴν ἠφάνισεν. Ἐκ δὲ τούτων οἱ Θούριοι τῷ βορρᾷ ἔθυσαν, καὶ ἐψηφίσαντο εἶναι τὸν ἄνεμον πολίτην καὶ οἰκίαν αὐῷ καὶ κλῆρον ἀπεκλήρωσαν, καὶ καθ' ἕκαστον ἔτος ἐπετέλουν αὐτῷ.

On land allotment D. Asheri, *Distribuzioni di terre nella antica Grecia*, *AAT* 1966, is fundamental.

portant aspect of religious and civic life. The god is here considered a real citizen; as such, he has the right to a house and a parcel of land. Probably this was (or became) usual in some public cults—those that were fully part of the life of the polis—even though this cannot be proved. But even gods had to live and needed maintenance. I assume that the same correlation between land and membership of the political community applied to both the citizens and the gods of the city. As there were 'civic cults', there were also some 'metic cults'. For example, in Athens the decree of 333 B.C. is well known (*IG* II^2 337 = Tod 189), in which merchants of Kition were allowed to have their temple of Aphrodite (as the Egyptians their temple of Isis). On the proposal of Lykourgos of Boutadai, they were granted a plot of land (ἔνκτησιν χωρίου) on which to erect the temple.

Zeus was, of course, an important 'citizen' in every Greek city, and so in Locri Epizephyrii too, where he had land and was involved in financial business. But the rich god had to lend money to the city in various circumstances. How important his loans were is revealed by the use of his money (fortifications, different forms of contributions and so on). The first editor of the Locrian archive estimated the whole sum as 44,000 talents (i.e. Sicilian talents; 1 talent = 1440 ounces). In spite of the many studies already published and others in progress, there are many open questions, such as chronology, the identification of the *basileus* and the interpretation of some words. The loans have been analyzed many times (recently by Migeotte), so that we can go over them quickly.[11]

The range of the income sources of this sanctuary was very wide: cultivated land near the borders, land beyond the River Halex, (raw) bricks, *pithoi*, iron collections and booty funds. Some scholars have thought that Zeus' treasure was really the state treasure, even though the polis system of accounting and that of the temple were different. However, in Locri, too, the city institutions decided about treasure and loans; the *hieromnamones* seem just to have executed orders, and loans were only partly repaid, as far as we know. However, city and temple were two different institutions, even if strictly related.

If we consider the agricultural aspects, we can see that, both here and in Heraclea, there is no clear evidence of a pastoral economy. The estate is normally leased. There is at least a *misthoma* to be paid in kind. Text no. 16 quotes 65 medimnoi of barley as the rent of borderland, in this case land increased by the river (added to lands already rented). The controversial expression *hiaran misthoma*, about which some adventurous speculations have been made, probably refers to payments for sacred land. The total amount of this is not in kind, but in money, precisely 20 talents. If the value given in tab. 16, i.e. 1 medimnos of barley = 1 talent, 33 stateres and 15 litrai, may be applied to the *hiaran misthoma*, the rent will be less than 20 medimnoi. Various explanations are possible: sacred land of small extent, low rent or peculiar features of the plot.[12] More expensive are the *kataboloi tas gas*, an essential part of Locrian finances. Cereals are often mentioned, such as *pyros* and *kritha* (tablets 4, 15, 16, 25, 28, 30 and 31; *pyros*: 5, 23, 30 and 31; *kritha*: 16, 23, 30 and 31), and then the broad beans (tab. 5) and *hygroi karpoi* (tablets 15, 23, 30 and 31).

It should once more be noted how important for the city was the food-supply problem: one text (tab. 5) mentions a decree of the Council and the popular assembly ordering a price reduction for wheat and broad beans.[13] Temple estates seem to have been included in responses to risk and crisis in the food supplies of the Greek cities.

Leases of sanctuary properties are in my opinion involved in an epigraphical text from Sicily dating from the 5th century B.C.[14] A man called Archon, his sister and his children owe to the god (that is to the temple) a certain sum; to be free, they must pay this sum and the

[11] De Franciscis (supra n. 1); *Le tavole di Locri* (Atti del colloquio Napoli 1977), Rome 1979 (papers by De Franciscis, M. Gigante, J. Blomqvist, M. Torelli, E. Pozzi Paolini, N.F. Parise, D. Musti and A. Landi); F. Costabile, 'Finanze pubbliche. L'amministrazione finanziaria templare', in Pugliese Carratelli (supra n. 9), 103–114; L. Migeotte, 'Sur les rapports financiers entre la sanctuaire et la cité de Locres' in *Comptes et inventaires dans la cité grecque* (Actes du colloque en l'honneur de J. Tréheux, Neuchâtel 1986), Neuchâtel & Genève 1988, 191–203. See also D.M. Lewis, 'Preliminary notes on the Locrian archive', *Klio* 52, 1970, 247–253; D. Musti, 'Città e santuario a Locri Epizefiri', *PP* 29, 1974, 5–21; C. Ampolo, 'Fra economia, religione e politica: tesori e offerte nei santuari greci', in *Anathema* (Atti del convegno Roma 1989) (= *Scienze dell'Antichità* 3–4, 1989–90 (pr. 1991), 271–279.

[12] So for Torelli (in *Le Tavole di Locri*, supra n. 11, for example, 106f.) and Musti (ibid, 222, more cautious), *hiaran misthoma* is a "canone fisso pagato dalle addette al *lupanar*". Against such interpretation previously, S. Pembroke in *Annales E.S.C.* 25, 1970, 1270.

[13] This is good evidence of price regulation by the city authorities, at least during times of crisis. The conclusions of Garnsey (supra n. 9), 272, on this specific point must be modified. See Ampolo, 'Il pane quotidiano delle città antiche fra economia e antropologia', *Opus* 5, 1986, 143–151. In Locri (tab. 15), some grain was sold every day.

[14] G. Manganaro, 'Tavolette di piombo inscritte della Sicilia greca', *ASNP*, s. 3, 7, 1977, 1329–1349; *SEG* 27, 1977, 657. I reproduce here the text as edited by Manganaro:

interest (*syn tōi tokōi*), not in kind (that is, food, *broton*) but in statues and furniture. I do not think that Archon was a supplier of the temple; it seems more probable, especially if we compare the text with the payments in barley mentioned in the *tabulae Heracleenses*, that this man was simply a tenant who normally paid in kind (or some guarantor) and did not pay what he had to. In such a case, the Attic law contained sanctions against all the family of the insolvent man: "Those who do not pay the rents of the sanctuaries of the goddess Athena, the other gods and the eponymous heroes shall suffer loss of civic rights, themselves, and their family, and their heirs, until such time as they pay" ([Dem.] 43.58). If I am right, we have here a sanctuary estate, rent paid in kind, and debt payment by *agalmata* and furniture for the temple. This is a good example of an economic circulation in which money is not the predominant feature.

Carmine Ampolo
Università degli Studi di Pisa
Dipartimento di Scienze Storiche
del Mondo Antico
Via Galvani 1
I-56100 PISA

[θε]ὸς Τύχα – Ἄϱχο̄ν ὀφε̄́λει τᾶι Θεο̃ι – ΤΤ-
[σὺ]ν το̄ι τόκο̄ι κεφάλο̄μα – ΙΔΔΔΔΗΤ⊥⊥⊥-
[το]ύτο̄ – οὐ βϱο̄τὸν, ἀλλὰ πϱιάσσθο̄ – ἀγάλμα-
4 [τα] καὶ σκέα πϱιάσσθο̄ τούτο̄ το̄ ἀϱγυϱίο̄ κα-
[ὶ] μ[ν]έας Ͱίκατι ὀφε̄́λει τᾶι Θεο̃ι – καὶ Ͱα ἀ-
δελφε⟨ὰ⟩ Ἄϱχο̄νος ὀφε̄́λει καὶ τὰ χϱε̄́μα-
τα τὰ αὐτ⟨ᾶ⟩ς καὶ τὰ Ἄϱχο̄νος τοῦτο τὸ
8 ἀϱγύϱιον καὶ τὰ παιδία ὀφε̄́λοντι
Κύπυϱα Σαισο̄ ἐλεύθεϱοι αὐταυτᾶ-
ν καί παιδί⟨α⟩· ὅτι τὸν χϱε̄́σταν Ἄϱ-
χο̄να, ἐπεί κ' ἀποδοῖ τοῦτο τὸ ἀϱ-
12 γύϱιον τ⟨α⟩νικαῦτα ἐλεύθεϱος
ἔσστο̄-

Robin Hägg

Sanctuaries and Workshops in the Bronze Age Aegean

In the framework of a symposium dealing with the economics of cult in the ancient Greek world, I fear that my contribution will go outside what may have been intended and expected, both chronologically and geographically. What I intend to do is to survey a number of cases in different regions in the Bronze Age, where we can see indications of a more of less close association between religious cult and the production of goods in workshops. Sometimes (1) this association can be clearly seen in the spatial juxtaposition of buildings for cult (or ceremony) with workshops, such as metallurgical installations. In other cases (2) a find complex of cultic character includes such unexpected items as unfinished objects, unworked raw material or scrap material, tools and implements; in yet other cases (3) an excavated workshop has yielded primarily objects for sacred use. However, actual workshop installations have been found in very few cases.[1] Such finds may indicate in different ways that the production of certain goods was associated with, or under the control of, a religious institution. I shall cite examples from Minoan Crete of the Protopalatial and Neopalatial periods, from mainland Greece of the Mycenaean period and from Cyprus of the Late Bronze Age.

In the cave of Arkalochori, in central Crete, S. Marinatos found a great number of metal objects, especially double axes, swords and daggers; some of the swords of thin foil were obviously made as votives.[2] There was a total of at least 100 double axes, of which 26 were of gold and 7 of silver. Some of the axes were inscribed in Linear A,[3] which would indicate that the activity performed here was somehow connected with the upper level of society. Since Marinatos noted that a number of the weapons appeared to be unfinished and that the votives included objects interpreted as ingots (so-called bun ingots), he suggested that the cave might have been a smithy. However, neither tools nor installations for the working of metal were found; thus the cave itself, at least as far as excavated, could not have functioned as a working area. The dedication of unfinished objects and of ingots may, however, point to some kind of close relationship between the cult performed in the cave and a metal workshop perhaps, but not necessarily, situated close by in the area. This hypothesis may be supported by the parallels from Bronze Age Cyprus and Iron Age Greece to be discussed below.

Quite different is the situation in Quartier Mu at Malia, a Protopalatial, administrative, building complex, in which the remains of three separate workshops for a highly specialized production were found.[4] The excavator, J.-C. Poursat, has suggested that these workshops, for sealstones, for pottery decorated with moulded appliqués and for cast metal, respectively, were working to supply the needs of the religious cult. In this case, unfortunately, the actual sanctuaries that were served by the workshops have not been found; they may have been situated on the upper floor somewhere in the same complex,[5] in the town or, perhaps, in the contemporary palace.[6]

---

[1] A useful discussion of the criteria for identifying workshops in a Bronze Age culture is to be found in I. Tournavitou, 'Towards an identification of a workshop space', in *Problems in Greek prehistory. Papers presented at the Centenary Conference of the British School at Athens, Manchester, April 1986*, Bristol 1988, 447–467.

[2] J. Hazzidakis, 'An Early Minoan sacred cave at Arkalokhori', *BSA* 19, 1912–13, 35–47; S. Marinatos, *Prakt* 1935, 212–220; cf. *idem*, 'Zur Frage der Grotte von Arkalochori', *Kadmos* 1, 1962, 87–94.

[3] A. Furumark, 'Linear A and Minoan religion', *OpAth* 17, 1988, 51–90, esp. 58, with refs.

[4] J.-C. Poursat, 'Ateliers et sanctuaires à Malia: Nouvelles données sur l'organisation sociale à l'époque des premiers palais', in *Minoan society. Proceedings of the Cambridge colloquium 1981*, Bristol 1983, 277–281; *BCH* 102, 1978, 831–834; B. Détournay, J.-C. Poursat & F. Vandenabeele, *Fouilles exécutées à Mallia: Le Quartier Mu* II (ÉtCrét, 26), Paris 1980, 116–132; *BCH* 106, 1982, 621; 107, 1983, 821.

[5] As indicated by the finds from the area adjacent to the metal workshop, among them snake tubes and fragments of offering tables fallen from above (cf. *BCH* 107, 1983, 821).

[6] Poursat (supra n. 4), 280, thinks that in the Protopalatial period there was a religious administration separate from the royal administration of the palace.

In the palace of Zakros, it is generally recognized that the west wing had a predominantly religious function;[7] however, in addition to the ceremonial rooms and the storage areas, especially the so-called 'treasury' containing bins that were found filled with stone chalices and other valuable objects, there is clear evidence also of the existence of workshops. Next to the treasury of the shrine, Platon found a workshop equipped with a bench for the working of steatites and polychrome stalactites.[8] On the upper floor, there had been storage areas for valuable, imported, raw materials, such as elephant tusks and bronze ingots of the ox-hide type; on that storey, there were also looms and workshops for other kinds of production.[9]

These three examples from Minoan Crete are likely to be representative of a phenomenon of wide occurrence: workshops for the production of precious objects, especially for sacred use. What we cannot see is whether such workshops had an additional, 'surplus', production also for 'secular' needs or whether they were producing exclusively for the sanctuaries.

On the Greek mainland, the so-called Cult Centre of Mycenae offers the best example of the association of cult with workshop production. This complex, dated in the LH IIIB period (basically the 13th century B.C.), was thought by G.E. Mylonas to be the main cult area of Mycenae.[10] Among the finds were tools, raw materials and partly worked pieces of valuable raw material, such as ivory. These types of finds were concentrated in three areas:[11] the basements of the so-called Megaron, the open area north of the Room with the Fresco and the 'Shrine' (room 32). I quote E.B. French:[12]

> It should be pointed out that the lighting in both the basements and the 'Shrine' seems quite inadequate for indoor workshops. It could be that both these areas dispensed materials which were then worked in the open area to the North and possibly on other parts of the site as well. The artisan would return both the finished object and the scrap material to store when he finished. The presence of the small clay objects usually known as gaming counters could be connected with such a scheme as counters or tallies.

This seems to be a system in which the sanctuary, as owner of valuable materials, handed them out to artisans, who worked the pieces and delivered the finished objects back to the sanctuary. Most of the indoor rooms with such finds are, however, rather storage rooms than actual workshops. Because of the high value of the raw materials used, the objects manufactured must usually have been of small size.

A confirmation of the association of Mycenaean sanctuaries with production is yielded by the Linear B tablets from Thebes, Pylos and Knossos, as analyzed, for example by S. Hiller.[13] The word *wo-ko*, one of the designations for 'sanctuary' in the language of the tablets, is identical with the later Greek word *oikos*, 'house'. There are several examples of a deity, male or female, designated as the 'owner' of an *oikos*. However, according to Hiller, the main function of an *oikos* does not belong to the cultic sphere, but to the economic: it has a work force (often listed on the tablets) and is engaged in the production of some kind of commodities (textiles and corselets in the known instances). Hiller draws a parallel to the Oriental system of so-called 'temple economy', while stressing that the *oikos* system constituted only *one* sector of the Mycenaean economy, and perhaps quite a restricted one.[14]

In Cyprus of the Late Bronze Age, we find several cases of a close association between religious cult and production, in this case, especially metal-working. One of the clearest examples is offered by the sanctuaries at the northern edge of the inhabited area of Kition, excavated by V. Karageorghis.[15] In the period between the end of the 13th and the beginning of the 12th centuries B.C. (levels II–III), this building complex (plan in *Fig. 1*)[16] comprised workshops and storage areas associated with copper production between Temple 1 to the south, the city wall to the north and 'Temenos A' to the east. Among the finds were quantities of copper slag, thick layers of ashes, pits containing slag, fragments of

---

[7] N. Platon, *Zakros: The discovery of a lost palace of ancient Crete*, New York 1971; J.W. Graham, *The palaces of Crete*, rev. ed., Princeton, N.J. 1987, 251.

[8] S. Chrysoulaki & L. Platon, 'Relations between the town and palace of Zakros', in *The function of the Minoan palaces. Proceedings of the Fourth International Symposium at the Swedish Institute in Athens 1984* (ActaAth-4°, 35), Stockholm 1987, 77–84, esp. 81.

[9] N. Platon, *Prakt* 1963, 174; cf. L. Platon (supra n. 8), 81.

[10] G.E. Mylonas, *The cult center of Mycenae* (Pragmateiai tes Akademias Athenon, 33), Athens 1972 (text in Greek and English); W.D. Taylour, 'New light on Mycenaean religion', *Antiquity* 44, 1970, 270–280.

[11] E.B. French, 'Cult places at Mycenae', in *Sanctuaries and cults in the Aegean Bronze Age. Proceedings of the First International Symposium at the Swedish Institute in Athens 1980* (ActaAth-4°, 28), Stockholm 1981, 41–48, esp. 45.

[12] French (supra n. 11), 45.

[13] S. Hiller, 'Mykenische Heiligtümer: Das Zeugnis der Linear B-Texte', in *Sanctuaries and cults* (supra n. 11), 95–125, esp. 99–103.

[14] Hiller (supra n. 13), 103.

[15] V. Karageorghis, *Kition. Mycenaean and Phoenician discoveries in Cyprus*, London 1976; *idem*, *Excavations at Kition*, V: *The Pre-Phoenician levels*, Nicosia 1985.

[16] After Karageorghis 1976 (supra n. 15), fig. 11.

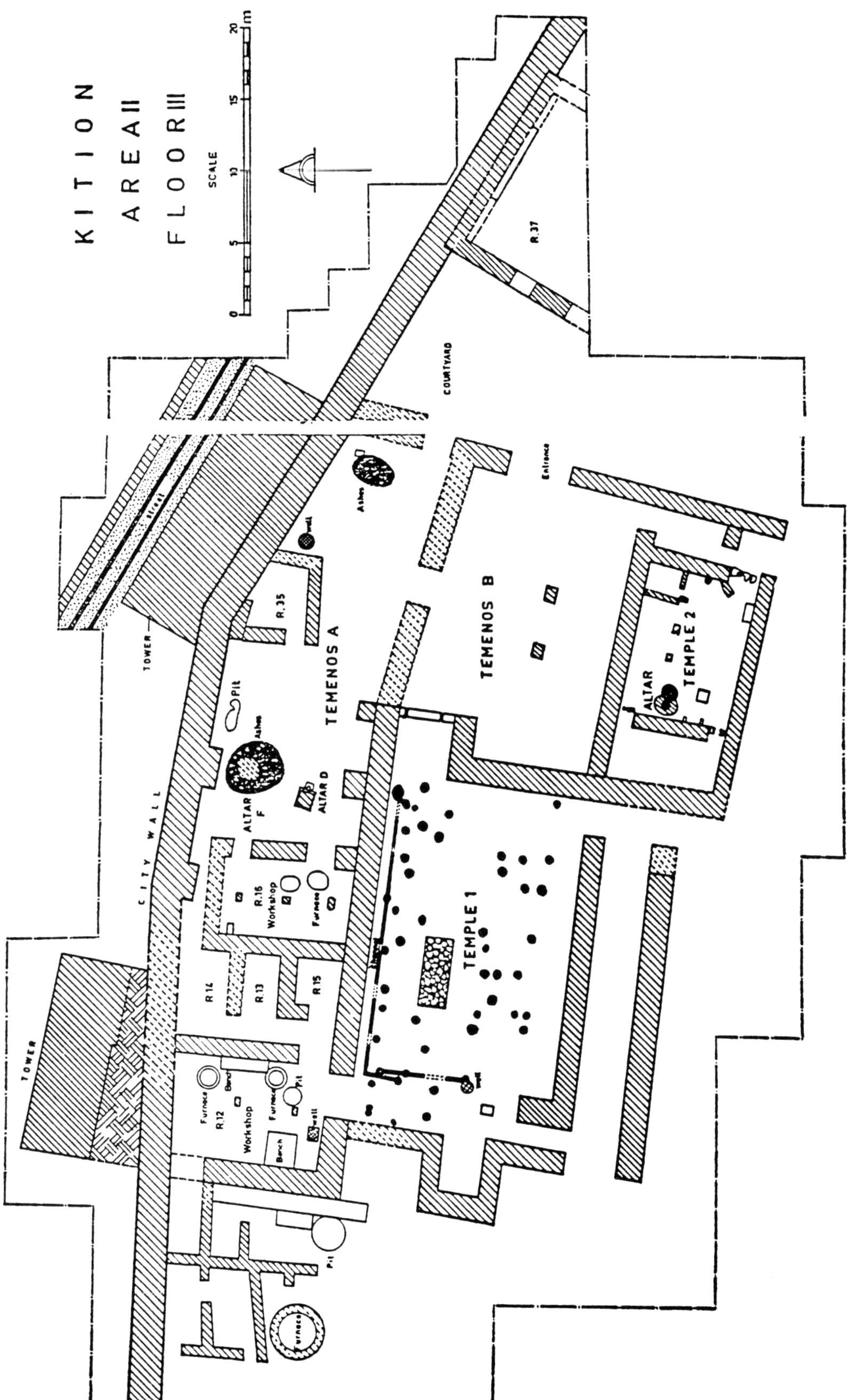

Fig. 1. Kition, Area II: Sanctuaries and workshops.

tuyères and crucibles and even furnaces. Other equipment connected with the metallurgical activity consisted of stone querns and pounders probably used to crush the minerals.[17] Since loomweights, spindle whorls and other tools were found in adjacent storerooms, it looks as if a variety of other crafts were also performed here in the immediate proximity of the temple.

Similar observations have been made at other sites in Cyprus, where metallurgical installations and religious structures have been found in close association: at Enkomi and Athienou,[18] and perhaps Kalopsidha,[19] to mention the clearest cases. Some finds give further evidence of a symbolical kind for what may be seen as a divine protection of the copper production: miniature bronze ingots occurring as votives and the famous bronze statuettes of the Ingot God and the Horned God, both from Enkomi. On the basis of all these finds, A.B. Knapp[20] has proposed a historical explanation, in which religious ideology is seen as internal to the economy and to the social relations of production. He suggests that newly-emerged elites in Cyprus manipulated and secured their domination over the production and distribution of copper by adopting the religious symbolism of the Ingot God etc.[21]

Whether we consider Knapp's hypothesis as basically correct, or accept it only partially, there is no doubt in my mind that the situation in Cyprus was radically different from what we can see in the Aegean. While the metallurgical production associated with religion in Cyprus was of great economic importance and must be thought to have operated primarily to supply "secular" needs, the sacred workshops in the Minoan and Mycenaean cultures appear to have had as their main, although perhaps not exclusive, aim to produce equipment of precious materials for sacred use. This is the situation both at Malia in the Protopalatial period and at Zakros in the Neopalatial period and probably—on an even more modest scale—at Mycenae in the Late Bronze Age. To me, it looks as if Hiller may have gone a little too far with his hypothesis of a temple economy of an Oriental type in Mycenaean Greece and that we should take heed of his own *caveat*,[22] that the production associated with the religious institutions was in reality only a minor sector of the Mycenaean economy.

I have given a few glimpses of the relationship between religious cult and the production of goods in a Bronze Age world, where the scarcity, or often complete absence, of written sources leaves us very much in the dark as to what was really going on. Even so, in spite of our incomplete understanding of the processes, these phenomena belong undoubtedly to the broad topic of 'the economics of cult in the Greek world'.

Robin Hägg
Swedish Institute at Athens
Mitseon 9
GR-117 42 ATHENS

[17] Karageorghis 1976 (supra n. 15), 72–74.
[18] A.B. Knapp, *Copper production and divine protection: Archaeology, ideology and social complexity on Bronze Age Cyprus* (SIMA-PB, 42), Göteborg 1986, with previous bibliography.
[19] P. Åström, 'Votive deposits in the Late Cypriote Bronze Age', in *Gifts to the gods. Proceedings of the Uppsala symposium 1985* (Boreas, 15), Uppsala 1987, 177–179.
[20] Knapp (supra n. 18).
[21] Knapp (supra n. 18), esp. Chapter 4.
[22] Hiller (supra n. 13), 103.

Christina Risberg

Metal-Working in Greek Sanctuaries

The working of metal is attested at various sanctuary sites in Greece, such as the sanctuary of Poseidon at Isthmia, where bronze and possibly also iron were worked.[1] W. Rostoker and E. Gebhard think that there is evidence of a bronze foundry working in the vicinity of the temple during the 5th and early 4th centuries B.C. The material found includes debris from bronze-casting and some metal scrap.[2] At Nemea a bronze foundry, dated to the second half of the 5th century, is assumed to have been at work. A small furnace and material indicating bronze-working have been found to the south of the temple.[3]

At Olympia, metal production is widely attested from the Late Geometric period onwards.[4] There are also indications of metal-working, mainly in bronze from Delphi,[5] Delos,[6] the Heraion on Samos,[7] Aigina,[8] Bassae,[9] and Aetos on Ithaka.[10] It seems likely therefore that the working of metal was one of the various activities taking place in Greek sanctuaries.[11]

My aim will be to show that metal production in sanctuaries existed as early as late Geometric times and to raise the issue of how this production was organised: Who was doing the producing? What was being produced? Where did the production take place? For whom were the products intended?

Although more often than not the remains of metal working are incomplete and sometimes difficult to interpret, the evidence can nevertheless, if used cautiously, give us an insight into the organisation and economy of Greek sanctuaries. Before presenting my argument, I would like to point out that at this early stage of my work I have far more questions than answers and the results must remain tentative.[12]

The following abbreviations have been used:

Heilmeyer 1969 = W.-D. Heilmeyer, 'Giessereibetriebe in Olympia', *JdI* 84, 1969, 1–28.

The Greek renaissance = *The Greek renaissance of the eighth century B.C.: Tradition and innovation*, ed. R. Hägg (Acta Ath-4°, 30), Stockholm 1983.

As we know, although metal production flourished at *Olympia* (*Fig. 1*), in archaic and later times, to date no remains of actual workshops have been found from the

[1] W. Rostoker & E.R. Gebhard, 'The sanctuary of Poseidon at Isthmia: Techniques of metal manufacture', *Hesperia* 49, 1980, 347–363.

[2] Rostoker & Gebhard (supra n. 1), 350–352, 361.

[3] S.G. Miller, 'Excavations at Nemea, 1976', *Hesperia* 46, 1977, 1–26, esp. 19f.

[4] Heilmeyer 1969; A. Mallwitz & W. Schiering, *Die Werkstatt des Phidias* (OlForsch, 5), Berlin 1964, 42–46, esp. 45; W.-D. Heilmeyer, G. Zimmer & G. Schneider, 'Die Bronzegiesserei unter der Werkstatt des Phidias in Olympia', *AA* 1987, 239–299.

[5] P. Perdrizet, *FdD* V. *Monuments figurés. Petits bronzes, terres cuites, antiquités diverses*, Paris 1908, 97, fig. 339; C. Rolley, *FdD* V:3. *Les trépieds à cuve clouée*, Paris 1977, 82f., 86.

[6] W. Deonna, 'Notes d'archéologie délienne', *BCH* 62, 1938, 209–235, esp. 209f.; S.H. Langdon, *Art, religion and society in the Greek geometric period: Bronze anthropomorphic votive figurines*, Diss., Indiana University 1984, 318, n. 153; C. Rolley, in *Études déliennes* (*BCH* suppl. 1), Paris 1973, 491–524.

[7] U. Jantzen, *Griechische Greifenkessel*, Berlin 1955, 57–60; G. Kopcke, 'Heraion von Samos: Die Kampagnen 1961/65 im Südtemenos', *AM* 83, 1968, 250–314; U. Gehrig, 'Frühe griechische Bronzegusstechniken', *AA* 1979, 547–558.

[8] P. Wolters, 'Forschungen auf Ägina', *AA* 1925, 2–11; *idem*, *Gnomon* 1925, 46–49.

[9] N. Yalouris, 'Δοκιμαστικὴ ἀνασκαφὴ εἰς τὸν Ναὸν τοῦ 'Επικουρίου 'Απόλλωνος Βασσῶν, *Prakt* 1959, 155–159; *idem*, *Ergon* 1959, 106–109; *idem*, 'Problems relating to the temple of Apollo Epikourios at Bassai', in *Greece and Italy in the Classical World, Acta of the XI International Congress of Classical Archaeology*, J.N. Coldstream & M.A.R. Colledge, eds., London 1979, 89–104, esp. 91.

[10] S. Benton, 'Further excavations at Aetos', *BSA* 48,1953, 253–361, esp. 343 and 352.

[11] The production of pottery for use in the sanctuary is also often assumed. A. Foley, *The Argolid 800–600 B.C.* (SIMA, 80), Göteborg 1988, for example 72, 73 and 74; U. Kron, 'Kultmahle im Heraion von Samos archaischer Zeit. Versuch einer Rekonstruktion' in *Early Greek cult practice*, R. Hägg, N. Marinatos & G. Nordquist, eds. (ActaAth-4°, 38), Stockholm 1988, 135–147.

[12] I hope to treat these questions more fully in my forthcoming dissertation.

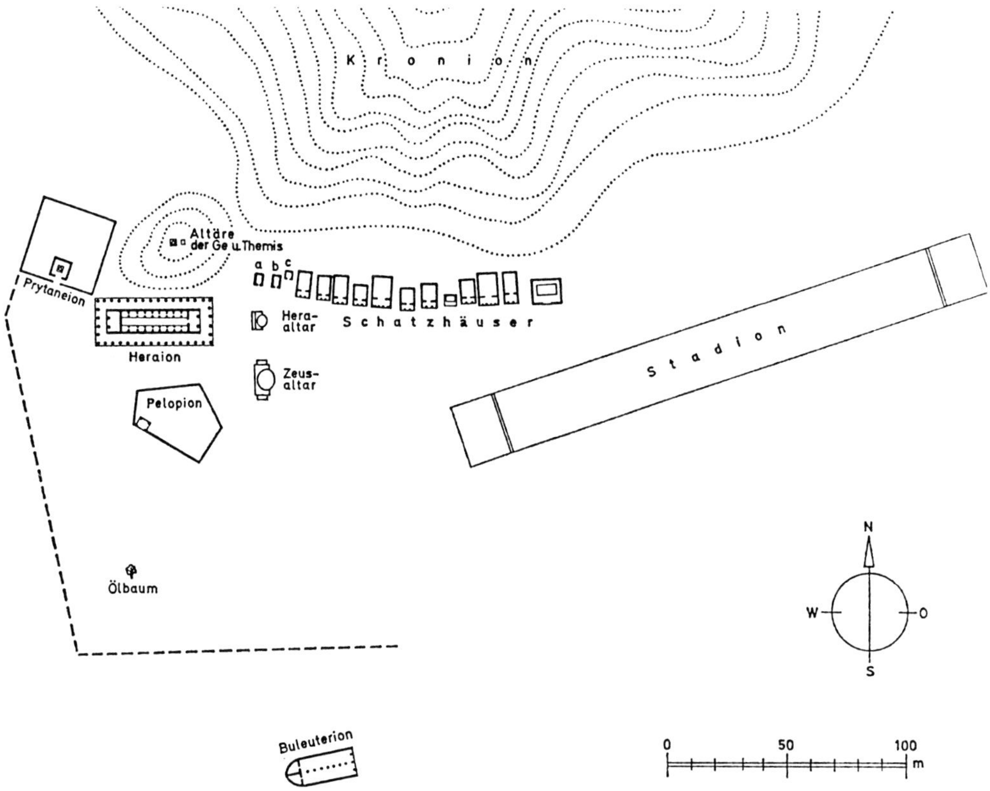

Fig. 1. The sanctuary area of Olympia during the 6th and early 5th century B.C. After H.-V. Herrmann, *Olympia. Heiligtum und Wettkampfstätte*, München 1972, fig. 74.

Geometric period.[13] Despite this, the examples of misshapen castings, together with some other remains of bronze-casting, have led several scholars to assume a local production of Geometric bronzes. In his publication of the bronzes and small finds from Olympia, A. Furtwängler published a number of misshapen bronze figurines, and their existence convinced him that many of the bronze votives were actually manufactured at Olympia.[14]

The unsuccessful castings of horses, birds and women have been found in the same layers as whole figurines.[15] This fact led K.A. Neugebauer to conclude that the unsuccessfully cast votives had been given by people of limited means who could not afford the perfect ones.[16] But this opinion has been disputed by, for example, Heilmeyer as not being tenable.[17]

W.-D. Heilmeyer, the scholar mainly responsible for drawing attention to this material, mentions other fragments of bronze votives and unsuccessful castings of miniature tripod vessels. He also maintains that bronze-working took place at Olympia and that at least the miniature bronzes, and perhaps also the larger tripod vessels, were manufactured there.[18]

Most of the material mentioned has been found in the northern part of the sanctuary, i.e. in the Altis. This has led Heilmeyer to assume that the place of production was situated in this area as well, on or below the terrace of the treasuries.[19] There are also indications of metal-working in the area of the stadium from the Late Geometric period.[20]

[13] Heilmeyer 1969, 1; *idem*, *Frühe olympische Bronzefiguren. Die Tiervotive* (OlForsch, 12), Berlin 1979, 52.

[14] A. Furtwängler, *Die Bronzen und die übrigen kleineren Funde von Olympia* (*Olympia* IV), Berlin 1890, 29 and 37.

[15] Heilmeyer 1979 (supra n. 13), 35.

[16] K.A. Neugebauer, *Staatliche Museen zu Berlin. Katalog der Statuarischen Bronzen im Antiquarium*, I. *Die minoischen und archaisch griechischen Bronzen*, Berlin & Leipzig 1931, 51f., nos. 132–134.

[17] Heilmeyer 1969, 1.

[18] Heilmeyer 1969, 2–5; Heilmeyer *et al.* (supra n. 4), 266–268; M. Maas, 'Die geometrische Dreifüsse von Olympia', *AntK* 24, 1981, 6–20, esp. 18.

[19] Heilmeyer 1969, 4f., 21; *idem* (supra n. 13), 35.

[20] H. Born & A. Moustaka, 'Eine geometrische Bronzestatuette im originalen Gussmantel aus Olympia', *AM* 97, 1982, 17–23.

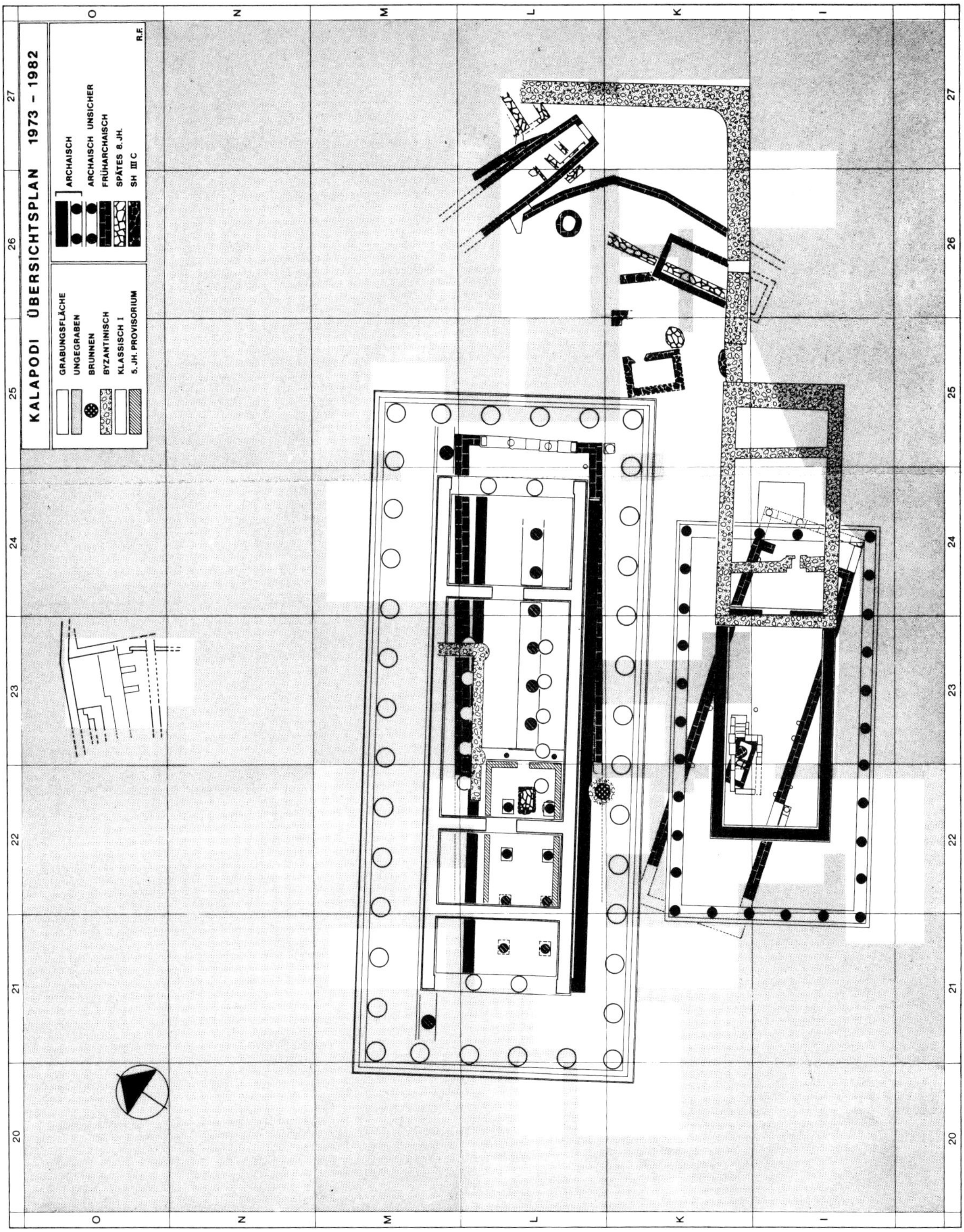

Fig 2. The sanctuary at Kalapodi. After R.C.S. Felsch, *AA* 1987, fig. 3.

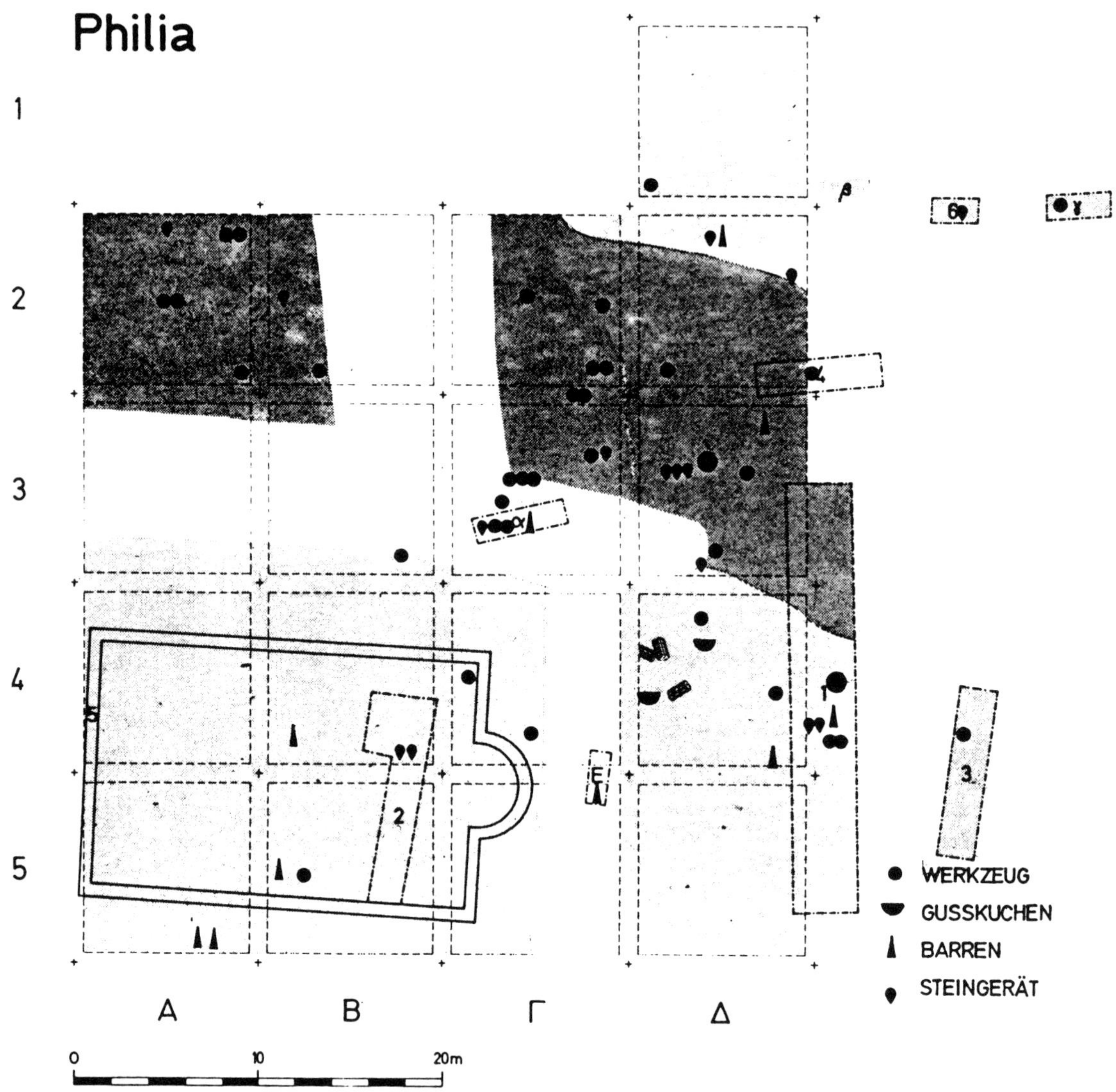

Fig. 3. Distribution of finds related to metal-working at the sanctuary of Athena Itonia at Philia. After K. Kilian, in *The Greek renaissance*, fig. 2.

At the sanctuary of Artemis and Apollo at *Kalapodi* (*Fig. 2*), the evidence of metal-working seems to indicate that bronze and iron artefacts were manufactured at least from the later half of the 8th century.[21] On a closer inspection, the evidence of metal-working in the Late Geometric period amounts to one unsuccessfully cast male figurine.[22]

The preliminary publications of the excavations at Kalapodi mention both constructions and finds of debris from bronze casting which may be evidence of Late Geometric metal-working at this sanctuary.[23] Unfortunately, these finds are not referred to again in later publications of the excavations. Whether this was due to a reinterpretation of the evidence or a mere omission of this material is unknown to me.

At *Philia* in Thessaly (*Figs. 3–4*), in the sanctuary of Athena Itonia, there have also been found remains which

[21] R.C.S. Felsch, 'Zur chronologie und zum Stil geometrischer Bronzen aus Kalapodi', in *The Greek renaissance*, 123–129.

[22] Felsch (supra n. 21), 123.

[23] H.W. Catling, *AR* 1980–81, 24; G. Touchais, 'Chronique des fouilles en 1979', *BCH* 104, 1980, 625.

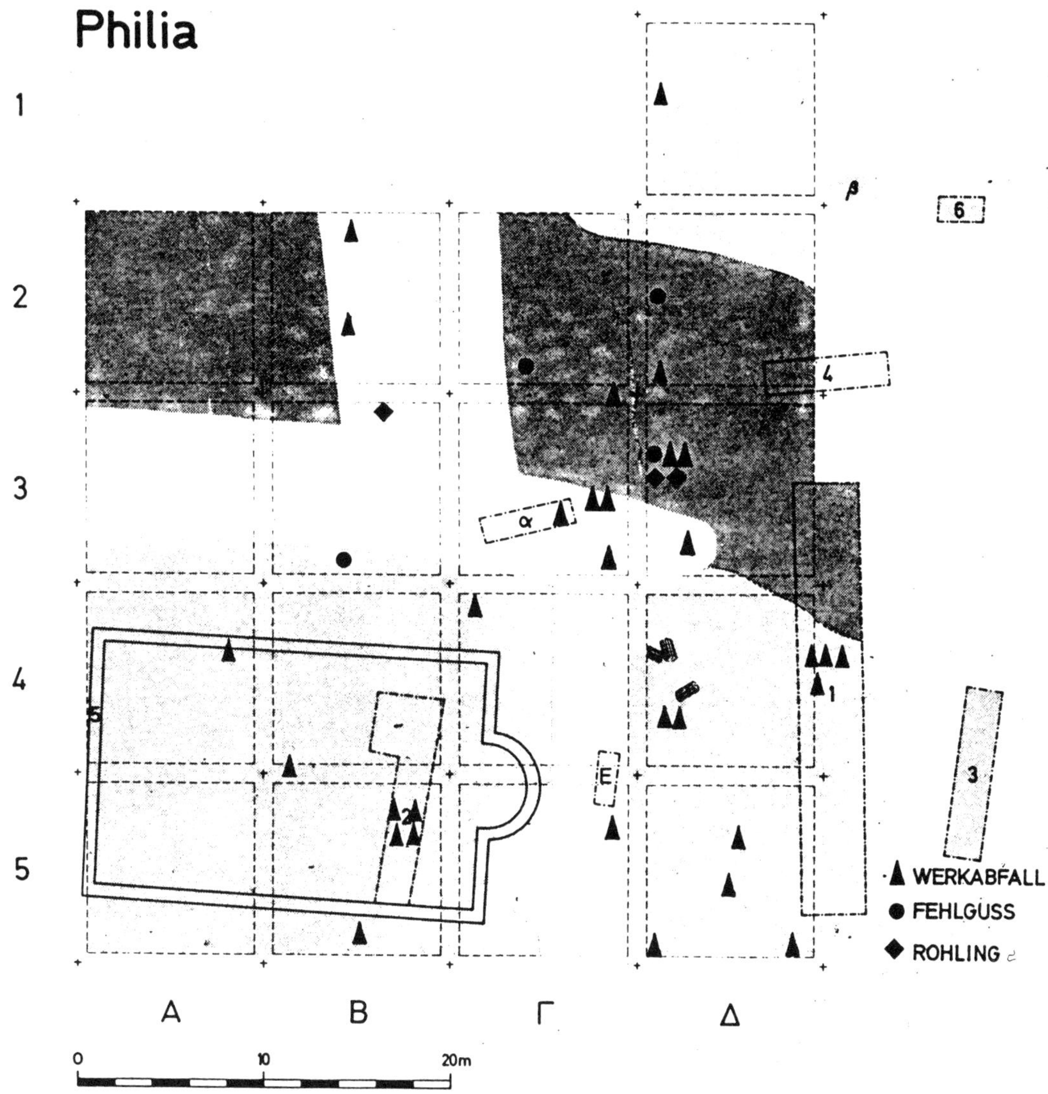

Fig. 4. Distribution of finds related to metal-working at the sanctuary of Athena Itonia at Philia. After K. Kilian, in *The Greek renaissance*, fig. 3.

have been interpreted by K. Kilian as indications of both bronze- and iron-working in the vicinity of the sanctuary.[24] The remains consist of misshapen castings, casting debris, partly finished artifacts and also some raw material. Kilian also draws attention to some stone implements and tools found at the site which could be indicators of metal production. According to Kilian, these remains point to a local fabrication of votives, weapons and also things for everyday use, such as dress-pins and knives.[25]

A building found to the east of the temple of Apollo at *Eretria* (*Fig. 5*), has been tentatively interpreted by the excavators as a bronze-smith's workshop.[26] The building, a mud-brick construction on a stone socle, has been dated to the second half of the 8th century. Inside the building was a pit, measuring 0.35 m in diameter and

[24] K. Kilian, 'Weihungen aus Eisen und Eisenverarbeitung im Heiligtum zu Philia (Thessalien)', in *The Greek renaissance*, 131–146.

[25] Kilian (supra n. 24), 145.

[26] A. Altherr-Charon, 'Chantier du temple d'Apollon', in C. Krause, 'Eretria. Grabungen 1979–80', *AntK* 24, 1981, 70–87,

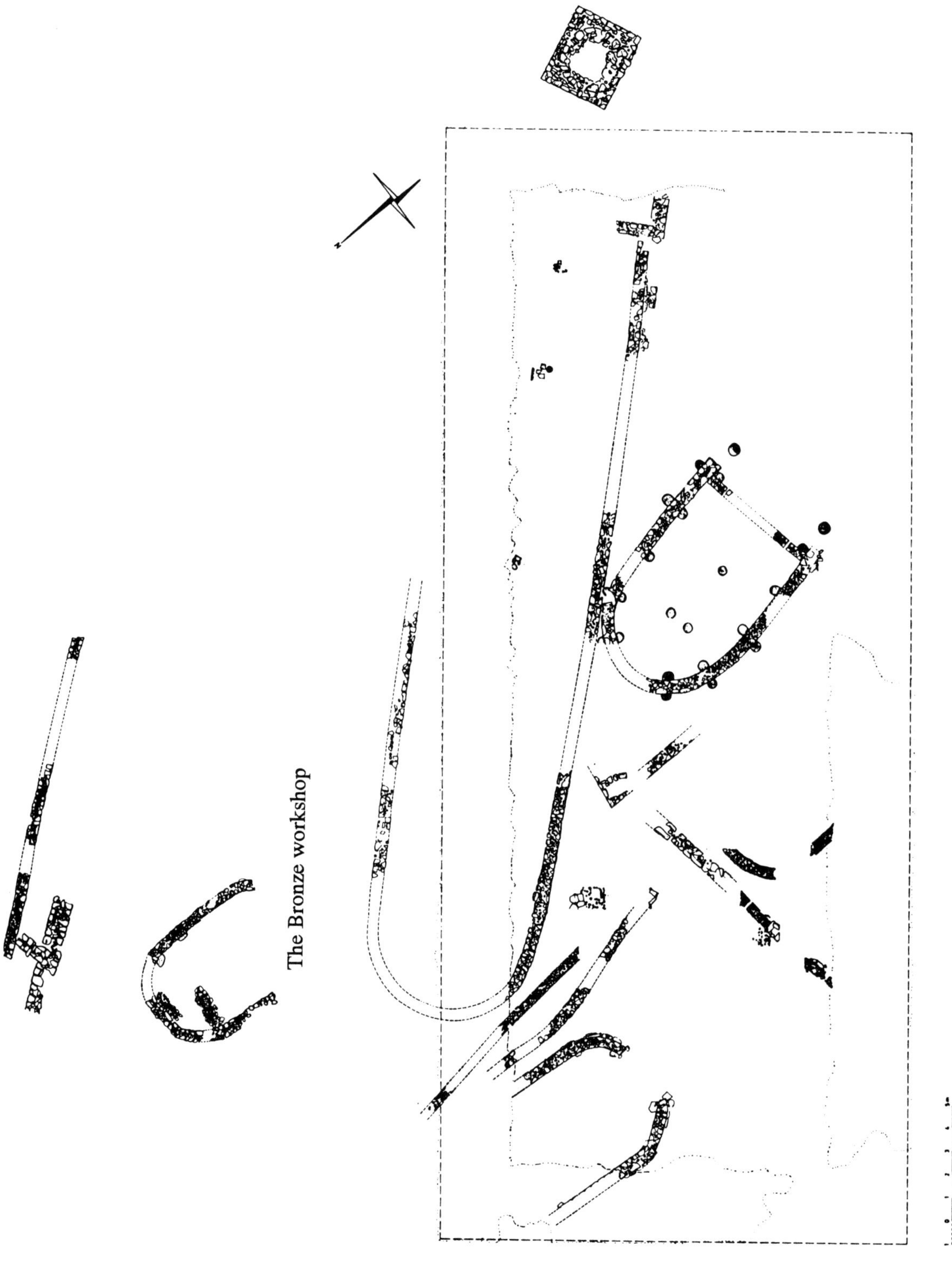

Fig. 5. The sanctuary of Apollon at Eretria. After *BCH* 106, 1982, fig. 122.

0.25 m in depth. The excavators believed this to be a casting pit and found in it ashes, burnt clay, slag and shapeless pieces of bronze. At the rear end of the building were also found stone pavements which could have been used as foundations for a workbench or may have served as a workplace.[27] The interpretation of this building as a workshop must for the time being remain tentative and await further publication.

This is perhaps also the place to mention the goldsmith's hoard found some 150–200 m to the north of the sanctuary of Apollo.[28] The hoard, weighing *c*. 510 g, had been placed in a skyphos with a lid. It was composed of sheet metal, gold ingots, gold wire and gold foil, together with pieces of electrum and shapeless pieces of jewellery. The skyphos was found underneath the foundation wall of an absidal house dated to *c*. 700 B.C., which may or may not have been the workshop of the unfortunate goldsmith who never returned to retrieve his material.

While the evidence of metal-working at sanctuaries in the Late Geometric period may not seem at all copious, it is nonetheless present in the archaeological material in the form of debris from the production of castings, tools and implements used in the manufacture of weapons and other metal products. We also have the unsuccessful cast figurines, which are perhaps the most ubiquitous indicators of metal production. When found in isolation, however, they must be used with caution as evidence of metal-working.[29]

The workshops at sanctuaries, as indeed workshops almost anywhere during this period, have left very few traces in the archaeological record. This is probably due to their being of a not very stable nature, constructed, as they were, only for temporary use. Another possible reason is the, in many cases, extensive, rebuilding activities that took place in most Greek sanctuaries in later periods. The find of a workshop at Eretria is a rare instance for almost any period and especially so for the Late Geometric period.[30]

Now to the question as to who were the craftsmen, who worked the metal at the sanctuaries and what relation, if any, they had to the sanctuary. The idea of independent, itinerant craftsmen setting up shops temporarily at the various sanctuaries seems to be the explanation favoured by most scholars who have discussed this question.[31] In the case of Olympia, Heilmeyer is inclined to ascribe the production of votives to itinerant craftsmen coming to the sanctuary for the duration of a festival and afterwards returning to their homes—whether this was the area around Olympia or further afield, such as the Argolid or in Lakonia.[32]

A slightly different picture must be assumed for Eretria and some other sanctuaries, since these were connected with settlements.[33]

A number of questions remain as to who supplied the metal to be worked—the craftsman himself or the presumptive customer? The latter is a system which is known from other cultures.[34] Perhaps there was even some sort of central agency handing out metal, as may have been the case in Mycenaean times?[35] How was the work paid for in a non-monetary economy? In an oikos type of economy, such as is reflected in the Homeric poems, almost all production, and many of the craftsmen also, were part of an integrated economic system and no payment was required.[36] Is this the type of economy that we can expect to have functioned in the Late Geometric period? C.G. Starr does not think that the craftsmen

---

esp. 81f.; *eadem* & S. Amstad, 'Chantier du temple d'Apollon', in C. Krause, 'Eretria. Ausgrabungen 1981', *AntK* 25, 1982, 150–160, esp. 154–158; A. Mazarakis Ainian, 'Geometric Eretria', *AntK* 30, 1987, 3–24, esp. 11f.

27 Altherr-Charon & Amstad (supra n. 26), 154–156.

28 P.G. Themelis, 'An 8th century goldsmith's workshop at Eretria', in *The Greek renaissance*, 157–165; *idem*, ''Εργαστήριο χρυσοχοΐας τοῦ 8ου αἰ. π.Χ. στὴν 'Ερέτρια', *AAA* 14, 1981, 185–208; Mazarakis Ainian (supra n. 26), 6–9.

29 Heilmeyer 1969, 4.

30 The best-preserved and most complete workshop from this period is the one at Pithekoussai: G. Buchner, *AR* 1970–71, 63–67; J. Klein, 'A Greek metalworking quarter. Eight century excavation on Ischia', *Expedition* 14, 1971, 34–39; D. Ridgway, *L'Alba della Magna Grecia*, Milano 1984, esp. 105–109.

31 Heilmeyer 1969, 2f., 21; *idem* 1979 (supra n. 13), 52; on itinerant craftsmen, see M.J. Rowlands, 'The archaeological interpretation of prehistoric metalworking', *WorldA* 3, 1971, 210–224, esp. 214.

32 Heilmeyer 1979 (supra n. 13), 35.

33 Yalouris 1979 (supra n. 9), 90.

34 On the question of raw material supplied by the customer, see Rowlands (supra n. 31), 211.

35 S. Hiller, 'Allgemeine Bemerkungen zur JN-Serie', *SMEA* 55, 1972, 51–72; A. Leukart, 'Autour de ka-ko na-wi-jo: quelques critères', and S. Hiller, 'Ka-ko na wi-jo. Notes on interdependence of temple and bronze in the Aegean Bronze Age', in *Colloquium Mycenaeum, Actes du sixième colloque international sur les textes mycéniens et égéens tenu à Chaumont sur Neuchâtel du 7 au 13 septembre 1975*, E. Risch & H. Mühlestein, eds., Neuchâtel & Genève 1979, 183–187; 189–195 respectively. For the organisation of metal production and its relation to sanctuaries in Bronze Age Cyprus, cf. A.B. Knapp, *Copper production and divine protection. Archaeology, ideology and social complexity in Bronze Age Cyprus* (SIMA-PB, 42), Gothenburg 1986.

36 F. Eckstein, *Handwerk*, 1. *Die Aussagen der frühgriechischen Epos* (= *ArchHom*, Kap. L 1), 1974, 29–38; M.M. Austin & P. Vidal-Naquet, *Economic and social history of ancient Greece: An introduction*, London 1977, 141–143.

mentioned in the works of Homer and Hesiod were anything but independent workers.[37] Did the sanctuaries function as markets for goods other than those used in the sanctuary? Oswyn Murray seems to think so, but how is this to be checked?[38]

As predicted I have only a lot of questions to offer as my contribution to this symposium. I can only hope that some of them are the right questions and that answers may someday be found to some of them.

Christina Risberg
Dept. of Classical Archaeology and Ancient History
Gustavianum
S-753 10 Uppsala

[37] C.G. Starr, *The economic and social growth of early Greece 800–500 B.C.*, New York 1977, 81.

[38] O. Murray in the discussion following the paper by K. Kilian (supra n. 24), 147.

Discussion

Ingrid STRÖM: It would be very rewarding if you go on to study the metal-producing sanctuaries in all their aspects.

CR: I would like to point out that the four sanctuaries which I have studied from the late Geometric period, where metal production took place, are in fact sanctuaries to Apollo, in one case to Apollo and Artemis, and at Olympia we have of course the sanctuary of Hera. This, I think, is in agreement with Ingrid Ström's studies.

Carmine AMPOLO: Il semble qu'il y ait des sanctuaires à cette époque, par exemple celui de Zeus à Locres, qui obtiennent des loyers provenant du fer.

CR: One problem when working with this question is that the remains are difficult to find, firstly for the archaeologist in the field and, secondly, also for the researcher, since a lot of material is kept in store-rooms and never published. I hope that with this communication I can at least bring attention to this kind of material.

Ingrid Strøm

Obeloi of Pre- or Proto-Monetary Value in the Greek Sanctuaries

It seems to be generally acknowledged that the Greek coinage, based on drachmai and obeloi, each drachme, a handful, worth six obeloi, had its origin in a monetary-value system based on iron spits, collected in sixes.[1]

According to ancient literary sources, King Pheidon of Argos, whose reign is placed in the 8th or 7th century B.C., established standard measures in the Peloponnese, introducing the Greek silver coinage of Aeginetan standard, and dedicating iron spits to the Argive Heraion as examples of the now outdated currency.[2] As everybody knows, a large collection of iron spits was found during the American excavations of the Argive Heraion in the late 19th century.[3]

Today, the Western Anatolian electrum coins of Lydian standard, which—as already inferred by Herodotus—are considered the earliest coins, are usually dated to the second half of the 7th century B.C., followed some time after 600 B.C. by the Aeginetan silver coins.[4]

Leaving aside all speculations about King Pheidon and the origin of Greek coinage, I should like to look at the information we have at our disposal today on the iron spits, their primary function and the prerequisites for their use in a monetary-value system. These aspects, of course, have been studied many times before, in particular by scholars such as I.N. Svoronos, Mrs. Oikonomides, Uta Kron, Bruno d'Agostino, Andreas Furtwängler, and—not least—Paul Courbin.[5] Nevertheless, it may be profitable to look once again into the evidence.

Presumably, the iron obeloi were given their monetary

Abbreviations:

AH = Ch. Waldstein, *The Argive Heraion* I–II, 1902–1905.
Annales = *Annales, Economies, Sociétes, Civilisations.*
Coldstream, *GG* = J.N. Coldstream, *Geometric Greece*, 1977.
Courbin, *Annales* 14 = P. Courbin, 'Dans la Grèce archaïque. Valeur comparée du fer et de l'argent lors de l'introduction de monnayage', *Annales* 14, 1959, 209–233.
Courbin, in *Greek Renaissance* = P. Courbin, 'Obéloi d'Argolide et d'ailleurs', in *Greek Renaissance*, 149–156.
Cult Practice = *Early Greek cult practice. Proceedings of the Fifth International Symposium at the Swedish Institute in Athens 1986*, eds. R. Hägg, N. Marinatos & G.C. Nordquist (ActaAth-4°, 38), 1988.
d'Agostino, 'Tombe principesche' = B. d'Agostino, 'Tombe "principesche" dell'Orientalizzante Antico da Pontecagnano, *MonAnt*, Ser.Misc. 2, 1, 1977.
Furtwängler, 'Obeloi' = A. Furtwängler, 'Zur Deutung der Obeloi im Lichte samischer Neufunde', in *Tainia. Roland Hampe zum 70. Geburtstag*, eds. A. Cahn & E. Simon, 1978.
Greek Renaissance = *The Greek renaissance of the eighth century B.C.: Tradition and innovation. Proceedings of the Second International Symposium at the Swedish Institute in Athens 1981*, ed. R. Hägg (ActaAth-4°, 30), 1983.
Strøm, *Problems* = I. Strøm, *Problems concerning the origin and early development of the Etruscan Orientalizing style*, 1971.
Sympotica = *Sympotica. A symposium on the symposion*, ed. O. Murray, 1990.

[1] Cf., for example, *Der kleine Pauly*, s.v., 'Drachme' and 'Obolos' (H. Chantraine, 1967 and 1972); Ch. Seltman, *Greek coins*, 2nd ed. 1955, 33ff.; Coldstream, *GG*, 148, and below, nn. 5 and 29.

[2] For King Pheidon of Argos, his enterprises and the date of his reign, cf. *CAH* III, 3, 1982, 338f. with references to ancient literary sources (N.L. Hammond); R.A. Tomlinson, *Argos and the Argolid*, 1972, 81ff. and 188ff.; L.H. Jeffery, *Archaic Greece*, 1976, 134ff.; Coldstream, *GG*, 154ff.; and A. Foley, *The Argolid 800–600 B.C.* (SIMA, 80), 1988, 49ff.

[3] *AH* I, 61f., fig. 31 and p. 77. Cf. also below, n. 5 (almost all references) and n. 29.

[4] Her. 9.94. C.M. Kraay, *Archaic and Classical Greek coins*, 1976, chapters 2 and 3; R.W. Wallace, 'The origin of electrum coinage', *AJA* 91, 1987, 385ff., with references (n. 1) to the current discussion on the chronology of the earliest electrum coins. According to A. Bammer, *Das Heiligtum der Artemis von Ephesos*, 1984, 167ff. and 227, the so-called Foundation Deposit A in Ephesos, in and around which the earliest electrum coins were found, should not be considered an original deposit, but is correlated with Basis B and consequently is also dated to the period of Early Corinthian pottery (EC). Bammer and other scholars date EC pottery *c.* 610–590 B.C. (op. cit., 186). I still prefer Payne's date of *c.* 625–600 B.C. (cf. *Acta Arch* 32, 1961, 187, n. 47) and Strøm, *Problems*, 109ff.; Kraay (op. cit., p. 43), dates the earliest Aeginetan coinage to the second quarter of the 6th century B.C., J.H. Kroll & N.M. Waggoner ('Dating the earliest coins of Athens, Corinth and Aegina', *AJA* 88, 1984, 325ff.) more generally to the 6th century B.C. (Conclusions, p. 339).

[5] Selected literature on iron obeloi: I.N. Svoronos, 'Obeloi si-

value, because they were already used in a specific function in sets of six, each set being already standardized and, therefore, representing a specific value.

The appearance of iron spits in standardized units may not in itself be evidence of a monetary-value system, as their primary function would be likely to exist beforehand and continue alongside their function in a monetary-value system. Only their contexts can tell whether the particular obeloi should be considered as examples of a proto-monetary-value system or not.[6] However, the use of iron obeloi in standardized units is an inevitable prerequisite for their proto-monetary value. Thus, one should look for the origin of this monetary-value system in circles where such standardized units of the iron obeloi were already established as a result of their primary function. Presumably also, the proto-monetary system of iron obeloi was introduced at a time and by administrative bodies that felt the need for a common economic standard, because they had reached a certain level of organization and had dealings in common. One should not expect the geographical area into which the system was introduced to be too restricted or such a need would hardly have arisen.

What, therefore, was the original function of the iron obeloi, in which contexts do we find them, what is their chronology and their distribution area, above all, at the time preceding early Greek coinage?

The iron spits were used for the roasting of meat and, in early Greece, we find them in two main contexts, in tombs and in sanctuaries.

In Greek tombs we find them together with fire-dogs. The dead persons were warriors who, judging from their burial contexts, were, in general, of a high social status.[7] In like combinations, the iron spits are found over large areas of the Mediterranean.

The earliest examples of iron spits come from 11th-century Cypriot tombs and there are Cypriot burial contexts similar to the Greek ones around 700 B.C. and later. The spits are in some cases found in the numbers of 12 or 18, i.e. in multiples of six. Their length varies; some measure less than 1 m, others about 1.50 m.[8]

In Greece, the earliest iron spits in tombs are from 10th-century Crete and the contexts of warriors' tombs with fire-dogs and iron obeloi are known from the 9th and the late 8th centuries B.C., but there seems to be no information about the numbers and length of the spits.[9]

There is one recorded find from Euboea, small fragments of one or a few iron spits from a funeral pyre at Lefkandi, dated to the Sub-Protogeometric Period, i.e. the 9th century B.C. The metal remains represent a banquet service, as well as a warrior's equipment.[10]

In Argos, we have three warriors' tombs with fire-dogs and iron spits, all dated to the late 8th century B.C. The spits were found in the numbers of six and twelve and their original length was 1.65 m.[11] Courbin agrees with Furtwängler that the numbers of six and twelve are due to the duodecimal system being generally accepted in early Greece and refers to the number of drinking cups in one of the tombs likewise being twelve.[12] Nevertheless, multiples of six show a systematization which was apparently connected with the meals of the upper-class warriors in 8th-century Argos, both with the roasting of meat and with the wine-drinking. In general, the burial contexts indicate actual banquet services.[13]

---

deroi', *JIAN* 9, 1906, 192ff.; Courbin, *Annales* 14, 209ff.; W. Kendrick Pritchett, 'The Attic stelai II', *Hesperia* 25, 1956, 178ff., esp. 312f.; M. Caramessini-Oikonomides, 'Sideroi obeloi', *AAA* 1, 1969, 436ff. U. Kron, 'Zum Hypogaeum vom Paestum', *JdI* 86, 1971, 117ff., esp. 131ff.; Coldstream, *GG*, 146ff.; B. d'Agostino, 'Grecs et 'indigenes' sur la côte tyrrheniénne au VIIe siecle', *Annales* 32, 1977, 3ff., esp. 9ff.; *idem*, 'Tombe principesche', 9ff., General Discussion, 18ff.; Furtwängler, 'Obeloi', 81ff.; Courbin, in *Greek Renaissance*, 149ff.; J.N. Coldstream, in V. Karageorghis (ed.), *Archaeology in Cyprus 1960–1985*, 49, 51 and 54.

[6] Although I accept O. Murray's distinction between a 'pre-monetary' and a 'proto-monetary' system, I disagree with his statement (*Greek Renaissance*, 156) that the standardization of iron spits can only have been arrived at through a proto-monetary system.

[7] Coldstream, *GG*, 146ff.; G. Bruns, *Kücherwesen und Mahlzeiten* (= *ArchHom*, Kap. Q), 1970, 31ff.; the latest list is in A.J.M. Ainian, 'Early Greek temples: their origin and function', in *Cult Practice*, 105ff., esp. 118, n. 48.

[8] Coldstream, *GG*, 146ff. and nn. 20–22; *idem*, in Karageorghis (supra n. 5), 51 and 54. For the varying lengths of the Cyprus spits, see V. Karageorghis, 'Note on sigynnae and obeloi', *BCH* 94, 1970, 35ff. esp. 38–41.

[9] Coldstream, *GG*, 146ff. and n. 22; *idem*, in Karageorghis (supra n. 5), 51; *AR* 1978–79, 47 and 49.

[10] Lefkandi, Pyre 13, *BSA* 77, 1982, 240.

[11] Argos, Tomb 45. P. Courbin, 'Une tombe géométrique d'Argos', *BCH* 81, 1957, 322ff., esp. 367 and 373ff.; *idem*, *Tombes géométriques d'Argos*, I (1952–1958) (Études Péloponnésiennes, 7), 1974, 40 and 136 (12 obeloi, fragmentary).
Argos, Tomb 1. Courbin, *Annales* 14, 219ff.; *idem*, *Tombes géométriques* (supra), 11, 13 and 136; *idem*, in *Greek Renaissance*, 152ff. (six obeloi).
Argos, Tomb 18. E. Protonotariou-Deïlaki, *Les Tumuli d'Argos*, 1980, 43ff., pl. Γ 11; *eadem*, *ASAtene* 60, 1982, 45; Courbin, in *Greek Renaissance*, 155 (six obeloi).
For the length of the Argos obeloi, cf. Courbin, in *Greek Renaissance*, 152 with nn. 25 and 155. Cf. also Foley (supra n. 2), 95f. with references also to Argos tombs with one or two obeloi.

[12] Courbin, in *Greek Renaissance*, 156.

[13] The Argos tombs contain craters as well as skyphoi. In *Greek Renaissance*, 156, K. Kilian suggests that the iron spits were used for funeral meals and in Karageorghis (supra n. 5),

The tradition of warriors' tombs with iron spits and fire-dogs may have developed in Cyprus and from there spread to Crete, Euboea, and Argos; at the two last-mentioned places, at least, they form part of banquet services. In the Aegean, this tradition seems to have died out around 700 B.C.

In the late 8th or early 7th centuries B.C., the same custom was adopted in Etruscan Italy, possibly directly from Cyprus, as we have no evidence for a like tradition in the Greek colonies in Italy.[14] It is represented in Etruria itself,[15] in Latium[16] and in Etruscan Campania.[17]

In Etruscan Italy, we do not find the same standardization of iron spits as in Argos, either as regards their numbers or their length. For example the two, almost contemporary, Pontecagnano tombs, Nos. 926 and 928, contained 13 and 10 spits, respectively. According to d'Agostino, the well-preserved Pontecagnano spits measured between 1.58 and 1.60 m; on the other hand, the bronze spits in Tomba Regolini-Galassi vary in length around 1 m.[18]

Most iron spits in Greece and Italy, in tombs as well as in sanctuaries, are of the same general types, cast solid with a square or rectangular section, usually 1–2 cm wide. At one end, they finish in a spike, at the other in a flat plate, either lance-head-shaped or rounded (oval or circular); the first-mentioned type sometimes has a central hole. Another form of plate is open and ring-shaped.[19]

As pointed out by Courbin, the warriors' tombs in Argos indicate a standardization as regards the numbers and the length of the spits and apparently also their weight. Although stating "that the obeloi were used for meat in the tombs and had no monetary value in this context", Courbin maintains that the Argos obeloi were used as a proto-monetary-value system.[20] Not only the contexts of the Argos tombs form an argument against

---

54, Coldstream sees a connection with Homeric banquets for the fire-dogs and obeloi in tombs. Cf. also H. Drerup, *Griechische Baukunst in geometrischer Zeit* (=*ArchHom*, Kap. O), 1969, 126f. and Furtwängler, 'Obeloi', 59, n. 31.

[14] The only iron spits I know about in the Greek colonies in Italy are the finds in the hypogaeum in Paestum, cf. below, p. 44 and n. 24 and the spits listed in the Torricella inscription, cf. below, p. 49 and n. 61, in both cases connected with sanctuaries.

[15] K. Kilian's list of iron spits and fire-dogs in Italy ('Weihungen aus Eisen und Eisenverarbeitung im Heiligtum zu Philia (Thessalien)', in *Greek Renaissance*, 133f. n. 15 and fig. 6), comprises also a few Italic local finds of iron spits outside the Etruscan area. The fire-dogs had a wider distribution in Etruscan Italy than is inferable from Kilian (cf. Strøm, *Problems*, n. 482). To his list of the finding places of iron spits in *Etruria* should be added:

Cerveteri. L. Pareti, *La Tomba Regolini-Galassi*, 1947, 298, nos. 276–280 (small fragments of numerous iron spits). Nos. 256–264 are spits of the same type, but in bronze, varying in length between 87 and 110 cm.

Quinto Fiorentino. Tomba della Montagnola, *StEtr* 33, 1965, 521.

Populonia. Tomba dei Flabelli, *MonAnt* 34, 1931, pl. XIII and p. 307f. Fragments of six obeloi are illustrated, but the exact number of spits is not given, nor are their lengths.

[16] *Etruscan Latium*:

Castel di Decima, Tomb 15, *NSc* 1975, 289, nos. 61–64, figs. 61 and 66. Fragments of four spits of uncertain lengths, but exceeding 1 m. This is apparently the only tomb with iron spits in Etruscan Italy definitely dated before 700 B.C. Tomb 152, ibid. nos. 40–41, 317ff., figs. 102 and 104. (Fragments of two spits).

Palestrina, Tomba Bernardini? Although there are fire-dogs in the Bernardini Tomb, there are no certain examples of iron spits preserved. The objects (F. Canciani & F.-W. v. Hase, *La Tomba Bernardini di Palestrina*, 1979, p. 60, no. 90 and pl. 52,1) are definitely not spits; their projections show that they were meant for fastening to a different kind of material.

[17] *Etruscan Campania*:

Arenosola. Fragments of iron obeloi have been found in Tombs 18, 43, 88 (and possibly 80). Tomb 43 is the richest of the 7th-century tombs and contains fragments of one iron obelos and two fire-dogs. In Tomb 18, there are fragments of one iron obelos and in Tomb 88 possibly of two; the largest fragment measures *c.* 75 cm. I wish to thank MA Helle Horsnæs (Copenhagen), who is shortly going to publish the Arenosola necropolis, for this information.

Pontecagnano. Tombs 926 and 928, d'Agostino, *Annales* 32, 1977, 9ff.; d'Agostino, 'Tombe principesche', loc. cit. Tomb 926, cat. nos. R3–R15, p. 10 and figs. 2–5, pls. II–III. Tomb 928, cat.nos. R 9–18, p. 13, figs. 13 and 15–16 and pls. XIII–XIV. For the length of the obeloi, varying between 1.58 and 1.60 m, cf. p. 20. According to d'Agostino, no. R 17 measures only 1.50 m. The catalogue numbers are not given in the figures, but the last spit but one in the illustrations from Tomb 928 (cf. fig. 15 and pl. XIV) is presumably cat. no. R 17. It is smaller than the others, but it seems to be broken.

Apparently, the tradition of placing iron obeloi in the tombs continued in Pontecagnano into the 6th century B.C., not always confined to warriors' tombs. On exhibition in the museum of Pontecagnano, there are two more tombs with iron obeloi, both dated later in the 7th century B.C. Tomb 1697 has fragments of two obeloi and Tomb 5946 has two well-preserved obeloi, measuring considerably less than 1 m. The tomb, which also contains two fire-dogs, is a woman's burial. In the magazines of the museum are at least two more tombs with iron obeloi, Tomb 5014 from the late 7th century B.C. and Tomb 6034, perhaps dated to the 6th century B.C. The obeloi which I have seen under restoration measure *c.* 1.35 m from the former tomb and *c.* 1 m from the latter tomb; their number is not certain. I thank the director of the museum, Luca Cerchiai for letting me see these finds and informing me about the contexts.

[18] Cf. above n. 15, Cerveteri. Apart from the early warriors' tombs in Pontecagnano, the obeloi here seem to vary in length, cf. above n. 17.

[19] Furtwängler, 'Obeloi', 84ff. and fig. 4.

[20] Courbin, *Annales* 14, esp. 228ff. and *idem*, in *Greek Renaissance*, esp. 155ff.

the theory. It seems to me that Late Geometric Argos in itself was much too restricted an area to have the need for and the profitable use of a proto-monetary-value system. At this time, the late 8th century B.C., iron spits in tombs are recorded only at one other place in Greece, namely in Crete. Nor do we have any evidence that the tradition of iron obeloi continued in Argos. There is a difference in time of more than a century between the Argos spits and the replacement of spits of proto-monetary-value by coins of Aeginetan standard. Courbin seems to overcome the difficulties by suggesting that the Argos finds should be viewed in connection with the Argive Heraion spits, the whole Argolid representing the area of the proto-monetary-value system. However, he shows—and in my opinion quite correctly—that the Argive Heraion obeloi are about 15 cm smaller than the Argos spits, measuring only about 1.50 m.[21] The Argive Heraion spits, therefore, do not fit into the same proto-monetary-value system. I see this fact as a serious contradiction and do not find Courbin's explanation of the difference as a kind of devaluation of an earlier established monetary-value system convincing.[22]

Courbin's studies of the iron obeloi are invaluable and all further studies must build on his fundamental results. The Argos spits were definitely used in standardized units by the upper-class warriors of this settlement in the late 8th century B.C. Their forming part of a banquet service seems evident and it must be in this function that they were made up in sets of six and multiples of six in Argos as well as in Cyprus. However, for the above reasons, I do not accept the iron obeloi in the Argos tombs as a sign of an already established proto-monetary-value system in late 8th century Argos.[23]

As pointed out also by Courbin, the length of the iron obeloi at the Argive Heraion has a counterpart in another sanctuary, the obeloi found in a late 6th century context in the hypogaeum at Paestum. Here were five obeloi wrapped up in cloth and placed on a table, one in the middle and two on each side. Each obelos measured 1.49 m. On either side of the table were placed bronze hydriae and amphorae containing organic material. The sacrificial nature of the context is evident; apparently we have here a pempobolon accompanied by food offerings. Whatever the correct interpretation of the hypogaeum at Paestum may be—and there are a number of suggestions—it remains a fact that it was situated inside a sanctuary, the main deity of which was Hera.[24]

Usually, the standard of weight of the iron obeloi is considered more important than the standard of length, but today it is almost impossible to determine and compare their original weight, owing to the varying degree of oxidization.[25] Also, I wonder what originally determined the standard of obeloi and drachmai. A standard of weight is fundamentally important for coins made of precious metals, but, for the iron objects of every-day use which preceded them in monetary value, a standard of weight cannot originally have had any significance. The obeloi were primarily made with the specific function in view of roasting the meat and, for this particular use, a standard of length seems practical. If the manufacture was well organized, the weight would correspond to the length, but this is likely to have been a secondary circumstance. Metal production existed in early Greek sanctuaries as well as in settlements[26] and an organized manufacture would at both places produce standard implements. The metal value of the obeloi is likely to have been originally determined by their standard length and may even not have lived up to the exact standard measures of later periods.[27] As suggested by Courbin, the correspondence in length of the iron obeloi could be significant. The iron obeloi of the Argive Heraion and those of the Heraion at Paestum correspond in length, about 1.50 m, as just mentioned. However, a comparison with the obeloi from the early tombs of the two nearby sites, Argos and Pontecagnano, respectively, seems to indicate that there is no geographically determined area for a standard length of the obeloi, the spits at one site measuring 1.65 m, at the other 1.58–1.60 m.[28] This cor-

[21] Courbin, in *Greek Renaissance*, 151f. I quite agree with Courbin that the present condition of the Argive Heraion spits cannot be used as an argument against the measures taken at the time of excavation (Furtwängler, 'Obeloi', 93).

[22] Courbin, in *Greek Renaissance*, 156.

[23] In this conclusion, I agree with, among others, Bruno D'Agostino, 'Tombe principesche', 20ff. and Furtwängler, 'Obeloi', 89.

[24] Kron (supra n. 5) and M. Bertarelli Sestieri, 'Nuove ricerche sull'Ipogeo di Paestum', *MEFRA* 97,2, 1985, 647ff. (with new analyses of the organic material of the context; the bronze vases do not contain honey, but a mixture of animal and vegetal fats). Courbin compares the lengths of the obeloi from the two sanctuaries (*Greek Renaissance*, 154) and stresses the fact that both were Hera sanctuaries.

[25] Cf. esp. A.M. Woodward, 'The iron spits and other coins', in R.M. Dawkins (ed.), *The sanctuary of Artemis Orthia at Sparta* (*JHS* Suppl. Paper, 5), 1929, 391ff.

[26] Cf. the most recent list of sanctuaries with metal production in this publication (Christina Risberg, 'Metal-working in Greek sanctuaries'). Most sanctuaries have bronze production, and Athena Itonia at Philia has iron production from the Late Geometric period onwards (cf. Kilian, in *Greek Renaissance*, 131ff.).

[27] Even the early electrum coins show variations in their metal value, although their weights are regularized, because their metallic alloys vary (cf. Wallace, supra n. 4).

[28] Cf. above, nn. 11 and 17, the warriors' tombs.

respondence in length of the obeloi from the two geographically distant Hera santuaries may, therefore, open up a new possibility. Instead of looking for an area with a standard value of iron obeloi defined by geographical boundaries, one should perhaps look for an area defined by religious relations?

Turning now to the sanctuaries, in the Argive Heraion we have the one find of obeloi, the monetary value of which is widely accepted, the bundle of iron spits found together with an iron bar.[29] Courbin reconstructs the number of iron spits as 96; they were bound together with two iron wires and the plates of the obeloi were stuck into a lead disc. The iron bar was broken below and measured in its fragmentary state 1.15 m, with a weight of 73 kg. The upper part of the bar reminds us in its shape of the lance-head form of one known type of iron obeloi. Svoronos and Courbin regarded the iron bar as a kind of canon for the obeloi,[30] but it may just as well be interpreted as a bar of the raw material used for the manufacture of the obeloi.[31] If this is a correct interpretation, we apparently have a corresponding dedication in the region from the Hellenistic period. At the time when the independent coinage of Argos was abandoned in the second century B.C., bronze bars and flans were dedicated at a temple in the Agora of Argos, presumably as examples of the outdated currency.[32] A corresponding interpretation seems to be the most likely one for the Argive Heraion obeloi, based on the character of the find itself.

The iron obeloi and the iron bar at the Argive Heraion were excavated near the place where the altar was presumably situated already in the Geometric period[33] and must also for this reason be regarded as a votive dedication, possibly of official character. Interpreted as a votive dedication of the outdated currency at the time of the introduction of the Aeginetan coinage in the Argolid, the Argive Heraion find corresponds perfectly with the literary information about Pheidon's offering, except for his chronology. If the interpretation is correct, the dedication—whoever was responsible for it—took place some time in the 6th century B.C.[34]

Two more obelos offerings in Greek sanctuaries have been considered dedications of monetary value by some scholars. One is the offering to Apollo in Delphi by the Thracian female slave and hetaira, Rhodopis in Naucratis, of a tithe of her earnings in the form of iron obeloi, mentioned by Herodotus. The numbers and length of the obeloi are not known, but as Herodotus characterizes them as ox-bearing, they cannot have been small. They were placed behind the altar. A fragment of the Rhodopis inscription is dated to the 6th century B.C. and the chronological information about her indicates a date in the first half or around the middle of the 6th century B.C., when a monetary dedication of iron spits would be oldfashioned, but not necessarily anachronistic.[35] As Rhodopis dedicated a tithe of her earnings, the iron spits she offered must have had a specific monetary value and I agree with Courbin that this is an example of iron spits in a monetary-value system.[36]

The third possible, proto-monetary dedication of iron spits is preserved in an inscription stele from Perachora. Together with other inscriptions, the stele in a re-used condition framed the hearth of the so-called Hera Limenia Temple, presumably a 6th century hestiatorion, as shown by Tomlinson. The stele had traces of cuttings for clamps along its side, probably for holding a handful of obeloi in a vertical position. The stele was cut for its re-

[29] Cf. above nn. 3 and 5. In *Greek Renaissance*, 149f., Courbin summarizes the preceding discussion about the proto-monetary significance of the find. Since Svoronos' publication, the most thorough modern studies of this find have been made by Courbin, in *Annales* 14, and *Greek Renaissance* with detailed illustrations (cf. esp. *Greek Renaissance*, 153ff., figs. 5–11, of which fig. 7 is a drawing with measurements of the iron bar). Also Furtwängler, 'Obeloi', 93ff. accepts the Argive Heraion find as a monetary dedication, although he considers it to be a symbolic offering.

I wish to thank Mrs. Oikonomides for the great help which she gave me during my studies of this find in the National Archaeological Museum of Athens in 1984.

[30] Svoronos (supra n. 5), 198 and Courbin, in *Greek Renaissance*, 152.

[31] Furtwängler, 'Obeloi' 93ff. with reference to R.J. Forbes *Bergbau, Steinbruchtätigkeit und Hüttenwesen* (=*ArchHom*, Kap. K), 1967, 32, although Forbes here refers to the iron obeloi, not to the bar.

We do not know how the bar was shaped at the other end and there may have been practical reasons for its specific form, just as for the so-called, ox-hide ingots of the Aegean Bronze Age.

[32] H. Consolaki & T. Hackens, 'Un atelier monétaire dans un temple argien?' in *Etudes argiennes* (*BCH* Suppl., 6), 1980, 279ff., esp. 284ff. The conclusions (with a question mark) are on p. 292.

[33] For the altar of the early Argive Heraion, cf. *ActaArch* 55, 1988 (publ. 1989), 176f. (I. Strøm).

[34] Cf. above p. 41 and nn. 2 and 4, the chronology of Pheidon and the Aeginetan coinage. The chronology has, of course, always been the main obstacle to connecting the dedication with the reign of King Pheidon.

[35] Her. 2.135. E. Mastrokostas (in *Geras A. Keramopoullou*, 1953, 635ff., pl. 31) publishes the inscription and quotes the ancient literary sources on Rhodopis (642ff.). According to these, Rhodopis was a contemporary of the brother of Sappho, born in the late seventh century B.C., as well as of Amasis, who reigned from *c*. 570–525 B.C. A thorough discussion of the dedication with earlier references is also given by Furtwängler, 'Obeloi', 91f.

[36] Cf. Courbin, in *Greek Renaissance*, 151.

use and the inscription is only partly preserved, opening with the words: Δϱαχμα εγō Ͱēϱα λευϙ[ōλενε---]

On epigraphical criteria, Jeffery dates it between *c.* 600 and 550 B.C.[37] Considering its find context, I do not accept the inscription as one of proto-monetary value, but at least it tells us that a drachma of obeloi was a fixed standard in the Archaic Hera sanctuary, most likely connected with banquets in the hestiatorion.

Both inside and outside the same building, the hestiatorion in Perachora, iron spits were found in considerable numbers, although too fragmentary and corroded for any conjectures to be made as to their numbers and sizes.[38]

Also the two other, above-mentioned sanctuaries, the Argive Heraion and the Apollo sanctuary at Delphi, have yielded separate finds of iron spits[39] and so have other Greek sanctuaries.[40]

In the cella of the 7th century Apollo Temple at Halieis, numerous obeloi are recorded as having been found behind the cult base, the adjoining room containing goats' horns and animal bones, iron knives, swords, and spears.[41]

At the site of Artemis Orthia at Sparta, there is a large number of fragments of iron obeloi with handle plates of the lance-head shape, some of which were found east and south of the altar, others at different points of the sanctuary. The obeloi are said to begin to be frequent in the strata with Protocorinthian pottery but are not known from the earliest strata with Geometric pottery only. They continued through the deposits of Laconian I but did not appear together with definitely Laconian II pottery.[42] In general, these observations seem to imply a period covering the greater part of the 7th century B.C., presumably starting around 700 B.C.[43]

In the Heraion of Samos there are several finds of iron obeloi which, however, differ in construction from the other Greek obeloi. They were not made of solid iron, but of a 1–3 mm thick, iron plate which was bent into a square section, originally covering a wooden staff, a construction which has counterparts in Cyprus. The handle plates, on the other hand, are similar to the types known from other sites in Greece and Italy. They are all fragmentary, but Furtwängler considered them to be longer than 1 m in most cases.[44] There is at least one certain example of the Samos obeloi being connected with an animal sacrifice like the Paestum obeloi. By a path leading to the sea, south of the altar of Hera, a boukranion was buried around 600 B.C., together with three obeloi, a triobolon.[45]

In the Athena Itonia sanctuary at Philia in Thessaly, the iron obeloi were likewise found near the roads of the sanctuary and interpreted as remnants of animal sacrifices in correspondence with the Samos finds, presumably dating from the Late Geometric period onwards.[46]

There are several obelos fragments in the Hera-Zeus sanctuary of Olympia, one of which has an Archaic inscription to Zeus in a formula known in Olympia from weapon offerings. The published Olympia spits differ from the above-mentioned types in ending in a half-

---

[37] J. Wade-Gerry, in H. Payne *et al.*, *Perachora* I, 1940, 257ff., no. 1, pl. 36c and pl. 132, iii; L.H. Jeffery, *The local scripts of Archaic Greece*, 1961, 131, no. 17, pl. 20; discussion of the stele and the inscription, 122ff., absolute chronology p. 124. P.A. Hansen, *Carmina Epigraphica Graeca Saeculorum VIII–V a.Chr.*, 1983, 188f., no. 354, with other references and a thorough discussion of the arrangement of the inscription. A.W. Johnstone, *Supplement 1961–1987*, to L.H. Jeffery, op. cit., 1990, 440.

For the interpretation of the so-called Hera Limenia Temple in Perachora as a hestiatorion, cf. R.A. Tomlinson, 'The upper terraces at Perachora', *BSA* 72, 1977, 197f. On p. 200, he connects the spits with the function of the dining-room. *Idem*, 'The Perachora hestiatorion' in *Sympotica*, 95ff.; on p. 98, the building is dated to the late sixth century B.C.

[38] *Perachora* I, 187ff., cf. Tomlinson 1977 (supra n. 37), 200.

[39] Separate finds of iron spits in the Argive Heraion (*Hesperia* 21, 1952, 183) and in Delphi (*BCH* 69, 1944–45, 37).

[40] I follow Furtwängler ('Obeloi', 86, n. 22) in leaving out the iron objects from Aetos on Ithaca and a strange, fragmentary bronze object from a bronze workshop in a sanctuary for an unknown deity at Anthedon in Boiotia. From Furtwängler's list, 89, n. 32, I find reason to leave out only the iron fragments interpreted as spits from the Apollo Temple at Dreros. Without illustrations, their identification cannot be certain (cf. *BCH* 60, 1936, 227, and *Perachora* I, 138).

To his list should now be added A. Cambitoglou, *Archaeological Museum of Andros. Guide to the finds from the excavations of the Geometric town at Zagora*, 2nd ed. 1991, 98, no. 320, iron spit, fragments, from the temple (Inv. 1879); for the chronology of the temple (second quarter of 6th century B.C.) and identification of the deity (presumably Athena), cf. p. 84.

[41] Cf. Ainian (supra n. 7), 118, n. 47 and fig. 19.

[42] Woodward (supra n. 25), 391.

[43] Boardman's chronology of the Artemis Orthia stratigraphy (*BSA* 58, 1963, 1ff.), which lowered considerably the absolute chronology given by the excavators, has now been revised, owing to the correspondence with the Menelaion stratigraphy (cf. *BSA* 79, 1984, 34f. and *AJA* 91, 1987, 388). The excavator's absolute chronology of Laconian I should, therefore, now be only slightly lowered.

[44] Cf. Furtwängler, 'Obeloi'; for the length of the spits, cf. p. 86. The published, dated contexts of the Samos obeloi are as follows: late 7th century B.C., late 7th or early 6th century B.C., and around 600 B.C. (cf. op. cit. nn. 20, 21 and p. 97).

[45] Furtwängler, 'Obeloi', 97f. and pl. 18.

[46] Kilian (supra n. 15), 131ff., esp. 133. Distribution of iron obeloi in the sanctuary, fig. 1. The finds are dated from the Late Geometric period onwards, 131. Cf. also Furtwängler, 'Obeloi', 97.

moon-shaped plate.[47] Apart from Olympia, this type of obeloi seems in Greece to be known only from the two Zeus sanctuaries at Dodone[48] and Nemea. At the last-mentioned site alone, they were found in secure contexts. One is a votive deposit of the first half of the 5th century B.C. and the other a deposit of the third quarter of the 6th century B.C. The latter deposit comprised a discus, a jumping weight, a fragmentary strigil and two javelin points and was interpreted by the excavators as a votive dedication of an athlete, probably a pentathlete.[49] These obeloi seem to differ from the other obelos finds in the Greek sanctuaries, not only in type, but also as regards contexts. They may perhaps represent a different tradition.

Obeloi are still present in the Greek sanctuaries in the Classical period; for example, one was placed together with other votive offerings in the 5th-century altar to Artemis Elaphobia at Kalapodi in Phocis;[50] and they are known from inscriptions in the Athena sanctuary on the Acropolis of Athens and the Apollo sanctuary on Delos, at the latter site even in the Hellenistic period.[51] However, from the above-mentioned contexts, their main period of functioning in large quantities seems to be the 7th century B.C., perhaps beginning in the late 8th century B.C. or around 700 B.C. and lasting until sometime in the first half of the 6th century B.C.[52]

The distribution of the iron obeloi in the Greek sanctuaries forms a specific pattern. They are known from sanctuaries over almost the whole of Greece, although with a predominance of sanctuaries on the Greek Mainland. Apart from the Zeus sanctuaries, where they may represent a different tradition, they are primarily restricted to sanctuaries of Apollo, Artemis, Athena and Hera and seem in particular to be connected with Hera sanctuaries. There are two examples of votive dedications of iron obeloi as proto-monetary value and in one other inscription we find the expression, drachma, although not as a monetary dedication.

The contexts indicate the function of the obeloi in the roasting of the meat. Obeloi were definitely used in the Greek sanctuaries as cult implements for animal sacrifices. In this capacity, their numbers were two, three or five.[53] As these numbers do not conform with the monetary-value system of drachmai, consisting of six obeloi, it is hardly conceivable that iron spits in sanctuaries could give rise to the Greek proto-monetary-value system from their function as sacrificial implements.[54]

From the obelos finds in the Argos tombs, we gathered the information that iron obeloi were used in banquet services in Greece in sixes or multiples of six.[55] From the late Archaic period onwards, banquet halls are just as common in Greek sanctuaries as in Greek settlements and we have signs of early Greek temples having been arranged for common meals,[56] although there is no evidence that this comprised the Near Eastern banquet tradition, including wine. In some of the sanctuaries, in particular, the Hera sanctuary at Perachora and the Apollo sanctuary at Halieis, the contexts of the iron obeloi indicate their use as banqueting implements and at the former site we have an inscription, including the word "drachma".[57] Moreover, from other Greek inscriptions we learn that drachmai or obeloi in sixes were

[47] H. Weber, 'Eisengerät', in *OlForsch* 1, 1944, 166f., pl. 71. For the votive inscription, cf. also Furtwängler, 'Obeloi', 95, n. 68, with a reference to *OlBer* 8, 1967, 86ff. (E. Kunze).

[48] C. Carapanos, *Dodone et ses ruines*, 1878, pl. 53, 14 and Furtwängler, 'Obeloi', 86, n. 22.

[49] *Hesperia* 52, 1983, 79f., pl. 23*f*, and *Hesperia* 53, 1984, 181, pl. 37*d*, in the former case found together with an athlete's equipment.

[50] *AA* 1980, 89ff., figs. 71–72; fragmentary iron spits were also found outside the building (op. cit., p. 96). For the identification of the cult, cf. *AA* 1987, 681ff., Conclusions, p. 687.

[51] The inventory of the Treasurers of Athena on the Acropolis, *IG* II^2 1425, line 407, here in the number of 42 obeliskoi, listed immediately after Laconian craters and thus possibly as part of a banquet service. For the Delos inscriptions, cf. references from Pritchett (supra n. 5), 312f. Also in some of the Delos inscriptions, the obeliskoi form part of a banquet service. Pritchett's article is one of three in which are published the inscription stelai recording the sale of the confiscation of the personal property of Alcibiades and others in 415–414 B.C. It shows that iron obeloi or obeliskoi (the terms are used at random) formed part of the household properties of the upper classes of Athens in the Classical Period.

[52] The relevant find contexts are those of Halieis, Perachora, Samos, Sparta, and possibly Philia (cf. above nn. 37–38, 41–44 and 46). Although the Perachora hestiatorion may be later, the inscription stone with clamps for holding obeloi is dated to the first half of the 6th century B.C. (cf. above n. 37).

[53] Cf. esp. Kron (supra n. 5), 151 ff. and Furtwängler, 'Obeloi', 94ff.

[54] In this part of his conclusions, I agree with Furtwängler, 'Obeloi', 98, but I do not see the sacrificial function of the iron obeloi in the sanctuaries as the only possibility.

[55] Cf. above p. 42 and nn. 11 and 13.

[56] Cf. Ainian (supra n. 7), 116ff. and B. Bergquist, 'Sympotic space: a functional aspect of Greek dining rooms', in *Sympotica*, 37ff. One should perhaps leave out the Kommos Temple, which the excavators take to have been built by Phoenicians (cf. J.W. Shaw, 'Phoenicians in Southern Crete', *AJA* 93, 1989, 165ff.). *Sympotica* contains several articles of importance also for the theme of banquets in sanctuaries, besides that of B. Bergquist, especially O. Murray, 'Sympotic history', 3ff.; P. Schmitt-Pantel, 'Two models of civic institutions in the Archaic city', 14ff.; and N. Bookidis, 'Ritual dining in the sanctuary of Demeter and Kore at Corinth: some questions', 86ff. Cf. also above, n. 37 (R.A. Tomlinson) and below, n. 64 (A. Rathje).

[57] Cf. above, p. 45f. and nn. 37–38 and 41.

Fig. 1. H. Roehl, *Inscriptiones Graecae Antiquissimae*, 1882, pp. 66f.

closely connected with banquets in the Near Eastern tradition. Three inscriptions are especially important, one is dated to the 4th century B.C., the two others to the first half of the 6th century B.C.

The first example is an inventory from Chostia in Boeotia, listing the equipment of three Hera sanctuaries, at Thespiae, Siphae and Kreusis. Although the inscription was published by N. Platon in 1938, the correct interpretation was not given until 1980, when R.A. Tomlinson pointed out that all the listed objects formed part of a banquet service: lebetes, obeliskoi, cups, klinae, tables, craters, oinochoae, strainers, mortars, plates, knives, foot-baths etc. This inventory is important not only because the obeliskoi are recorded in drachmai, but also because of their constant correspondence with the number of lebetes. In the Heraion of Thespiae were 35 lebetes and 35 obeliskon drachmai, in the Heraion of Siphae were three lebetes and three obeliskon drachmai and in that of Kreusis two lebetes and two obeliskon drachmai.[58]

The Chostia inscription confirms that a system of drachmai of obeliskon was connected in the sanctuaries with banquets of the Near Eastern type and informs us of their regular relation to the lebetes (which in banquets were used as containers of wine),[59] one lebes being accompanied by a drachme of obeloi. It seems possible that the reason for this regular system is to be found in the arrangements of banquets in subgroups of persons, each group possibly sharing one lebes of wine and six meat spits.[60]

[58] N. Platon & M. Feyel, 'Inventaire sacré de Thespies trouvé à Chostia (Beotie)', *BCH* 62, 1938, 149ff., pl. XXVIII; R.A. Tomlinson, 'Two notes on possible hestiatoria', *BSA* 75, 1980, 221ff.; *idem* in *Sympotica*, 99.

[59] For the lebes and its function in banquets, cf. G.M.A. Richter & M.J. Milne, *Shapes and names of Athenian vases*, 1935, 9f. with illustration, and D.A. Amyx, 'The Attic stelai III', *Hesperia*, 27, 1958, 163ff., esp. 199f.

[60] When the banqueters took up a reclining position, using klinai, each unit sharing one lebes may have been made up of six persons on three klinai. In her article in *Sympotica*, n. 56, B. Bergquist stresses the subdivision of the banqueting rooms for a spatial division into functional subgroups. R.A. Tomlinson, in *Sympotica*, 99, suggests that reclining at banquets was already a feature in the 7th century B.C.

Of the two 6th-century inscriptions, one comes from an Artemis sanctuary, situated near Torricella, about 30 km SE of Taranto in southern Italy. The most plausible interpretation is that of an inventory, comprising a banqueting equipment, besides other implements. Here we see the same correspondence in wine-drinking and meat-roasting, one lebes and six meat spits made of iron.[61]

According to Raubitschek, one more inscription connects lebetes and drachmai. It is an inscribed stone base found at Krisa near Delphi in the early 19th century. Today it is lost. It has a joint dedication to Athena and Hera. The site was excavated in the 1930's by French archaeologists and yielded nothing later than the Mycenaean Age. As the nearby village of Krisa has several inscriptions transferred at some date from Delphi, it has been suggested that the inscription was originally placed in the Athena Pronaia sanctuary at Delphi. The inscription is boustrophedon, covering two sides of the stone in three lines. The letters were not deeply cut and were difficult to distinguish because of their irregularity and the cracks in the stone (*Fig. 1*).[62] The relevant word consists of seven letters, of which five are clear: δϱα[. .]ας. Raubitschek reconstructs the word as "drachmas" and reads the whole inscription as follows:

Τάσδε γ' 'Αθαναίαι δϱαχμὰς Φανάϱιστος ἔθεκε
*h*έϱαι τε *h*ος καὶ κε̂νος ἔχοι κλέϝος ἄπθιτον αἰϝεί.

Raubitschek's reconstruction of the crucial word as "drachmas" seems to be confirmed by the drawing of the base itself. On its top is a small, round hole, well suited for holding a drachma of iron spits. As the base is broken, there may have been one more similar hole and at least the inscription—if Raubitschek is correct—mentions drachmas in the plural. On either side of the small hole were two large, rounded cuttings, which Raubitschek suggests served for inserting bronze kettles, i.e. lebetes, giving references to similar cuttings with such a purpose in other sanctuaries.[63] This inscribed stone base seems to support the above-mentioned evidence of a close functional and numerical relation between lebetes and drachmai of obeloi in Greek sanctuaries.

To sum up, in the Greek sanctuaries, the iron obeloi evidently had a cultic function besides that of serving for animal sacrifices, namely exactly the same function as is known from the Late Geometric Argos tombs, the roasting of the meat for banquets. For this purpose, they were likewise used in sets of six, i.e. in drachmai of obeloi, and each set was used together with one lebes, which presumably held the wine, according to the Near Eastern banquet tradition. In this connection, the term "drachme" is used in the Greek sanctuaries in inscriptions from the first half of the 6th century B.C., i.e. in exact accordance with the terminology of the Greek proto-monetary system which survived in the Greek coinage. In contrast with the use of iron obeloi in the Argos tombs, as we know them today, there is no break in the function of the obeloi in the sanctuaries where they are plentiful from not later than around 700 B.C. (probably shortly earlier) and down into the first half of the 6th century B.C. Moreover, it is in the sanctuaries that we have the few certain examples of obeloi in a proto-monetary-value system, in the Argive Heraion and—in my opinion—also in the Apollo sanctuary at Delphi.

The sanctuaries which used the iron obeloi in the period in question are distributed over almost the whole of Greece, although especially over the Greek Mainland. Their distribution does not form a pattern which makes it possible to connect them with any known group or league of settlements. The only pattern observable in the distribution of the iron obeloi seems to be one of a religious character. The sanctuaries with iron obeloi, in actual finds as well as inscriptions, are primarily those of Apollo, Artemis, Athena, and Hera, the obeloi in the Zeus sanctuaries possibly belonging to a different tradition. In two Hera sanctuaries, geographically distant, the obeloi appeared to have been manufactured in the same length and thus indicate a correspondence also in weight and metal value; moreover, their lengths differed from those of the obeloi found in warriors' tombs in nearby settlements. In the Greek sanctuaries, the metal production, which must be seen as a prerequisite for an independent, organized manufacture of obeloi, is known from the Late Geometric period onwards.

---

[61] F.G. Lo Porto, 'Due iscrizioni votivi arcaiche dai ditorni di Taranto', *PP* 232, 1987, 39ff. The inscription stone in question is illustrated (*Fig. 1*). It is published as a votive dedication, but the opening words are missing. In comparison with the Chostia inscription, I find an inventory more likely. It lists a ritual household service, the ritual character being given by the word στϱόφις, i.e. στϱόφιον, a ritual band. The greater part of the equipment fits into a banquet service, but there are certain implements of a different character. Cf. also Johnstone (supra n. 37), 463, "... an inventory (?) of perhaps 550–525 ...".

[62] H. Roehl, *Inscriptiones Graecae Antiquissimae praeter Atticas in Attica Repertas*, 1882, 66f. The inscription was found by H.N. Urlichs in the 1830's and was already destroyed by 1844. For later excavations of the site, cf. *RevArch* 1937, 129ff. and *BCH* 61, 1937, 466f.

The reconstruction of the partly missing word as 'drachmas' is given by A.E. Raubitschek, 'Another drachma dedication', *YCS* 11, 1950, 295f. The stone measured when published, 65 cm in width and 1 m in length. Each round cutting measured *c*. 50 cm; they were not very deep and their surface was rough.

[63] Raubitschek (supra n. 62), n. 6.

However, do we have reason to presume that the adoption of the Near Eastern banquet tradition in the Greek sanctuaries with which the iron obeloi are clearly to be connected took place as early as the first known appearance of iron obeloi in the sanctuaries? At least the inscriptions combining lebetes or cauldrons and obeloi are from the 6th century B.C. or later.

Recently, the Danish scholar Annette Rathje, has interpreted the North Syrian griffon cauldrons of bronze with siren attachments and placed on conical stands in the two Palestrina tombs of the first half of the 7th century B.C., Tomba Barberini and Tomba Bernardini, as parts of banquet services, the cauldrons, in her opinion, holding either wine or water or both. This was the time, when the Near Eastern banquet, including wine, was introduced into Italy.[64] In Greece we have examples of identical types of North Syrian bronze cauldrons, dated to the last quarter of the 8th century B.C. and reaching into the first quarter of the 7th century B.C., and the same absolute chronology is given to the North Syrian bronze cauldrons with animal handles, likewise well-known in Greece.[65] I find it legitimate to give the same interpretation of the North Syrian cauldrons found in Greece, as of the North Syrian cauldrons found in Italy. For these cauldrons, which also in Greece must be taken as a sign of the Near Eastern banquet tradition, their function later on replaced by Greek lebetes, we find a distribution pattern which corresponds with that of the iron obeloi from Greek sanctuaries. The cauldrons are not known from any secure Greek tomb context, but are found in sanctuaries over almost the whole of Greece, primarily in sanctuaries of the following deities, Apollo, Artemis, Athena, and Hera, including the sanctuary at Olympia, where there were main cults for both Hera and Zeus.[66]

The Near Eastern banquets were apparently introduced into this group of Greek sanctuaries around or shortly before 700 B.C. In Greek settlements, as well as in Greek sanctuaries, iron obeloi were used for banquets in sets of six and in a standard manufacture, but only the sanctuaries seem to fulfil the requirements of continued use into the 6th century B.C. and a wide distribution pattern.[67] Moreover, only in the sanctuaries have we found contemporary evidence, of the term "drachme" being used in connection with iron obeloi, as well as of iron obeloi in a context of proto-monetary value.

On the basis of the above archaeological and epigraphical evidence, I see the transition to the proto-monetary-value system of drachmai consisting of six obeloi as most likely having taken place in the group of Greek sanctuaries in question some time in the 7th century B.C. and possibly early in that century, standard units of iron obeloi already having been established previously in close connection with the introduction of the Near Eastern banquets.

The need for a proto-monetary-value system should presumably be seen in connection with external contacts. Not only the North Syrian bronze cauldrons, also other kinds of Near Eastern imports of the same period found in Greek sanctuaries seem to indicate that this group of sanctuaries may have had co-ordinated relations with the Near East in the late 8th and early 7th centuries B.C. or, at least, were in close contact regarding the acquisition of imported vessels which had a function in their cult life.[68] In a sphere where iron obeloi were in constant use in standardized units, it would be natural to relate economic dealings with this commonly accepted standard, drachmai of iron obeloi.

The above conclusions imply that the Greek sanctuaries in question had an independent economy and a high level of organization in the late 8th and the early 7th century B.C. The same preconditions should be required for the contemporary Greek settlements, should the inven-

[64] A. Rathje, 'A banquet service from the Latin city of Ficana', *AnalRom* 12, 1983, 7ff.; *eadem*, 'I keimelia orientali', *OPUS* 3,2, 1984, 341ff.; *eadem*, 'Manners and customs in Central Italy in the Orientalizing period: influence from the Near East', *Acta Hyperborea* 1, 1988, 81ff. and *eadem*, 'The adoption of the Homeric banquet in Central Italy in the Orientalizing period', in *Sympotica*, 279ff.

[65] For the North Syrian localization of both types of bronze cauldrons and for their absolute chronology, cf. H.-V. Herrmann, *AM* 99, 1984, 28 and *OlBer* 11, 1981, 78.

[66] The North Syrian cauldrons have recently been studied by O.W. Muscarella, 'Greek and Oriental cauldron attachments: a review', in *Greece between East and West, 10th–8th centuries B.C.*, New York 1990, ed. G. Kopcke (in press). In the same publication, I have studied the specific aspects of the function and the distribution pattern of the two groups of North Syrian cauldrons in question. The title of my paper is 'Evidence from the sanctuaries'.

There is one find of a hammered griffon protome (which I still regard as North Syrian) from the Zeus sanctuary at Dodone and according to O.W. Muscarella, there are fragments of griffon protomes and a siren attachment in the Poseidon sanctuary at the Isthmia; however, they are unpublished and the latter, at least, is not a North Syrian original (cf. reference from my above-mentioned paper, nn. 27 and 30).

[67] The geographical area for the above-mentioned sanctuaries with iron obeloi made by the same technique comprises regions which later used the Aeginetan standard for coins, the Peloponnese, Phocis and Thessaly, and as regards iron obeloi in inscriptions, the sanctuaries of Athens, Boiotia and Delos (cf. above nn. 51 and 58). As the Samos obeloi differ in technique, they cannot have been used in the same system of standard value.

[68] Cf. above n. 66.

tion of the proto-monetary-value system be attributed to one or a group of them, which the evidence does not favour. In both cases, we must admit that our information on the economic and organizational aspects of the early Greek communities is slight, regarding the period in question. Also, our insight may be somewhat distorted owing to a general tendency to use evidence from the sanctuaries for results regarding the settlements and the emerging city-states. One example is the building of monumental temples.[69] I think that the evidence on which the above conclusions are based calls for more and separately viewed, detailed studies of the economic, political, and social role of the early Greek sanctuaries in the crucial period.

Ingrid Strøm
Tornmarksvej 95
DK-5491 BLOMMENSLYST
Denmark

[69] It seems to me to be urgent that the studies of sanctuaries and settlements should be separated, in order that we may understand the relations between sanctuary and settlement during the period, when the city-state emerged; cf. my paper above n. 66 and earlier studies in *OPUS* 3, 1984, 355ff., and *ActaArch* 59, 1988 (1989), 173ff., esp. 199f.

Discussion

Jacques TRÉHEUX: En ce qui concerne l'inscription de Pérachora, on voit qu'il s'agit de drachmes qui ont été offertes à la déesse, et peut-être que c'est le donateur qui parle — *ego*. Vous avez bien rappelé que les oboles de l'Héraion d'Argos n'ont pas été trouvés dans un temple, ils n'ont pas été trouvés ni dans le plus ancien temple, ni dans le plus récent; ils ont été trouvés devant le temple, n'est-ce pas?

IS: They are found in connection with the altar, not in connection with the temple.

JT: Dans ces conditions, on est tenté de faire de ces *oboloi* des *oboloi* pour la préparation des viandes, pour des viandes grillées à partir des victimes de l'autel. Et pourtant ce sont des *oboloi* qui sont liés et qui paraissent avoir une fonction monétaire, une fonction de « pre-value ». Il y a là un problème. La deuxième question que je vous poserai, c'est que les *oboloi* ne sont pas liés aux sanctuaires de toutes les divinités, mais qu'on les trouve surtout dans les sanctuaires de trois divinités que vous avez énumérées, quatre plutôt, Apollon, Artémis, Athéna et Héra. Est-ce que vous avez une idée sur la raison pour laquelle ces sanctuaires reçoivent de façon privilégiée la consécration d'*oboloi*?

IS: There are certain relations between Apollo and Artemis; there is definitely a certain relation between Apollo and Hera. In connection with the Greek colonization, we often find Hera and Apollo. And actually I think, in this dedication from Krisa, we have a connection between Hera and Athena. I think you possibly should look back to the gods of the Mycenaean age.

JT: Je pense à la connection entre Héra et Apollon et Artémis; en principe, Héra est la mère putative de ces jumeaux, même si elle n'est pas la mère réelle. Avec Athéna, je comprends moins. On pourrait aussi remarquer que les *oboloi* sont six ou douze et par conséquent correspondent à la division de la drachme.

IS: There may be a question about what kind of relations the sanctuaries had. Apart from the Zeus sanctuaries where the oboloi are different, they are almost only found in these sanctuaries. We have exactly the same distribution pattern with imports of North Syrian cauldrons.

JT: Est-ce qu'il n'y avait pas d'*oboloi* dans les inventaires de l'Asclépieion?

Sara ALESHIRE: No.

Michael Vickers

The Metrology of Gold and Silver Plate in Classical Greece

The ancients were materialistic, very materialistic indeed, and they paid great attention to matters concerning precious metal—most of which was kept in the form of plate, and most of which has in turn been melted down time and again since antiquity. Students of the classical past, by contrast, have tended to dwell on what has actually survived, whether to please a wealthy collector, or to exhalt the contents of their museums and exhibition catalogues. The bulk of what has survived is, to be brutally frank, material which no one could be bothered to recycle: ceramic, marble and scraps of bronze. The intensity with which such material has been studied, especially after the middle of the eighteenth century, has tended to be increased by a moralizing attitude towards precious metal which has prevailed among those who work in universities and museums, and which is only slowly giving way to a more realistic assessment.[1]

It requires a great effort to put such anachronistic considerations behind us, and to attempt to look at antiquity through the eyes of the ancients, using their scale of material values. This is an exercise of fundamental importance if we are to understand what antiquity was like. We do not have to share the values in question, but we should at least be in a position to recognise them for what they are. Only recently, an eminent scholar has stated that: "We need shed no tears for the loss of the great essays in gold and ivory",[2] in the context of the chryselephantine statues of Zeus and Athena Parthenos at Olympia and Athens. Instead, we are invited to think of ceramics as "best plate" exported for their "intrinsic value".[3] They are not views which I think anyone in antiquity would have understood, but the degree to which the underlying philosophy has come to be widely accepted can be illustrated by the following anecdotal-cum-statistical evidence.

We know enough about the cost of various commodities in the fifth and fourth centuries to be reasonably certain that the ratio between the prices for painted pottery, bronze, silver and gold was in the order of 1 : 10 : 1000 : 10,000.[4] For some years now I have asked audiences, mostly academic, to guess at what the ratio might have been. They record the results on slips of paper, which I save. The median of the guesses to date is 1 : 6 : 15 : 25. Bronze is fairly accurate, but silver and gold are out by factors of 66.6 and 400 respectively. The time was when I should have scored equally badly, and indeed should have regarded the matter with a certain unlachrymose indifference, but an increasing awareness[5] that the ancients were far from indifferent to the intrinsic value of precious metal has made me look at the material evidence as well as received wisdom with fresh eyes and not a little scepticism.

What evidence there is suggests that the cosy picture we are usually given in archaeological handbooks of Athenian aristocrats, potters and pot-painters entertaining each other to their symposia may be erroneous. Rather, there seems to have been, even at Athens, a polarisation of the kind mentioned by Plato: "In every city

---

1 M. Vickers, 'The impoverishment of the past: the case of classical Greece', *Antiquity* 64, 1990, 455–463; cf. *idem*, 'Value and simplicity: eighteenth century taste and the study of Greek vases', *Past and Present* 116, 1987, 98–137.

2 J. Boardman, *Antiquity* 62, 1988, 381.

3 J. Boardman, *The Greeks overseas*, London 1980, 17.

4 For the ratio of pottery to silver, see M. Vickers, 'The influence of exotic materials on Attic white-ground pottery', in *Ancient Greek and related pottery*, ed. H.A.G. Brijder (Allard Pierson Series, 5), Amsterdam 1984, 90, n. 26; of bronze to silver, M.J. Price, 'Early Greek bronze coinage', in C.M. Kraay & G.K. Jenkins (eds.), *Essays in Greek coinage presented to Stanley Robinson*, Oxford 1968, 103; of silver to gold, D.M. Lewis, 'New evidence for the gold-silver ratio', ibid. 109; cf. D.W.J. Gill, 'Pots and trade: spacefillers or objects d'art?', *JHS* 111, 1991, 29–47.

5 M. Vickers, 'Demus's gold *phiale* (Lysias 19.25)', *AJAH* 9, 1984 (pr. 1988), 48–53; *idem*, 'Persian gold in Parthenon inventories', *REA* 91, 1989, 249–257. I owe much to: H.A. Cahn, 'Die Gewichte der Goldgefässe', *AK* 3, 1960, 26–29; D. von Bothmer, 'A gold libation bowl', *BMMA* n.s. 21, 1962–63, 155; D.M. Lewis, 'Temple inventories in ancient Greece', in M. Vickers (ed.), *Pots and pans. A colloquium on precious metals and ceramics in the Muslim, Chinese and Graeco-Roman worlds, Oxford 1985* (Oxford Studies in Islamic Art, 3), Oxford, 1986, 71–81.

there are two cities: the rich and the poor".[6] This has been overlooked in favour of a tendency to view Greek material culture solely from the point of view of the poorest members of society, to view prices and values in terms of what an artisan might earn—a drachma a day for the skilled laborer, half that for the unskilled—and to edit out of the popular image of ancient Athens the idea that the rich might have lived lives of luxury, or at least respectable gentility.

A tale told about Socrates well expresses the wide disparity which existed between the rich and the not-so-rich in 5th century Athens:

> When Socrates heard one of his friends remark how expensive [Athens] was, saying "Chian wine costs a mina, a purple robe three minae, a quarter of a litre of honey five drachmas", he took him by the hand and led him to the grain market. "Four litres of grain for an obol"; then to the olive market, "a litre of olives for two coppers"; then to the clothes market, "a tunic for 10 drachmas! The city is cheap".[7]

There was clearly a level of society within which it was natural to speak in terms of minae,[8] with silver drachmas as the small change.[9] At the other end of the social scale it was possible to obtain a substantial amount of grain, and hence the means of survival, for one six-hundredth of a mina.[10] The most expensive item here is expressed in terms of drachmas. I have explored some of the implications of this in a recent paper in the *American Journal of Archaeology*.[11] There were indeed persons who lived on a mina standard: a visit to a high-class prostitute might cost one mina,[12] or five,[13] or even ten;[14] a cheap one could cost as little as an obol–or less.[15] I took the liberty of attempting to convert ancient prices to modern—no longer a difficult matter now that the price of gold has ceased to be artificially pegged. By taking the price of gold, and making due allowance for the difference in the silver-gold ratio between antiquity and the present, it was possible to work out that late in 1989 a mina was equivalent to $350, and a drachma to $3.50. Socrates' friend's three mina robe was thus equivalent to a $1000 dollar suit, and the obol's worth of grain (four litres) would have cost the equivalent of 60 cents.

Some silver vessels exquisitely decorated with gold-figure decoration and found more than fifty years ago in the fifth-century graves at Duvanli in Bulgarian Thrace are surely Attic.[16] The *kantharos* (*Fig. 1*) weighs two and a half Attic minae, and the *phiale* (*Fig. 2*) exactly one mina.[17] That the *phiale* was made at Athens is clear not simply on account of its weight, but because—at least according to Theophrastus—the *apobates* race represented on it was only practiced in Attica and Boeotia.[18] We hear of silver vessels being given as prizes at games at Marathon[19] and Sicyon,[20] specifically silver *phialai* for horseracing at Sicyon, perhaps *phialai* resembling the Duvanli specimen.

Available evidence suggests that painted pottery vessels cost between 750 and 1000 times less than their silver analogues.[21] If, in contemporary terms, the one mina silver *phiale* cost the equivalent of $350, a pottery version of the same shape (*Fig. 3*),[22] and *mutatis mutandis*, bearing the same kind of decoration, would have cost between 35 and 45 cents. That such a figure is not illusory can be shown by a commercial graffito (*Fig. 4*) on the underside of a pot in Oxford attributed to J.D. Beazley's "Achilles Painter" (*Fig. 5*) which may be read as 4 items for 3.5 obols,[23] which gives a price of 0.88 obol, or 51 cents. This is slightly higher than a price found on a pelike in Göttingen which is marked with a price of 16.5

[6] Plat. *Rp.* 422e.

[7] Plut. *Mor.* 470f.

[8] 1 mina = 430 grams, approximately 1 pound of silver. Eupolis, for example, speaks of a 10 mina gem stone as a paradigm of luxury (*fr.* 202 K–A). The median value of fourteen houses reported in the Attic orators is 20 minae (W.K. Pritchett, 'The Attic stelai, part II', *Hesperia* 25, 1956, 275). The values of slaves given in the orators are usually given in minae, and vary between half a mina and 30 minae (ibid. 277). The details of Demosthenes' estate and income are given in talents and minae; business debts and loans were expressed in minae (Dem. 33.6–8; 34.7). We hear of an 80 minae dowry (Dem. 30.20).

[9] 1 drachma = approximately 4.3 grams of silver (but see nn. 48 and 85 below); there were 100 drachmas to the mina.

[10] There were 6 obols to the drachma.

[11] M. Vickers, 'Golden Greece: relative values, minae and temple inventories', *AJA* 94, 1990, 613–625.

[12] Ath. 13.583c; 584c.

[13] Ath. 13.581b.

[14] Ath. 13.581b.

[15] Ath. 13.569f; Eup. *PCG* 247.3.

[16] *Kantharos*, Plovdiv 1634: C. Danov & T. Ivanov, *Antique tombs in Bulgaria*, Sophia 1980, pl. 9; *Phiale* Plovdiv 1515: ibid. pl. 16; D.E. Strong, *Greek and Roman gold and silver plate*, London 1966, pl. 15b.

[17] D.W.J. Gill, 'Luxury vases', *Omnibus* 15, March 1988, 10–12.

[18] Theophr. *ap.* Harp. *s.v. apobates*.

[19] Pind. *Ol.* 9.90.

[20] Pind. *Nem.* 9.51.

[21] Cf. Vickers (supra n. 4), 90, n. 26; Gill (supra n. 4).

[22] Kiel B 651: B. Freyer-Schauenburg, 'Eine attisch rotfigurige Phiale in Kiel', in E. Böhr & W. Martini (eds.), *Studien zur Mythologie und Vasenmalerei: FS Konrad Schauenburg*, Mainz 1986, 115–120, pl. 19. I am grateful to Dr Freyer-Schauenburg for supplying a photograph and for permission to publish it.

[23] Münzen und Medaillen, *Auktion* 70, 1986, 75, no. 216; Vickers (supra n. 11), 616f., figs. 3–4: discussed more fully by Gill (supra n. 4). I am grateful to Dr Gill for allowing me to read his paper before publication.

Fig. 1. Silver *kantharos* decorated with gold-figure ornament, from Duvanli, Thrace. Plovdiv, Archaeological Museum (Courtesy of the Bulgarian Committee for Culture).

Fig. 2. Silver *phiale* decorated with gold-figure ornament., from Duvanli, Thrace. Plovdiv, Archaeological Museum (Courtesy of the Bulgarian Committee for Culture).

Fig. 3. Pottery *phiale* decorated with red-figure ornament. Kiel, Archäologisches Institut (Museum photograph).

Fig. 5. Attic red-figure pottery *pelike* in the Ashmolean Museum, Oxford (Museum photograph).

Fig. 4. Graffito on the underside of a *pelike* in the Ashmolean Museum, Oxford (Museum photograph).

obols for 32 pieces (or 30 cents each).[24] And such prices are not out of line with the general run of prices. An amphora attributed to Beazley's "Berlin Painter" bears a price of 7 obols,[25] the highest price known for a figured bell-crater is 4.5 obols,[26] and no pot bears a price of more than three drachmas.[27] In a world where the rich thought in terms of minae, and regarded a drachma as a "trifling sum"[28] such prices are of little account.

There is a tendency to regard the finds on classical sites not so much as the detritus left over from the past as a fair cross-section of the artefacts that were in use in antiquity. Ceramics in particular have fallen prey to what Anthony Snodgrass has called the " 'positivist fallacy', which assumes that the importance of a class of evidence for antiquity stands in some relation to the quantity to which it survives to be studied today".[29] Such naive positivism has come to figure large in modern ceramic scholarship. Thus, R.M. Cook maintains that "... it should be possible to compare the prosperity of contemporary settlements and sanctuaries by the amount and quality of the pottery found in them".[30] If this were indeed the case, we should perhaps judge Olympia to have been twice as wealthy as Delphi, since eight or nine attributed red-figure pots are attested from the one site and four from the other.[31] Olympia may well have been the richer, but this is not the way to establish the fact. Better perhaps to consider both sanctuaries very rich indeed, and recognise that pottery, even "fine pottery" did not figure large in ancient value systems.

So, I come before you as a repentant Beazleyite, and one who has come belatedly to understand that in the eyes of the ancients it was gold and silver that really mattered. Whether in the home or in public sanctuaries, wealth was regularly kept in the form of vessels of precious metal, and this raises another issue which has been well outlined in a related context by C.R. Dodwell: "In descriptions of the radiant trappings of society there was no difference between Anglo-Saxon poetry and those pedestrian sources for Anglo-Saxon history—the annals, the legal wills and the chronicles. What we discover, in fact, is that the poets were not dreaming up gilded visions but delineating the tastes of the world around. It was a world which both in the religious and secular spheres savoured resplendence".[32] I used to believe that when Aeschylus or Pindar refer to divine or mortal wealth in terms of "gold-wrought and silver cups"[33] or a "solid gold bowl, the peak of possessions"[34] that they may have been making poetical flights of fancy. But now that it is generally agreed— as it is by all who have recently discussed the matter—that the rich used plate; now that the picture of at least Athenian society includes a level of consumption which we might properly describe as luxurious, we can begin to think of poetic accounts of great splendour at religious festivals as perhaps reflecting reality.

Euripides' *Ion* provides a case in point. The Servant's speech at lines 1122ff. describes the erection of a tent 100 feet square adorned with rich tapestries, in which the guests are entertained with wine served from craters in gold and "silver inlaid" cups whose size increased as time went by. While this passage is rarely discussed as evidence for Greek symposia,[35] there is no reason for not taking it as such. The square tent has the shape of the dining rooms in which symposia were usually held.[36] The Lesche of the Cnidians at Delphi, whose walls were adorned with permanent reminders of valorous deeds in the form of Polygnotus' paintings, was in the shape of a double dining room: two squares side by side, which would have accomodated 30 or so people reclining on couches.[37] Ion's tent would have accommodated more than sixty couches, but even his festivities must have been on a small scale compared with the occasion at Olympia in 416 when Alcibiades celebrated his unprecedented success in having his chariot teams placed first

[24] A.W. Johnston, *Trademarks on Greek vases*, Warminster 1979, 250, n. 1, Type 26F, no. 1.

[25] Johnston (supra n. 24), 159, Type 10F, no. 21, fig. 12p.

[26] Johnston (supra n. 24), Type 14F, no. 5.

[27] Prices marked on two large red-figure hydrias in Syracuse and Leningrad: Johnston (supra n. 24), 33, 113, 165. Hydrias were in any case generally more expensive than other pots, perhaps, it has been suggested, because their shape did not allow anything to be packed inside them (Gill, supra n. 4).

[28] Dem. 24.114; cf. 24.16. The identity tags on silver *hydriai* seem to have weighed 4 drachmas: D. Harris, 'Nikokrates of Kolonos, metalworker to the Parthenon treasurers', *Hesperia* 57, 1988, 329–337, esp. 332f. Thuc. 6.46.3 suggests how relatively cheap even silver might have been considered to be.

[29] A.M. Snodgrass, *Archaic Greece: the age of experiment*, London 1980, 126.

[30] R.M. Cook, *Greek painted pottery*, 2nd ed., London 1972, 277.

[31] J.D. Beazley, *Attic red-figure vase-painters*, 2nd ed., Oxford 1963, 1771, 1715.

[32] C.R. Dodwell, *Anglo-Saxon art: a new perspective*, Manchester 1982, 12.

[33] Aesch. *fr.* 184.

[34] Pind. *Ol.* 7.1–4.

[35] The only exception known to me: P. Schmitt-Pantel, *Le cité au banquet* (BEFAR) (forthcoming).

[36] R.A. Tomlinson, 'Ancient Macedonian symposia', *Symposium Ancient Macedonia, August 1968*, Thessaloniki 1970, 308–315; *idem*, 'Perachora: the remains outside the two sanctuaries', *BSA* 64, 1969, 155–258.

[37] R.A. Tomlinson, 'Two notes on possible *hestiatoria*', *BSA* 75, 1980, 221–228.

second and fourth by entertaining the entire company. It was on this occasion too that "the various states vied with one another in showing him honour. Ephesus pitched a magnificently adorned tent for his accommodation, Chios provided feed for his horses and a quantity of animals for sacrifice, and Lesbos provided wine and everything else necessary for giving lavish entertainment".[38] If it really was then that Alcibiades purloined the official plate belonging to the Athenian delegation,[39] yet another dimension can be added to the resplendence of the scene.

Back at Delphi itself, we know that at least the huge silver wine-crater dedicated by Croesus was regularly used at a religious festival,[40] and when the sanctuary was sacked by Phocians, the Delphians subsequently claimed to have lost 10,000 talents.[41] Even allowing for an inflated insurance claim, this would leave plenty of room even for "big cups" of gold and silver.

Herodotus gives us the weight of Croesus' gold wine-crater: eight and a half talents and twelve minae.[42] And at this point I want to introduce the theme of the rest of this paper. I believe that I have come across a phenomenon which I have not seen discussed until recently, though experience tells one that the idea must lie buried somewhere in earlier literature. I owe it to a remark of David Lewis's to the effect that some "peculiar Athenian weights" of gold objects on the Acropolis might be explained in terms of darics.[43] This made me look at other "peculiar weights" with a view to seeing if there is an underlying pattern. Not only does Lewis's observation hold good for a much wider range of gold vessels than he originally had in mind, but the same principle can also be applied to silver objects whose weights are awkwardly rendered in Attic drachmae, in that they can often be read in terms of Persian *sigloi*.[44]

An example of the phenomenon in a literary source is to be found in the pseudo-Demosthentic speech *Against Timotheus*, where "two *phialai* of Lycian workmanship", among other items, were in dispute. The plaintiff's father persuaded an associate "to accept the value of the *phialai*, as much as their weight amounted to, which was two hundred and thirty-seven drachmae.[45] 237 drachmae equals 180 *sigloi* at 5.66 grams, and we may surmise that the *phialai* weighed 90 *sigloi* each. Elsewhere in the same speech, we hear of a request made by Timotheus for a loan of "thirteen hundred and fifty-one drachmae and two obols; that was the exact sum he said he wanted".[46] 1351 drachmae 2 obols equals 1025 *sigloi* at 5.67 grams—the absolute top allowable weight.

Coming back to Croesus' gold crater at Delphi, we may assume in the light of Croesus' munificence elsewhere[47] that it was of solid gold. Herodotus was writing in the fifth century, and was probably recording the weight in terms of a contemporary standard. If this was the Attic standard, the crater will have been equivalent to 224.46 kilos, and thus very close to 2700 *karsha*.[48] Little is known about the pre-Achaemenid history of the *karsha*, but Herodotus' evidence perhaps points to its having been adopted from Lydia.

It is probably because the Athenian sources dominate our view of ancient Greece, that when weights of plate have been examined in the past, it was usually expected that an Athenian pattern would emerge.[49] Extant plate made to an Athenian standard is, however, extremely rare—the two pieces from Duvanli are exceptional; rather, most surviving plate appears to have been made to an Achaemenid Persian or to the closely related Thraco-Macedonian standard.[50]

Very many finds of gold and silver have been made in Bulgaria, in Central and Northern Thrace.[51] The bulk of them were hidden in an emergency which seems to have occurred between about 330 and 320, although I must confess that my inclination to think in terms of those

---

38 Plut. *Alc.* 12.1.

39 Plut. *Alc.* 13.

40 The *Theophania*: Hdt. 1.51.

41 Diod. 16.56; equivalent to more than 250 tonnes of silver.

42 Hdt. 1.50.

43 Lewis (supra n. 5), 77.

44 *Sigloi* were struck on two weight standards: an earlier one which ranged between *c.* 5.20 and 5.49 grams and a later, heavier standard of between *c.* 5.40 and 5.67 grams; the best summary is by S.P. Noe, 'Two hoards of Persian sigloi', *NNM* 136, 1956, 1–44, esp. 42.

45 [Dem.] 49.32.

46 [Dem.] 49.7.

47 Hdt. 1.50, 92; 6.124.

48 At 25.86 kilos to the talent (i.e. 4.31 grams to the drachma: cf. M. Lang, *OCD*[2] 1138), Herodotus' weight would be equivalent to 224982 grams; at 25.80 (4.3 grams to the drachma), 224460. The *karsha* weighed 83.3 grams (cf. A.D.H. Bivar, 'Achaemenid coins, weights and measures', *Cambridge History of Iran* 2, Cambridge 1985, 637). 224982 divided by 83.3 = 2700.86; 224460 divided by 83.3 = 2694.60.

49 E.g. Bothmer (supra n. 5), 155; A. Oliver, *Silver for the Gods*, Toledo Ohio 1977, 15.

50 For the possible use of the Thraco-Macedonian standard, see M. Vickers, 'Persian, Thracian and Greek gold and silver: questions of metrology', in A. Kuhrt & H. Sancisi-Weerdenburg (eds.), *Achaemenid history* 6. *Proceedings of the Eighth Achaemenid History Workshop, Groningen 1988* (forthcoming).

51 A. Fol, B. Nikolov & R.F. Hoddinott, *The new Thracian treasure from Rogozen, Bulgaria*, London, British Museum 1986, 10.

Fig. 6. Part of the Rogozen treasure (Courtesy of the Bulgarian Committee for Culture).

dates is coloured by the knowledge—which I owe to Isager and Hansen's important study—that there was a severe drought in the Aegean and surrounding areas at that time.[52] Panagyurishte is by far the richest hoard discovered so far, and its metrology was investigated in exemplary fashion by Herbert Cahn in 1960.[53] Cahn was able to show, by examining the weights of the various gold objects, that some were made in units of Persian darics, and others in units of Alexander staters, and he drew the conclusion that the amphora, rhyta, jugs and *phiale* were made about the time, in the latter part of the fourth century B.C., when the one unit of currency was being replaced by the other.

The Panagyurishte *phiale* with its heads of black youths has been associated, and surely rightly, with the *phialai Aithiopides* mentioned on fourth century inscriptions,[54] and the rows of acorns and beechnuts in turn associates it with the *phialai karyotai* also referred to in

[52] S. Isager & M.H. Hansen, *Aspects of Athenian society in the fourth century B.C.*, Odense 1975, 200–208; cf. J.M. Camp, 'Drought and famine in the 4th century B.C.', in *Studies in Athenian architecture, sculpture and topography presented to H.A. Thompson* (*Hesperia*, Suppl. 20), 1982, 9–17; P. Garnsey, *Famine and food supply in the Graeco-Roman world*, Cambridge 1988, esp. 145f.

[53] Cahn (supra n. 5), 26–29; cf. Strong (supra n. 16), 97, 102; J.G. Griffith, 'The siege scene on the gold amphora of the Panagjurischte Treasure', *JHS* 94, 1974, 38–42. For the Panagyurishte Treasure in general: D. Tsontschev, *Der Goldschatz von Panagjurischte*, Berlin 1959; I. Venedikov, *The Panagjurischte gold treasure*, Sofia 1961; Exhibition Catalogue, *Thracian treasures from Bulgaria*, London, British Museum 1976; Exhibition Catalogue Mainz, *Gold der Thraker: archäologische Schätze aus Bulgarien*, Mainz 1979, frontispiece and 180–188, 199, 200.

[54] N. Kondoleon, 'The gold treasure of Panagurischte', *Balkan Studies* 3, 1962, 185–200.

Table 1. Rogozen.

Catalogue Number	Shape & Inventory Numbers	Wt in grams	sigloi	Weight	T–M drachmai	Weight
1	*Phiale* B-590 22301	337.69	60	5.62	96	3.51
2	*Phiale* B-428 22302	253.52	45	5.58	72	3.49
3	*Phiale* B-586 22303	171.48	30	5.67	48	3.54
4	*Phiale* B-464 22304	182.83	33.33	5.52	53	3.47
5	*Phiale* B-514 22305	69.22	12.5	5.52	20	3.45
94	*Phiale* B-429 22394	178.04	32	5.56	52	3.42
95	*Phiale* B-543 22395	170.29	31	5.50	50	3.41
96	*Phiale* B-556 22396	67.92	12	5.66	19.5	3.48
97	*Phiale* B-465 22397	281.66	50	5.61	80	3.51
98	*Phiale* B-491 22398	50.78	9.5	5.39	15	3.41

fourth century temple inventories and which David Lewis has argued were akin to, indeed interchangeable with, *phialai balanotai* ("knobbed libation bowls").[55] All three categories appear to have been made to a hundred daric standard,[56] and it is interesting that the Panagyurishte *phiale* weighs exactly 100 darics (though it is inscribed "196 drachmas and one twenty-fourth").[57]

Although it has been suggested that such *phialai Aithiopides* were made at Athens,[58] is seems likely that we should look to the Achaemenid empire. Their metrology alone would not justify this, but their decoration recalls Herodotus' account of the sources of Persian tribute. Every two years, the Ethiopians sent to the Persian king "two measures of gold nuggets, two hundred ebony logs, five Ethiopian boys, and twenty large elephant tusks".[59] If there is an allusion of this kind being made, the four *phialai Aithiopides* recorded on the Athenian Acropolis from the 370s,[60] may be the fruits of Athenian diplomatic contacts with Persia in the years following the King's Peace.[61]

There is a fine example in New York of a *phiale kary-*

55 Lewis (supra n. 5), 77.
56 Lewis (supra n. 5), 77.
57 Cahn (supra n. 5), 27; Lewis (supra n. 5), 76; Vickers (supra n. 5), 50.
58 By Lewis (supra n. 5), 77.
59 Herodotus 3.97.
60 *IG* II^2, no. 1413, 7–8.
61 For a hundred daric *phiale* given to an Athenian by the Great King earlier in the fourth century, see Vickers (supra n. 5).

Fig. 7. Silver cup from Nymphaeum, Crimaea. Ashmolean Museum, Oxford (Museum photograph).

ote decorated with acorns and beechnuts.[62] It weighs exactly 90 darics, and I have suggested that its imagery may be a play on the Old Persian words for "wood", "gold" and "daric": *daru, *dariyaka, *darayaka*.[63] Again, both metrology and imagery combine to suggest a Persian origin for the type.

The 165 pieces of silver in the Rogozen hoard (*Fig. 6*) found in 1985 and 1986 and publicised with admirable speed by the Bulgarian authorities[64] have added a great deal to our knowledge of ancient silver plate. Nearly all the objects from Rogozen were *phialai* and jugs. Two groups, one of 100 objects, the other of 65, were found. When the Rogozen Treasure was in London, it was possible to weigh the individual pieces accurately, and with Dan Quillen, the Waynflete Professor of Pure Mathematics at Oxford, lending a guiding hand figures like those in *Table 1* emerged.[65] These figures are typical: with but a few exceptions the weights could easily be read in terms of Persian *sigloi* or the closely related Thraco-Macedonian drachmae—insofar as it is possible to do so at all given the damaged condition of some of the pieces.

No. 2 is a silver *phiale* with large lobes and a stylised floral pattern. Anyone would, I think, have attributed it to a Persian source, but it is good to have this apparently confirmed by the weight of 45 *sigloi*. The weight of No. 4, a very beautiful *phiale* decorated with Auge and Heracles, is a third of 100 *sigloi* which makes it fall easily into the Persian rather than the Thracian weight standard, and it is easy to imagine that it may have been imported from a Greek city on the western seaboard of Asia Minor. The *phiale* No. 97 decorated with stylised winged horned lions could just as easily be 50 *sigloi* as 80 Thraco-Macedonian drachmai, but its decorative scheme strongly suggests that it too was imported from Anatolia. Similar in conception, though probably earlier, is a silver *phiale* in the Metropolitan Museum decorated with a series of reliefs of the Great King walking on eagles' heads[66]—a golden eagle was, as Carl Nylander has reminded us, the standard of the Great King.[67] No one, I think, has ever doubted an Asia Minor provenance for this piece, and it is also interesting to note that its weight converts neatly to 45 *sigloi*. Indeed, many of the silver objects acquired during the past few years by the Metropolitan seem to have been made according ot a Persian *siglos* standard, and I am glad to say that Dietrich von Bothmer concurs with this view, having arrived at it independently.

Some of the pieces in both groups in the Rogozen hoard are badly damaged. Nevertheless, their total weight of 19.91 kilos is equivalent to 3600 silver *sigloi* whose average weight is 5.53 grams. Judging by a "slightly chipped" Achaemenid weight from Persepolis which weighs half the weight of the Rogozen hoard, and is inscribed "120 karsha" in Old Persian[68] and "20 minae" in Babylonian,[69] it seems likely that the Rogozen

[62] Bothmer (supra n. 5), 154–166; *idem*, 'A Greek and Roman treasury', *BMMA* n.s. 62, 1984, 86.

[63] Vickers (supra n. 5), 53, n. 23.

[64] 'Katalog na Rogozenskoto sakrovishte', *Izkustvo* 36 June, Sofia 1986; *Frakiiskii klad iz Rogozena*, Moscow, Pushkin Museum 1986; Fol, Nikolov & Hoddinott (supra n. 51).

[65] The figures are taken from M. Vickers, 'Panagyurishte, Dalboki, Lukovit and Rogozen: questions of metrology and status', in *The Rogozen Treasure*, ed. B.F. Cook, London 1989, 101–111.

[66] D. von Bothmer, 'Les trésors de l'orfèvrerie de la Grèce orientale au Metropolitan Museum de New York', *CRAI* 1981, 195f., fig. 2; *idem* 1984 (supra n. 62), 25, no. 18.

[67] Xen. *Anab.* 1.10.4; *Cyr.* 7.1.4; cf. C. Nylander, 'The standard of the Great King—a problem in the Alexander mosaic', *OpRom* 14, 1983, 19–37.

[68] R.G. *Old Persian*, New Haven 1950, 114, 157 [Wc].

[69] E.F. Schmidt, *The treasury of Persepolis and other discoveries in the homeland of the Achaemenians* (Oriental Institute Communications, No. 21), Chicago 1939, 62f., fig. 43.

hoard represented a notional load of 240 Persian karsha. A "round" overall weight was arrived at despite the damage and loss suffered by some of the pieces, and this in turn implies that all the silver objects were destined for the melting pot, the usual fate of silver through the ages from antiquity to the present day.[70]

The *phiale* weighing 33.33 *sigloi* is far from unusual. A silver cup (*Fig. 7*) from Nymphaeum in Oxford[71] also weighs a third of a hundred *sigloi*. It is also made of extremely pure silver (98.7%), and this too seems to have been the norm. Thus two silver beakers from the Thracian burial at Dalboki in Bulgaria[72] are made from 98.5% and 99.4% pure silver respectively.[73] Modern silver, at least in England and America, usually has an additive of 7.5% of copper to prevent wear and tear, and this has given rise to the view that since "pure silver is generally considered too soft for making vessels" this must have obtained in antiquity as well.[74] In fact, such considerations were secondary to purity,[75] something which is in principle closely linked with the apparent emphasis laid on the weight of plate.

There were three beakers found in the Dalboki tomb in 1879. Two are in Oxford (*Figs. 8* and *9*), but the third one is in Leningrad (*Fig. 10*).[76] It was only when Irene Saverkina of the Hermitage kindly provided the weight of the beaker in her keeping that the metrology of the three beakers began to make sense. Their total weight is 560 grams, which easily converts to 100 *sigloi* of 5.6 grams.

It also seems that the three beakers from Dalboki were a stacking set,[77] with the Leningrad piece fitting neatly between the two in Oxford (*Fig. 11*). If they had been kept in such a way, it would explain why one of the Oxford beakers has a relatively fresh surface, while the other one is somewhat abraded. Stacking sets, usually of *phialai*, occur frequently in inventories. But the important point is that the pieces have been made to a round figure. If plate did form a major part of a family or a sanctuary's liquid assets, then the apparent fact that gold and silver vessels were made up in round figures in terms of coinage standards perhaps provides the answer to the question which is often raised by numismatists in the face of the comparative paucity of fractional coinage, namely "Where was the small change?" If plate served in effect as large denomination bank notes, and a drachma was considered in some circles to be a "trifling sum", then the coins we have were probably the "small change".

There are one or two indications that plate could be regarded simply as bullion. Apart from temple inventories, we find Aristophanes referring in his *Babylonians* of 426 to a drinking vessel worth two minae. One character says "I owe a debt of 200 drachmas. How can I pay it?" His companion replies: "Here, take this silver cup and pay for it with that".[78] Even without Pollux's gloss,[79] it is clear that the vessel was simply worth its weight in silver. We might also compare Demosthenes' "gold vessels, weighing a mina each".[80] Decoration could naturally have added to the value of an object when it was new and fashionable,[81] but the value could not fall below the weight, assuming the metal was pure.

It was the weight which was crucial when officials came to compile the lists of objects in sanctuaries when handing over responsibility to their successors,[82] and there are several such lists extant. In my *AJA* paper, I examined the inventories relating to the Parthenon during the fifth century B.C.[83] (revising some of the figures which appeared in the proceedings of the Bordeaux conference on "L'or perse").[84] The list in *Table 2* gives an idea of the results obtained. Needless to say, the list only includes those objects for which complete weights are preserved: there are many for which weights are not given at all, or which only survive in fragmentary fashion. The weights as we have them are given in Attic drachmae (which I have taken to be the equivalent of 4.3

[70] Cf. G. Reitlinger, *The economics of taste* 2, London 1963, 14; H. Seemann & F. Ward, 'Silber, Metall für alle Tage', *Zeit Magazin*, 2 November 1984.

[71] M. Vickers, *Scythian treasures in Oxford*, Oxford 1979, pl. 13a.

[72] V. Prochorov, *Bolgarskiya raskopki bliz' Eski-zagr'i*, St Petersburg 1880; Oliver (supra n. 49), 30, no. 5; Catalogue, *Ermitazh: Antichnoe khudozhestbennoe serebro*, Leningrad 1985, 18f., no. 9; D.W.J. Gill, 'Classical Greek fictile imitations of precious metal vases', in Vickers (supra n. 5), 17, 24, fig. 26.

[73] Kindly analyzed by Zofya Stos-Gale by energy dispersive X-ray fluorescence.

[74] Strong (supra n. 16), 4.

[75] On the purity of Attic silver, see Polyb. 21.32.8 and 43.19.

[76] Leningrad Catalogue (supra n. 72).

[77] A suggestion I owe to my colleague Gerald Taylor.

[78] Ar. fr. 68 K–A.

[79] Poll. 10.85.

[80] Dem. 24.184.

[81] Cf. Pliny, *HN* 33.1.4.5: '... we have made gold and silver dearer by the art of engraving'.

[82] T. Linders, 'The purpose of inventories: a close reading of the Delian inventories of the Independence', in *Comptes et inventaires dans la cité grecque: Actes du colloque international d'épigraphie tenu à Neuchâtel 1986 en l'honneur de Jacques Tréheux*, ed. D. Knoepfler, Neuchâtel & Genève 1988, 37–47.

[83] Usefully summarised by W.E. Thompson in D.M. Lewis (ed.), *IG* I^3, pp. 305f., 318, 331f.

[84] M. Vickers, 'Persian gold on the Athenian Acropolis', *REA* 91, 1989, 249–257.

Fig. 8. Silver beaker from Dalboki, Thrace. Ashmolean Museum, Oxford (Museum photograph).

Fig. 9. Silver beaker from Dalboki, Thrace. Ashmolean Museum, Oxford (Museum photograph).

Fig. 10. Silver beaker from Dalboki, Thrace. Hermitage Museum, Leningrad (Museum photograph).

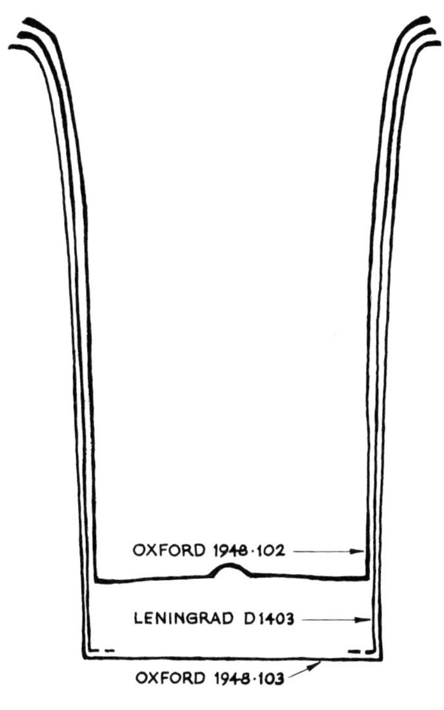

Fig. 11. The three silver beakers from Dalboki as a nesting set.

Table 2. Athens, Parthenon. Silver vessels.

Object and date of first appearance	Wt in Attic drachmae	Wt in grams	sigloi	Average weight of sigloi
a) Pronaos (*IG* I^3, pp. 305–6)				
(1) 3 *kerata*: 434/3	528	2265.12 (@4.29 grams)	400	5.66
(2) lamp: 434/3	38	163.40	30	5.45
(3) *poterion*: 430/29	25			
(4) 7 *phialai*: 429/8	700			
(5) 2 *phialai*: 428/7	200			
(6) 4 *phialai*: 427/6	329	1414.70	250	5.66
(7) Chalcidian *poterion* 427/6	40			
(8) 7 *phialai* 426/5	920	3956.00	700	5.65
(9) 4 *phialai* 425/4	420	1806.00	320	5.64
(10) *poterion* 425/4	40			
(11) 7 *phialai* 424/3	643 dr. 2 obols	2766.33	500	5.53

grams),[85] but while some are clearly "round" and are given in minae: at [4] 7 *phialai* at presumably 1 mina each, and [5] 2 *phialai* weighing 2 minae, presumably 1 mina each, others are clearly not. Among the earlier dedications in the Pronaos, for example, the 528 dr. at [1], the 38 dr. at [2], the 329 dr. at [6], the 910 dr. at [8] and especially the 643 drachmae 2 obols at [11] are so much out of keeping with some of the others that they invited a search for some other weight standard which might have been employed. But when the later Persian *siglos* standard is applied, we get 3 drinking horns weighing 400 *sigloi* [1], a lamp [2] weighing 30 *sigloi*, a set of four *phialai* [6] weighing a total of 250 *sigloi*,

[85] This is a slightly arbitrary procedure, in that e.g. the *kantharos* Plovdiv 1634 (*Fig. 1*) weighs 1073 grams (= 250 drachmae @ 4.29 grams), and the *phiale* Plovdiv 1515 (*Fig. 2*) weighs 428 grams (= 100 drachmae @ 4.28 grams), and inscriptions on two vessels from Verghina show them to have been based on drachmae of 4.29 and 4.28 respectively (M. Andronicos, *Vergina, the Royal tombs and the ancient city*, Athens 1984, 159).

seven *phialai* [8] weighing 700 *sigloi* (probably 100 each), four *phialai* [9] weighing 320 *sigloi* (perhaps 80 each), and a set of seven *phialai* [11] weighing 500 *sigloi*. The last mentioned is much "rounder" than 643 drachmae 2 obols. This pattern appears to exist throughout the rest of the Parthenon silver, which is either made according to an Attic or a Persian standard—and the gold; this also appears to have been made according to the Attic or Persian standards, but either in terms of drachmae or darics.

The "peculiar Athenian weights" principle can thus be extended over a wider area than a few gold *phialai*. Quite what this means is another matter. In my *AJA* paper I was content to think that round figures in drachmas implied domestic production, and odd numbers which came up in *sigloi* or darics, foreign. But while this may often have been the case, the situation is perhaps rather more complex. There are, for example, recorded cases of gold and silver plate made in Attica by at least one Athenian craftsman which appear to have been made to the Persian standard. Thus Diane Harris has recently discussed three gold *phialai* inscribed with the name of Nicocrates of Colonus as maker which appear in an inventory list of the Treasurers of Athena for the year 319/8 B.C., and which together weigh 593 drachmas:[86] "593 drachmas divided by three renders an average weight of 197 drachmas each"[87]—or, one would suggest, 100 darics each.[88] Nicocrates' silver *hydria* of 313/2 weighing 1438 drachmas[89] was, moreover, equivalent to 1100 *sigloi*. It might seem therefore, that the use of a Persian weight standard does not automatically mean manufacture in the Persian empire, and this impression is borne out by an examination of oddly expressed weights in other inventories.

This report on "peculiar weights" is far from comprehensive,[90] nor can I claim necessarily to have come up with the right explanation every time, but I hope that it is clear that there are indeed some underlying patterns in the metrology of plate listed in the inventories. It may be thought that there is too great a subjective element in the procedure—that things ought to be more clear cut, with less variation in the average weights of the *sigloi* and darics.[91] All that one can say is that we are dealing with objects made by different craftsmen at different times, objects which will have experienced different kinds of wear and tear. A further complicating factor is that they will have been weighed with equipment of varying degrees of accuracy.

An inventory roughly contemporary with those of the Parthenon is the list of items in the keeping of the treasurers of the Other Gods (429/8 B.C.). Very few complete weights survive, but among them are those relating to quite large amounts of silver belonging to different Athenian cult-centres. There is a complete series between lines 65 and 79, and they are set out at *Table 3*.[92] While little can be done with the silver *phialai* of Hera or the silver of Datyllos, the figures for some of the other properties can easily be read in Persian terms. The four *karchesia* weighing one third of a myriad of *sigloi* and the silver of Olympian Zeus weighing 4500 *sigloi* are especially suggestive. Until recently, these figures would have been considered surprising in that they would appear to set at nought the provisions of the Coinage Decree. Now, however, a crucial inscription cut with three-bar sigmas and tailed rhos[93] has been shown to have been cut in 418/7,[94] and not in 458/7 as was generally thought, and as a consequence the arguments put forward by Harold Mattingly for a date after 429/8 for the Coinage, or Standards,[95] Decree can be seen to be fundamentally sound.[96]

An example of the apparent use of a Persian weight standard from a much later period is to be found in the list at *Table 4*, which summarises lines 73–85 of *IDélos* 442B. For line upon line, the weights of *phialai* in this inventory are given in round figures in drachmae, and usually in minae into the bargain. Then suddenly, one gets odd numbers like 139, 143, 138 and so on for a series of *phialai leiai*; odd numbers again for a series of *phialai karyotai*; and again for two *oinochoai*. Then the round figures in minae carry on. While the weights of the individual objects in these groups do not seem to

[86] Harris (supra n. 28), 330.
[87] Harris (supra n. 28), 330.
[88] Cf. the Panagyurishte *phiale* inscribed "196 drachmas and one twenty-fourth", and weighing 100 darics.
[89] *IG* II² 1480 A, 8–11; Harris (supra n. 28), 334f.
[90] Very helpful leads were to be found in T. Linders, 'Gods, gifts, society', in *Gifts to the Gods* (Boreas 15), Uppsala 1985, 116, n. 9, and *eadem* (supra n. 82).
[91] The weights of extant darics vary between 8.25 and 8.46 grams: E. Babelon, *Les Perses achéménides*, Paris 1893, 1–16.
[92] *IG* I³ 383, 65–79; T. Linders, *The treasures of the Other Gods in Athens and their functions*, Meisenheim 1975.
[93] *IG* I³ 11.
[94] M.H. Chambers, R. Gallucci & P. Spanos, 'Athens' alliance with Egesta in the year of Antiphon', *ZPE* 83, 1990, 38–63.
[95] Chambers, Gallucci & Spanos (supra n. 94), 55.
[96] For recent (but now somewhat redundant) discussions of the issues involved, see D.M. Lewis, 'The Athenian Coinage Decree', in *Coinage and administration in the Athenian and Persian empires* (The Ninth Oxford Symposium on Coinage and Monetary History), ed. I. Carradice, (BAR-IS, 343), Oxford 1987, 53–63; H.B. Mattingly, 'The Athenian Coinage Decree and the assertion of Empire', ibid., 65–71.

Table 3. Athens, Other Gods.

Line number/ object(s)	Wt in Attic drachmae	Wt in grams	Sigloi	Weight of sigloi
65 silver *phialai* of Hera in Xypetos Dionysou	860 dr. 1 ob.			
68–71 4 *karchesia*	4395 dr. 1 ob.	18899.27	3333.33	5.67
72–3 silver of Ge Olympia	494 dr.	2124.20	375	5.66
74–7 silver of Theseus	4270 dr.	18361.00	3250	5.65
76–7 silver of Datyllos	346 dr.			
78–9 Silver of Olympian Zeus	5931 dr.	25503.30	4500	5.67

Table 4. Delos.

Line number/ object(s)		Wt in Attic drachmae	Wt in grams	Darics	Weight of darics
73/2 *phialai*		200			
73–4/2 *phialai*		200			
75/*phiale*		100			
76/ring		3 obols			
76–7/16 *phialai*		1600			
77/4 *phialai*		400			
77/2 *phialai*		200			
78/16 *phialai*		1600			
78/4 *phialai*		400			
78/*phiale leia*		139			
79/*phiale leia*		143			
79/*phiale leia*		138			
79/*phiale leia*		140			
79–80/*phiale leia*		136			
80/*phiale leia*		135			
80/*phiale leia*		136			
	Total	970	4171	500	8.34
80–81/*phiale karyote*		198 dr. 3 ob.			
81/*phiale karyote*		196 dr. 3 ob.			
81/*phiale karyote*		192			
81/*phiale karyote*		196			
82/*phiale karyote*		190 dr. 4 ob.			
82/*phiale karyote*		190			
	Total	1163 dr. 4 ob.	5003.76	600	8.34
82/*oinochoe*		685			
82–3/*oinochoe*		679			
	Total	1364	5865.20	700	8.38
83/*phiale*		100			
83–4/16 *phialai*		1600			
84/4 *phialai*		400			
84–5/16 *phialai*		1600			
etc.					

Table 5. Delos.

Line number/ object(s)		Wt in Attic drachmae in 161B	Wt in *IDélos* 442B	% discrepancy
26–7/ Thericlean *kylix*		236	233	1.3
. . . .				
27–9/ 7 *phialai leiai*:				
1st		146		
2nd		142		
3rd		142		
4th		140		
5th		139		
6th		144		
7th		138		
	Total	991	970	2.1
30–31/ 6 *phialai karyotai*:				
1st		202		
2nd		204		
3rd		195		
4th		193		
5th		201		
6th		196		
	Total	1191	1163 dr. 4 ob.	2.1
31/ gold *phiale*		201	194	3.5
. . . .				
33/ 2 *oinochoai*				
1st		697 dr. 2 ob.	685	
2nd		685	679	
	Total	1382	1364	1.4

Line number/ object(s)	Inscribed weight	Weight as weighed	% discrepancy
108–9/ 5th crown	118 dr. 3 ob.[97]	122	2.9
109/ 6th crown	63	65	3
110/ 10th crown	95 dr. 3 ob.	96	3.8
111–12/ 11th crown	66 dr. 4 ob.	68	2
112/ 13th crown	82 dr. 3 ob.	83 dr. 3 ob.	1.2
112/ 15th crown	82 dr. 3 ob.	84 dr. 3 ob.	2.5
113–14/ 19th crown	82 dr. 3 ob.	82 dr. 4 ob.	0.2
114/ 20th crown	100	101 dr. 3 ob.	1.5

make much sense, the total weight in each category do so in terms of darics, viz. 500, 600 and 700: 1800 darics in all. The smooth *phialai* and the *oinochoai* were inscribed "[the property of] Delian Apollo [and] Delian Artemis", while the *phialai karyotai* (presumably a stacking set of six) were simply inscribed "[the property of] Delian Apollo".

These objects are somewhat exceptional in this inventory (apart from one or two gold vessels in the Temple of Artemis which might also have been made to a daric standard):[98] most figures are given in round figures in Attic drachmae, and when they are odd there is an obvious reason for it—rentals, wages, scraps of metal. The relatively complete Delian inventory of a century earlier (*IG* XI.2 161) has rather more "peculiar weights", but it

[97] *IG* XI.2 161B, 108 reads 113 dr. 3 ob., but this was a mistake. The weight given here is taken from *IG* XI.2 199B, 29. I am grateful to Professor Tréheux for bringing this to my attention (and see his paper elsewhere in this volume).

[98] One thinks in particular of the gold Thericlean at line 181 (233 drachmae: 120 darics @ 8.35 grams); the *phiale karyote* dedicated by the Naxians to Apollo at line 182 (194 drachmae: 100 darics @ 8.34 grams); and the fluted *phiale* in the same line (64 drachmae: 33.33 darics at 8.32 grams).

Table 6. Didyma.

Deity	Shape	Weight in drachmae	Weight in grams	Darics	Average weight in grams
Agathe Tyche	*Phiale karyote*	247	1062.10		
Osiris	*Phiale karyote*	190	817.00		
Leto	*Phiale karyote*	198 3 ob.	853.55		
		Subtotal	2732.65	330	8.28
Hecate	*Phiale aktinote*	113	485.90		
Artemis	Double deer head *rhyton*	161	692.30		
		Subtotal	1178.20	140	8.42
Apollo	Pair of double goat-stag[99] *rhyta*	318 3 ob.	1369.55	165	8.30
Zeus Soter	Horn	173 3 ob.	746.05	90	8.29
Theoi Soteiroi	*Oinochoe*	386	1659.80	200	8.30
Sotira	*Psykter*	372	1599.60	190	8.42
	Bread Platter	1088	4678.40	560	8.35
	Totals	3247 3 ob.	13,964.25	1675	8.34

Table 7. Samos, Heraeum.

Shelf number	Wt in Attic drachmae	Weight in grams	Darics	Weight of darics
Phialai, if gold:				
1	919 dr.	3,951.70	475	8.32
2	952 dr. 4 ob.	4,096.46	490	8.36
3	892 dr. 2 ob.	3,837.03	460	8.34
4	information incomplete			
5	911 dr. 3 ob.	3,919.45	470	8.34
6	944 dr. 3 ob.	4,061.35	485	8.37
7	927 dr. 2 ob.	3,987.53	475	8.39
8	937 dr. 2 ob.	4,030.53	480	8.40
9	894 dr. 4 ob.	3,847.06	460	8.36
10	907 dr.	3,900.10	470	8.30
11	953 dr. 2 ob.	4,099.33	490	8.37
12	905 dr. 3 ob.	3,893.65	465	8.37
13	929 dr.	3,994.70	480	8.32
14	956 dr.	4,110.80	490	8.39
15	890 dr. 2 ob.	3,828.43	460	8.32
16	953 dr. 5 ob.	4,101.48	490	8.37
17	information incomplete			
18	936 dr. 3 ob.	4,026.95	480	8.39
19	908 dr.	3,904.40	470	8.31
20	information incomplete			
21	information incomplete			

is a far from straightforward task to elucidate them, since the officials who carried out the weighing process seem to have done so with equipment that was seriously deficient. This can be shown by comparing (*Table 5*) the weights given for the vessels we have just discussed with those in *IDélos* 442B. The *phialai* and *oinochoai* mentioned at B 27–33 are overweight, but inconsistently. My guess is that the actual silver coins used in the weighing process were badly but differentially worn.[100] We can hardly accuse the officials of carelessness, for the inventory in question is given in scrupulous detail. Sometimes even, the weights inscribed on the objects are overridden and new, apparently greater weights given. This is clear from the information concerning the crowns in lines B 108–114. So, 161 is an uncertain tool to use

[99] The stone is now badly damaged, but early manuscript copies confirm the reading *tragelaphon*: see Petzl (infra n. 106).

[100] For a discussion of the techniques used, see C.H. Grayson, *Weighing in Ancient Greece* (Oxford D.Phil. thesis 1975).

Table 8. Imbros.

Line number/ object(s)	Wt in Attic drachmae	Weight in grams	Darics	Weight of darics
A. Gold				
17 *plastra*	27 dr.	116.10	14	8.29
18 *hormiskos*	64 dr. 4 ob.	278.06	33.33	8.34
19 12 small *lepidiskai*	3 dr. 5 3/4 ob.	[4 dr?]		
20 2 larger ones	19 dr. 3 ob.	83.85	10	8.39
21 *boubalia*	68 dr. 3 ob.	294.55	35	8.41

Line number/ object(s)	Wt in Attic drachmae	Weight in grams	Sigloi	Weight of sigloi
B. Silver				
22 *escharis*	309 dr.	1328.70	235	5.65
23 *libanotis*	91 dr	391.3	70	5.59
24 *kerykeion*	33 dr.			
25 *karchesion*	242 dr. 4 ob.	1043.46	185	5.64
26 4 *phialai*	60 dr.			
27 2 *phialai*	61 dr.			
28 2 *phialai*	62 dr.			
Total	183 dr.	786.90	140	5.62
29 4 *phialai*	50 +			
30 1 *phiale*	56 +			

Table 9. Rhodian Peraea.

Line number/ object(s)	Wt in Attic drachmae	Weight in grams	Darics	Weight of darics
18–24 *phiale* dedicated by 8 individuals	198	845.46 (@4.27 grams)	100	8.46
25–30 *phiale* dedicated by 5 individuals	147	632.1	75	8.43
31–37 *phiale* dedicated by 7 individuals	97 dr. 4 ob.	419.96	50	8.40

for metrological work, rich as it is in informative detail.

It is fascinating to learn there, for example, of Aristarchus the silversmith who had been employed to do odd jobs during the previous year: he was paid 2 drachmas for "attaching the handle of the silver crater which had fallen off"; the 3 obols' worth of coals, which is the next entry[101] was presumably part of the expenditure for the same job. Later Aristarchus was paid 1 drachma 1 1/2 obols "for making a cup",[102] and then paid 1 drachma for "repairing the handle of a bronze cothon", in connection with which a drachma's worth of coals and another of wax were used.[103]

About ten years before the earlier Delian inscription (in 288/87 B.C.), Seleucus I wrote a letter describing the gold objects he proposed to present to the shrine of Apollo at Didyma (*Table 6*).[104] Not only is the total weight given (3248 drachmae 3 obols; in fact, one drachma more than the total weight of the individual items), but the individual weights are mentioned as well. There are brief descriptions of the objects and an indication of the deities to whom they were dedicated. Individually the three *phialai karyotai* do not make for round

[101] *IG* XI.2 161A, 102.

[102] *IG* XI.2 161A, 107.

[103] *IG* XI.2 161A, 111–112.

[104] *IDidyma* 424; G. Petzl, 'Zum Brief Seleukos' I., C.B. Wells, Royal correspondence Nr. 5', in *Erol Atalay Memorial*, ed. H. Malay (Arkeoloji Dergisi Özel sayr, 1), Izmir 1991, 145–152.

Table 10. Didyma.

Line number/ object(s)	Wt in Attic drachmae	Weight in grams	Darics	Weight of darics
10–13 *hydria*	1490	6407	770	8.32
13–16 *phiale* dedicated by king Prusias	300			
17–18 *phiale* of Cyzicenes	100			
18–20 *phiale* of Krateros	90 [Milesian]			
20–22 *kanoun* of tribe of Asopis	500			
22–25 2 *prousides* dedicated by king Prusias	816*	3508.80	415	8.46
	836	3594.80	425	8.46
25–29 *libanotis*	[100 *chryseoi* + *embolon* of 40 dr. 3 ob.]			
29–31 . . REPIS of queen Kamasarye	[187 1/2 *chryseoi* (= 360 drachmae?)]			
32–33 vessel for berries	[100 chryseoi]			

* Line 24: *KAIEK*. Sherard, now destroyed; *triakonta*? Haussoullier; *<ek>kai<d>ek[a]*? Rehm.

numbers in darics (approximately 128, 98 and 103), but when they are taken together they add up to 330: a "round … number" in the ancient Near East according to A.H. Sayce.[105] *Phialai* are in any case weighed together in groups, and we have seen from the Dalboki beakers how several objects might be made together with a view of achieving a round common weight. These were clearly *phialai* decorated with acorns (*karyon* = nut), and we might well think of Seleucus' gifts as resembling the gold *phiale* in New York. The other vessels also appear to have been made according to an Achaemenid standard, but whether they came from a Persian source as booty or were made more recently according to a Persian weight standard is impossible to say.[106]

This raises a question which I have not yet been able to answer satisfactorily, namely the degree to which Achaemenid standards survived after the introduction of Alexander's gold staters. I suspect, however, that they did continue in use and that the reason may lie in part in the inherent conservatism of goldsmiths, and in part in Persian weights being considered *chic*, being thought fashionable, and thus appropriate for the materials with which the Achaemenid empire was associated. Similar considerations—of conservatism and fashion—may also have lain behind their earlier use in Athenian contexts.

This will doubtless have been the case with the shelvesful of *phialai* in the Samian Heraeum listed in 346 B.C. Although the material from which they are made is not specified, it is almost certainly gold. The weights are given by the treasurers in Attic drachmas (*Table 7*),[107] where they look odd. Converted into Persian darics they look somehow rounder. But they belong to a period before the fall of the Persian empire. The inventory from Imbros (*Table 8*)[108] dates from a period when we might have expected Persian weights to have ceased to be used (*c*. 250–200 B.C.), but they do nevertheless appear to be still current. Similarly, the inventory from the Rhodian Peraea of *c*. 200 B.C. (*Table 9*),[109] which presumably describes gold *phialai* rather than silver, suggests that the daric was still the unit in which plate might be made. Later still, in 180/79 B.C., we find two drinking vessels known as *prousides* apparently made in units of darics and dedicated at Didyma (*Table 10*)[110] by Prusias, the king notorious for luxury and effeminacy[111] after whom they were named. He had also dedicated a *phiale* which weighed three minae, which

105 A.H. Sayce, *The Ancient Empires of the East: Herodotos I–III*, London 1883, 177, n. 1.

106 *Tragelaphai*/"goat-stags" (cf. Petzl [supra n. 104], 148f.) do, however, sound Persian; cf. Ar. *Frogs* 937.

107 D. Ohly, 'Göttin und Basis', *AM* 68, 1953, 46–49.

108 J. Tréheux, 'L'inventaire des cléruques d'Imbros', *BCH* 80, 1956, 462–479; *idem*, 'Retour à Imbros et à Samothrace', in *Hellenika symmikta. Etudes d'archéologie classique* 7, Nancy 1992, 145f.

109 P.M. Fraser & G.E. Bean, *The Rhodian Peraea and its islands*, Oxford 1954, 20–22, no. 11.

110 *IDidyma* 463.

111 Ath. 11.496d.

Fig. 12. Silver Etruscan mirror. Ashmolean Museum, Oxford (Museum photograph).

was the most customary thing to do by this period.

A silver mirror in Oxford (*Fig. 12*) provides an index of the influence over both space and time of Achaemenid weight standards. It is an Etruscan mirror of the third or second century B.C.,[112] but its weight (at 552 grams) shows it to have been made to weigh 100 *sigloi*. It is this kind of artefact which causes me to think that Persian weights, like guineas in the British Isles, may have continued to possess some kind of *cachet* long after they had any official standing. And this object is not unique: I am no longer surprised to find Celtic torcs and bracelets,[113] or late Hellenistic jewellery apparently obeying metrological rules laid down centuries earlier. Quite what all this means for the economics of cult, I am not sure. It cannot be that the use of a Persian standard necessarily implies that an object was manufactured within the Achaemenid empire, still less that a donor was a Persian. For the moment an explanation which lies in part in the conservatism of the craftsmen and in part in the fashion sense of the consumer seems to be preferable to any other.[114]

Michael Vickers
Ashmolean Museum
OXFORD OX1 2PH

---

112 The mirror will be discussed more fully by Professor Nancy de Grummond in her forthcoming Oxford fascicle of the *Corpus Speculorum Etruscorum.*

113 E.g. the gold torc from Tayac, Gironde (Bordeaux, Musée d'Aquitaine, inv. 50172), which weighs 757.9 grams: equivalent to 90 darics @ 8.42 grams (Exhibition catalogue, *L'art celtique en Gaule*, Marseille, etc. 1983, 123, no. 144.

114 On the irrationality of fashion, see Reitlinger (supra n. 70).

Discussion

Jacques TRÉHEUX: Concernant le fond de vase sur lequel il y a une inscription — est-ce que ce graffite est ancien?

MV: Yes, and it means "four vessels for three and a half obols". Which works out at a price of less than an obol for one.

Ingrid STRÖM: Regarding one of the inscriptions, you said that possibly the drachma used for balancing was wrong—do you really think that they just took any old drachma to use for balancing? Don't you think they had standard weights for balancing?

MV: I depended on David Lewis's summary of an Oxford thesis, which was given to me verbally, saying that they used drachmas, i.e. actual coins to weigh the sacred objects each year. What I'm suggesting is that they may have used worn coins, which will have accounted for the discrepancy between the weight inscribed on an object and the weight that it actually achieved. There isn't a constant discrepancy. I'm suggesting that in the bag of coins that they used, some were worn and some weren't. And the ones they happened to use, at any given moment, were different ones.

TL: Actually I think there is at least one passage in the Delian inventories which definitely says that this was weighed against coins.

Sara ALESHIRE: There is an example in the fourth-century inventories of the Asklepieion, where there's a note saying: "these coins are old". Do you think that the practice of making remelted items to a Persian weight continued down into the 3rd century at Athens?

MV: I don't know, I haven't come across one, but there could be material that I should look at.

Cecilia Beer

Ethnic Diversity and Financial Differentiation in Cypriote Sanctuaries

Our written sources for the study of the circumstances in Cypriote sanctuaries are generally meagre. Also the epigraphic evidence is a limited source for the understanding of the finances of cult in ancient Cyprus. Even the architectural remains—what is left to us of temple buildings—are scanty. However, there is one category of finds, the votive offerings, which may be of help in suggesting the reconstruction of one part of the finances of cult. Even though the most valuable gifts to the sanctuaries, those of gold and silver, generally have not survived, there is one significant group of objects left, namely the votive sculptures.

The latter are particularly abundant in Cyprus from the Archaic to the Hellenistic periods. Sanctuaries are numerous all over the island, but especially in and around the city-states of Kition, Idalion, Golgoi and Tamassos. The differences in the character of the gifts, when identified as representations of deities, priests, priestesses, princes, soldiers, musicians, ordinary votaries (male or female), children or other, and the quality of the execution in terms of the finely carved, colossal, limestone statue or the mass-produced, terracotta figurine may reflect something of the financial status of the donors and perhaps also give some information regarding local diversities and the organization at the sanctuaries. The problem here is the reliability of the archaeological context (or the lack of it), as many of the interesting pieces derive from old excavations.[1] Nevertheless, I believe that, from a cautious scrutiny of the available evidence as a whole, both archaeological and epigraphical, we should be able to obtain some further information regarding the social strata of the donors in the sanctuaries. In turn, questions can be asked (if not answered) about the financial contribution (in kind or other) of individuals to the running of a sanctuary.

I shall make a survey of some sites (for example, Idalion, Golgoi and Kition) with their various sanctuaries and mixed populations and discuss the finds of votives, especially sculptures and their value as a source for an estimate of the financial status of individuals, groups of people and ethnic communities. A few inscriptions that relate to offerings or other organizational circumstances at the sites under investigation will also be considered.

It is a well-known fact that Cyprus was an island of ethnic pluralities and was exposed to an increase in eastern influences, chiefly Phoenician, through colonization and trade contacts from the 9th century onwards.[2] The epigraphic evidence reveals that the three main groups

The present article is a somewhat altered version of the paper read at the Uppsala symposium in September 1990.

Abbreviations:
Cahier = *Centre d'Études Chypriotes. Cahier,* Paris 1984–
CIS = *Corpus inscriptionum semiticarum*, I, Paris 1881–
Hermary, *Catalogue Louvre* = A. Hermary, *Catalogue des antiquités de Chypre. Sculptures* (Musée du Louvre, Département des antiquités orientales), Paris 1989.
ICS = O. Masson, *Les inscriptions chypriotes syllabiques. Recueil critique et commenté*, Paris 1961.
Idalion I = L.E. Stager, A.M. Walker & G.E. Wright, eds., *American Expedition to Idalion, Cyprus. First preliminary report: Seasons of 1971 and 1972* (BASOR, Suppl., 18), Cambridge, Mass., 1974.
KBH = Max Ohnefalsch-Richter, *Kypros, the Bible and Homer*, London 1893.
Kition III = M.G. Guzzo Amadasi & V. Karageorghis, *Fouilles de Kition*, III. *Inscriptions phéniciennes*, Nicosia 1977.
Masson & Sznycer, *Recherches* = O. Masson & M. Sznycer, *Recherches sur les Phéniciens à Chypre*, Geneva & Paris 1972.
SCE II–IV = E. Gjerstad, *et al.*, *The Swedish Cyprus Expedition*, Stockholm 1935–1948.

[1] On the Cesnola controversy, regarding pieces from the original Metropolitan Museum collection, see for example Clarence Cook, *Transformations and migrations of certain statues in the Cesnola Collection*, New York 1882; cf. also Olivier Masson, *ICS* , 19–27, on the early activities of excavators and collectors in Cyprus. The worst damage was probably created by Luigi Palma di Cesnola, since his irresponsible behaviour has lessened the credibility of his stated provenances and/or contexts of finds; see O. Masson, 'Cesnola et le trésor de Curium', *Cahier* 1, 1984, 16–25, and *idem*, 'Cesnola et le trésor de Curium (II)', *Cahier* 2, 1984, 3–14.

[2] Dates are B.C. when not stated otherwise.

[3] See the basic study and corpus of the Cypro-Syllabic inscriptions by O. Masson, *ICS* .

were the autochthonous Eteo-Cypriotes,[3] the Greeks and the Phoenicians.[4] Other ethnic groups, such as Hittites, Persians and Jews, have left little or no epigraphic traces and are less well known.[5] However, images of foreign individuals can sometimes be recognized from their dress, as will be shown below.

Idalion

I have chosen to look more closely at this site in particular, as a wealth of material has been found here and also because of the relative certainty about the find contexts.[6]

Although a city-state of renown already in antiquity, particularly because of a famous sanctuary for the worship of Aphrodite,[7] little is still known of the city itself. Historically, we know that Idalion existed as an independent kingdom at least in the 7th century,[8] was conquered by Kition about 450[9] and remained a Kitian subject until the final Ptolemaic take-over in 294. It is also now recognized that the wealth of the city was due to its involvement in the metal industry. The processed ore was brought to Idalion for refining, after having been smelted at one of the mining centres in the Troodos foothills.[10]

Excavations have concentrated on the ancient remains situated on the two hills, the Western and Eastern Acropoleis, as well as the Lower City in the plain between them. In each of these three places, more than one *temenos* have been found.[11]

Athena-Anat sanctuary on the Western Acropolis. This was identified by inscriptions, but the Swedish Cyprus expedition only found a few traces of architecture;[12] the remains of a temple precinct were dated from the Cypro-Geometric III period to the end of the Cypro-Archaic period, when it was destroyed, possibly in 450 (or 470).[13]

Even before 1850, some farmers are said to have found a number of metal objects on the Western Acropolis. These included weapons and objects of bronze, a bronze tablet, and twelve plates of gilded silver,[14] of which only two have been preserved and are now in the Louvre.[15] The latter are masterpieces (see *Fig. 1*) of Phoenician metalwork in Egyptianising style, dating to the 7th century.[16] A pair of bronze blinkers for horses with a Phoenician inscription saying BᶜNT, probably "by Anat", has been dated to the 7th century, also on stylistic grounds.[17] Another Phoenician inscription, on a spear head, consists of only the beginning LᶜNT, "for (or "to") Anat", and is rather later, possibly around 500.[18]

The longest, known, Cypro-Syllabic text is inscribed on the bronze tablet with handle from the Western Acropolis.[19] The inscription, dated to before the middle of the 5th century,[20] is a sort of contract and it relates how King Stasikypros "and the people of Idalion" would compensate a group of physicians who had treated the wounded without charge during an unsuccessful joint at-

4 For the Phoenician inscriptions in Cyprus generally, see Masson & Sznycer, *Recherches*; cf. also *Kition* III.

5 Some recent, demo-epigraphical investigations have been made in order to study the Semitic immigrant groups as well as other foreigners in Cyprus, see C. Bonnet, 'Les étrangers dans le corpus épigraphique phénicien de Chypre', *RDAC* 1990, 141–153; I thank Corinne Bonnet for letting me read her article in manuscript. Cf. also A. Dupont-Sommer, S. Hadjisavvas & H. Lozachmeur, 'Cinq stèles funéraires découvertes sur le site d'Ayios Georghios à Larnaca-Kition en 1979', *RDAC* 1984, 101–116, dealing with Phoenician inscriptions mentioning Jewish names; and I. Nicolaou, 'Cypriots in the East and West. Foreigners in Cyprus (Archaic to Roman period)', in *Acts of the International Archaeological Symposium "Cyprus between the Orient and the Occident"*, ed. by Vassos Karageorghis, Nicosia 1986, 423–436.

6 A renewed study of Max Ohnefalsch-Richter's unpublished manuscript *Tamassos und Idalion*, kept in the Antikenmuseum, Berlin, has given some extra information.

7 Several sanctuaries in the area have been attributed to a cult of Aphrodite, however, without epigraphic substantiation; the identifications are based altogether on the character of the votive statuary.

8 Mentioned on the prism of Esarhaddon (680–669 B.C.), where it is listed as one of the ten cities paying tribute to the Assyrians, see D.D. Luckenbill, *Ancient records of Assyria and Babylonia* 2, Chicago 1926, 266, § 690.

9 Miranda Marvin in *Idalion* I, XXV; the late date disagrees with the earlier opinions of Einar Gjerstad, *SCE* IV:2, 479, and Vassos Karageorghis, *Kition*, London 1976, 111, who placed the fall of Idalion in 470. However, cf. the arguments of Franz G. Maier, 'Factoids in ancient history: the case of fifth-century Cyprus', *JHS* 105, 1985, 34, particularly nn. 9–12. Maier seems rather to opt for a late date, although it is still debatable.

10 *Idalion* I, 152.

11 See *KBH*, pl. II.

12 *SCE* II, 626ff.

13 See supra n. 9.

14 For the circumstances of the discovery of the silver plates, which are somewhat contradictory, see Masson, *ICS*, 234, with references; cf. E. Gjerstad, *SCE* II, 618, who thinks that the bowls must have been found in the area around altar 40.

15 AO 20134 and AO 20135; for descriptions and references, see Markoe (infra n. 16), 169–171, Cy 1 and Cy 2.

16 For a study of the corpus of such plates, see Glenn Markoe, *Phoenician bronze and silver bowls from Cyprus and the Mediterranean*, Berkeley & Los Angeles 1985.

17 Masson & Sznycer, *Recherches*, 110.

18 Cf. Masson & Sznycer, *Recherches*, 110, n. 4, and p. 111.

19 See Masson, *ICS*, 235–244, no. 217; cf. Miranda C. Marvin in *Idalion* I, p. XXVf.

20 Or, to be cautious, rather before Idalion was definitely conquered by Kition.

Fig. 1. Gilded silver plate from the Western Acropolis, Idalion. Diam. 19.5 cm. 7th century B.C. Musée du Louvre, AO 20134. Photo: Courtesy of the Louvre, Département des antiquités orientales.

tack by the Medes (Persians) and the Kitians. The text is very detailed, and it is decided that one talent of silver *or* some land (specified) should be distributed to the physicians. The silver would be at the charge of the king and the city (i.e. its inhabitants) together, whereas the land would be taken from the king's property. The tablet with these instructions was deposited in Athena's sanctuary (says the inscription) with oaths swearing not to break the agreement.

Judging by the remains around the sanctuary, there seems to be an almost total lack of sculptural votives, perhaps they were of bronze and have disappeared.

I have described some of the fairly valuable objects offered in the sanctuary of Anat/Athena. Thus, the name of the deity is recorded in the inscriptions, but generally the names of the donors are not preserved. Who where they? The probably individual gifts, such as spearheads and *horse-blinkers* of bronze, as well as orientalizing silver plates, reveal a Phoenician, aristocratic, plausibly also a predominantly masculine presence in the sanctuary. The bronze tablet, on the other hand, was the result of a collective and public contribution, initiated by the King of Idalion, to a group of professionals invited to help members of the community.

The question is, was the sanctuary somehow involved in the collecting of silver (coins?) from the citizens of Idalion? Did it function as a treasury, perhaps where the public funds from the people's taxes were kept, or was it just a wartime pay office? Or was Athena invoked as a mere witness to the promise of the king and the people?

Lastly, did the sanctuary own any land? These questions cannot be answered at present.

Other finds associated with the Western Acropolis. A further votive object, hypothetically attributed to another temple on the Western Acropolis,[21] is a libation spoon of silver with a dedication to the goddess referred to as

[21] *KBH*, 17, no. 32, speaks of a primitive shrine or temenos of Aphrodite on the northern slope of the Western Acropolis and a certain Konstantinides excavated on the north-eastern side of the hill in 1908; see Masson, *ICS*, 234 and n. 4.

"Golgoia", i.e. Aphrodite.[22] The spoon is dated stylistically to *c*. 600-475 (Cypro-Archaic II).[23]

Other finds "on the next hill to the west of" the Western Acropolis point to an important cult of a mother goddess and/or goddess of fertility, the site of which was called "*temenos* of Aphrodite Kourotrophos" by Ohnefalsch-Richter.[24] Photographs in his unpublished manuscript[25] illustrate numerous *kourotrophoi* figures and *temple-boys* of limestone from this sanctuary. Other finds consist of numerous votaries, chiefly female, but their exact functions are not easy to define.

Aphrodite-Astarte temenos by the riverside. More varied is the statuary from Ohnefalsch-Richter's so-called Aphrodite-Astarte *temenos* by the Yalias River,[26] north of and almost one kilometre distant from the Acropoleis. Although there is some confusion in the preliminary reports of the excavator, since he does not always state precisely which Aphrodite sanctuary he is speaking about, it is possible to piece together the following picture. The statuary from the riverside sanctuary almost exclusively represents females, from small, mould-made, terracotta figures to over-life-size, partly hand-made statues. Many of the limestone sculptures are Egyptianising in type, others are standing, nude women with their hands on their breasts (goddesses?), or covering their *pudenda* with a shameful (or tempting?) gesture, *kourotrophoi*, musicians, and votaries of various kinds. Whether the votaries are just ordinary women or priestesses or prostitutes is not possible to make out. Many of them wear elaborate earcaps, heavy jewellery, probably expensive dresses and sometimes nose-rings, probably of gold.[27] Other individuals wear shoes with upturned toes, a fairly usual way of dressing among the terracotta representations.[28] Finally, there are a few temple-boys of stone (only three in Ohnefalsch-Richter's manuscript).

The character of the finds seems to justify Ohnefalsch-Richter's assumption that the cult practised was associated with a fertility goddess of the Aphrodite-Astarte type. More than a hundred pottery lamps of Phoenician saucer type (open shell shape) stress the Eastern impression of the sanctuary.[29] The ornate, not to say extravagant, way of dressing and wearing jewellery seen on several female sculptures was perhaps just a superficial fashion inspired by the neighbours of the Levant. On the other hand, could it not reflect the actual occupation and function of a group of women within the sanctuary? From the Old Testament, it appears that the *zonoth*, generally regarded as religious prostitutes and probably devotees of the Baal cult, could be recognized by their flashy array, scarlet garments, much application of cosmetics and a special distinguishing mark on the forehead.[30] However, other details, such as nose-rings and upturned-toe shoes, are more likely to indicate an ethnic display, in these cases possibly by Phoenicians and Anatolians (or Northern Syrians).

Aphrodite temenos on the Eastern Acropolis. A third, plausible, Aphrodite-type sanctuary is located on the Eastern Acropolis of Idalion.[31] The architectural structure, a walled *temenos*, is perhaps a sign of a more prosperous institution. So is also the presence of a series of votive (?) stele-capitals of limestone.[32] Again we find almost exclusively female votaries and many women of uncertain interpretation, some also with nose-rings. The male exceptions are three riders, a warrior with helmet and some fragments of chariots. Only a single tiny terracotta temple-boy is recorded from this site. The terracottas predominate in the finds, but there are also important stone sculptures.

---

[22] The spoon was bought by R. Hamilton Lang; see Masson, *ICS*, 234, and inscription 245, no. 219, with references.

[23] Masson, *ICS*, 245 and n. 3, who refers to E. Gjerstad.

[24] *KBH*, 18, no. 33, only mentioned briefly, and pl. II, no. 15.

[25] *Tamassos und Idalion* (supra n. 6).

[26] *KBH*, 399–402 and pl. II, no. 36; for plan see pl. VII; probably also the *temenos* of Aphrodite by the riverside drawn on pls. LVI and LVII.

[27] Cf. *KBH*, 267–269 and pl. LV, nos. 1, 3 and 4; five female heads with nose-ring, excavated in the riverside temple, are described in *Tamassos und Idalion* (supra n. 6). The archaeological record confirms this use, for example, *SCE* III, Lapithos tomb 406.

[28] According to *Tamassos und Idalion* (supra n. 6); cf. a couple of terracotta individuals from Ayia Irini; see E. Gjerstad, 'Supplementary notes on the finds from Ajia Irini in Cyprus', *Med MusBull* 3, 1963, 24f., and fig. 33.

[29] The lamps were probably one-beaked and found in a heap by the northern (main) entrance (marked E) to the big roof-less room where many of the votive statues were erected (some bases *in situ*); see *KBH*, pl. VII, points marked *la*.

[30] B. A. Brooks, 'Fertility cult functionaries in the Old Testament', *JBL* 60, 1941, 236f., with references. The problem of female votaries in Cypriote cults will be discussed further by the present author in 'Women in Cypriote cults: problems of identification and function' (paper read at the Cypriote congress in Göteborg, August 1991; forthcoming).

[31] Excavated by Ohnefalsch-Richter in 1888 and 1894; see *KBH*, 16 and pl. III, no. 8—the latter map was originally published in 'Ancient Idalion and neighbourhood', *The Owl* (Nicosia), 6 (Sat., Nov. 10), 1888, pl. I, and the site discussed on pp. 54f.

[32] A number of them (21 + 4 fragments) are discussed by O. Masson & A. Hermary, in 'Les fouilles d'Ohnefalsch-Richter à Idalion en 1894', *Cahier* 10, 1988:2, 8–10, pls. II:2–3, III:4–6, IV:7 and pl. V:9.

Fig. 2. Male colossal statue from the sanctuary of Apollo at Idalion; priest? Limestone, h. 1.04 m. About 480 B.C. London, British Museum, C 154. Photo: Courtesy of the Trustees of the British Museum.

Fig. 3. Female harp-player from the sanctuary of Apollo at Idalion. Terracotta, h. 30.7 cm. Early 6th century B.C. British Museum, inv. no. GR 1873.3-20.87. Photo: Courtesy of the Trustees of the British Museum.

According to Ohnefalsch-Richter's confused descriptions there was a second, small, shrine or *temenos* about 120-150 metres west of the major *temenos*, and within the oldest city-wall.[33] The character of the limestone votaries, all of them female and of Greek type, made him decide that also this sanctuary was dedicated to Aphrodite.[34]

Apollo-Reshef temple. The most important architectural remains, however,were discovered in the plain between the northern sides of the two Acropoleis. They are associated with "Lang's temple"[35] or the temple of Apollo-Reshef, whose cult is attested by mainly fairly late,

[33] *KBH*, 17, no. 31 and pl. III, no. 7. Cf. *The Owl* 6, 1888, 55: "To the N.W. of the tower, fig. 7, pl. I, on the slope there existed another sanctuary dedicated to Aphrodite, large life-size statues have been found there..."

[34] *KBH*, 17, n.***.

[35] Excavated by Robert (later Sir Robert) Hamilton Lang in the 1860's.

Phoenician dedications.[36] A bilingual inscription (Phoenician and Cypro-Syllabic)[37] on a marble statue base,[38] which probably once carried a now lost, bronze statuette, was found inside the temple and dated to the 4th century. The donor was the Phoenician prince Baalrôm, son to Abdimilk, in the 4th year of the reign of Milkyaton, King of Kition and Idalion,[39] and it is a dedication to the Phoenician god Reshef Mikal, here assimilated in the Cypro-Greek translation with Apollo Amyklos.[40]

Other important finds in this temple are numerous, life-size, limestone statues, now chiefly male and of high-quality carving. Outstanding is the large-chested, bearded man, wreathed with laurel and holding a spray in his left hand (*Fig. 2*), dating from the early 5th century. Are we right in assuming that he is the image of a priest, because of his imposing size and placement,[41] or is he just another votary, although perhaps a person of high rank and status? The question is difficult to answer without substantiating evidence in the form of an inscription (the lower part of the statue and the base are missing). However, since this statue is one of many originally between colossal size and life-size from the Apollo sanctuary, it is even more uncertain how to identify the man. Some colossal heads, deprived of their bodies, are similar to the "priest" with elaborate curls above the forehead, wreaths, moustaches and beards.[42] Other heads show both bearded men wearing turbans and female votaries in an Egyptianising head-dress with veil or head-cloth crowned by a thick, rolled turban; these women, in addition, wear quite a lot of jewellery, such as earrings, earcaps and thick or multiple necklaces.[43] Beside these huge stone images[44] were also several statuettes of limestone representing mostly male votaries carrying offerings, such as birds, small boxes (for incense?)[45] or *aryballoi*, and some of the so-called Herakles-Melqart type,[46] often considered representations of a deity.[47] Some medium-sized terracottas were also found in the *temenos*, both males[48] and more rarely females, for example, a harp-player (*Fig. 3*) in typical Idalion attire bedecked with jewellery and wearing earcaps.

Although no complete bronze statuettes of medium size have survived from the Archaic and Classical periods, there are traces of such statuettes being dedicated in the sanctuary.[49]

Judging by the preserved, small-size, bronze statuettes, we can guess that these were once numerous in the sanctuary. Most characteristic are the Egyptianising standing males from the mid-6th century, perhaps the ideal image of a worshipper.[50]

A few weights of bronze,[51] partially filled with lead, were obviously heirlooms and were probably dedicated from their aspect as treasured possessions to the deity.

Two treasures of silver coins were also found inside the temple.[52] The earliest was found under the well-paved floor of a chamber situated at the temple's north-eastern corner.[53] The hoard was thought by the excavator to have been originally contained in a bag and consisted of 48 coins, chiefly issues with Cypro-Syllabic legends from various Cypriote cities, but also some Kitian ones

[36] *CIS* I, 90–94, preserved in the British Museum, Western Asiatic Department (WAA 125.320), see Tatton-Brown (infra n. 38), 62, fig. 74. Also an inscribed, small, bronze base with dedication to Reshef the Mikal, see A. Caquot & O. Masson, 'Deux inscriptions phéniciennes de Chypre (deuxième partie)', *Syria* 45, 1968, 302–306.

[37] Masson, *ICS*, 246–248, no. 220.

[38] See Veronica Tatton-Brown, *Ancient Cyprus* (British Museum Publications), London 1987, 62, fig. 74.

[39] Masson, *ICS*, 247, opts for a date at the beginning of the 4th century.

[40] See Masson *ICS*, 246.

[41] See Lang 'Narrative ...' (infra n. 44), 36 and plan opposite p. 30.

[42] For example, F.N. Pryce, *Catalogue of sculptures in the Department of Greek and Roman Antiquities of the British Museum*, Vol. 1, part 2, *Cypriote and Etruscan*, London 1931, figs. 91, 92, 96 and 99.

[43] Pryce (supra n. 42), p. 103, C 271, and fig. 172 (C 275).

[44] R. Hamilton Lang said that there were not less than a thousand pieces, of which about 100 were of colossal size, and a fair proportion in a good state of preservation; cf. 'Narrative of excavations in a temple at Dali (Idalium) in Cyprus', *Transactions of the Royal Society of Literature*, 2nd series, 11, 1878, 42; *idem*, 'Reminiscences...', *Blackwood's Edinburgh Magazine* 1905, I, 623ff.

[45] For example, Tatton-Brown (supra n. 38), 38f., fig. 42, dressed in Greek fashion with chiton and himation draped over one shoulder, h. 98 cm and dated *c.* 475–450.

[46] See Tatton-Brown (supra n. 38), 49, fig. 56.

[47] Identified as the Greek hero Herakles, but often assimilated with the Phoenician god Melqart; cf. Hermary, *Catalogue Louvre*, 299.

[48] See O. Masson, 'Kypriaka VII. Le sanctuaire d'Apollon à Idalion (fouilles 1868–1869)', *BCH* 92, 1968, 391, figs. 12–13.

[49] Lang, 'Narrative...' (supra n. 44), 42: "the tiny feet in bronze, still adhering to some of the marble slabs, speak to us of works of art of the highest value...".

[50] Cf. Tatton-Brown (supra n. 38), fig. 11 (h. 22 cm); and Masson (supra n. 48), 395, figs. 18–20; fig. 21 is Oriental in type with a horned, fairly high and pointed, conical head-dress.

[51] See Tatton-Brown (supra n. 38), 20, fig. 16; weight in the shape of a couchant bull weighing 87.12 grams and conforming to the Mesopotamian standard; dated to the late 13th century; cf. Masson (supra n. 48), 394ff. and figs. 22 (lion) and 24 (same bull as before).

[52] See R. Hamilton Lang, 'On coins discovered during recent excavations in the island of Cyprus', *Numismatic Chronicle*, New Series 11, 1871, 1–18; *idem*, *Cyprus: its history, its present resources, and future prospects*, London 1878, 335.

[53] Lang, 'Narrative...' (supra n. 44), 40 and plan, p. 30*bis*.

with Phoenician legends dating from the early 5th century.

The later treasure was contained in two small ceramic jars, closed with lead at the top, and discovered in a chamber behind (north of?) the former one. The jars were placed underneath a "strangely-shaped conical stone".[54] Their contents consisted of 17 mainly Kitian coins with Phoenician legends and generally of small denominations. This part of the building, where the treasures were found, presented a problem of function to the excavator, who suggested that the rooms had been priests' chambers.[55]

If we are to believe Ohnefalsch-Richter's claims, there were at least five sanctuaries of Aphrodite at Idalion, and some of them seem to have been very close neighbours. Perhaps they were actually laid out pairwise, with one sanctuary for the Astarte aspect (involving temple prostitution?) and a less prosperous (?) one for the *kourotrophos*-side of the goddess?

Golgoi

Ancient Golgoi has been associated with a site just NE. of modern Athienou,[56] which is situated 12 kilometres NE. of Idalion. An inscription found at Golgoi attests that Aphrodite was worshipped there as *Paphia*.[57] Cypro-Syllabic dedications further attest to a major cult of Apollo.[58]

Golgoi was the centre of much archaeological activity in the 19th century and conflicting reports led to scholarly disputes about the locations of the major temples.[59] It appears relatively clear that there were two sanctuaries at Ayios Photios (3 kilometres SE. of Athienou), an eastern temple structure, measuring 18 x 9 metres,[60] and a western *temenos* of a more modest, open-air style.

That the site(s) was extremely rich in votive objects is clear from the results of the many missions to the site, and Luigi Palma di Cesnola is said to have removed 35,000 objects.[61] Although we cannot be quite certain, it is possible that most of Cesnola's finds of 1870 derived from the eastern sanctuary at Ayios Photios, of which the south-western angle had already been excavated by the French in 1862.[62] Many of the sculptures found here had been placed in different deposits after being dismembered and having their heads knocked off.[63] These circumstances make it even more hazardous to reconstruct the find contexts. It is, however, evident that, both at the proper sanctuary site of Golgoi,[64] north of Athienou, and at the other two at southern Golgoi-Ayios Photios, there were several important limestone sculp-

Fig. 4. Male head wearing "mitra", from Golgoi. Limestone, h. 43 cm. Early 5th century B.C. Musée du Louvre, AM 2835. Photo: Courtesy of the Louvre, Département des antiquités orientales.

[54] Lang, 'Narrrative...' (supra n. 44), 41.
[55] See Lang, 'On coins ...' (supra n. 52).
[56] See O. Masson, 'Kypriaka IX. Recherches sur les antiquités de Golgoi', *BCH* 95, 1971, 306 and map, fig. 1.
[57] Masson, *ICS*, 283, no. 262.
[58] Masson, *ICS*, 286ff., nos. 265–267, 275, 276 (*probably* Apollo), 284, 294 and 300.
[59] See the summing up by Masson, *ICS*, 276–281.
[60] Ohnefalsch-Richter, *KBH*, 15f.
[61] J.B. Connelly, *Votive sculpture of Hellenistic Cyprus*, Nicosia 1988, 77.
[62] See Hermary, *Catalogue Louvre*, 16, with references.
[63] Hermary, *Catalogue Louvre*, 16.
[64] Mainly excavated by the French in 1865; see Hermary, *Catalogue Louvre*, 17f.

Fig. 5. Priest with dove, from Golgoi. Limestone, h. 2.17 m. About 500 B.C. New York, Metropolitan Museum of Art, inv. no. 74.51.2466. After: A.E.J. Holwerda, *Die alten Kyprier in Kunst und Kultus*, Leiden 1885, pl. V, 18.

tures of life-size or colossal size.[65] It is sometimes thought possible to identify images of royalty (see, for example, *Fig. 4*)[66] or a hero (Herakles),[67] a priest (helped by the inscription) (see *Fig. 5*), musicians,[68] votaries (mostly male), dressed after the Greek fashion in chiton and himation,[69] and, apart from goddesses, a row of females of uncertain identification (generally of medium or small size), some in Egyptianising dress[70] and others of Greek kore type.[71] However, both the life-size and smaller *terracottas* of females wearing rich jewellery and having veiled heads with earcaps in a unique Cypriote style, particularly abundant at Idalion, are almost totally absent at Golgoi.

When it comes to the limestone statuary, the situation is the opposite. Single pieces from Golgoi appear to have been worked in styles very closely related to single pieces found at Idalion,[72] and indicate the use of itinerant artists for the large-sized sculptures. The majority of the sculptural representations from Golgoi from the mid-6th century through the Classical period adhere to a Greek dress-fashion of Ionic inspiration. Hairstyle and accessories may be locally influenced, but the overall impression is of a Hellenic standard.

Very few sculptured individuals are ostentatiously foreigners during the late Archaic and Classical periods. Only one statuette featuring a Persian is certainly from Golgoi (see *Fig. 6*).[73] The standing male wears a short, woolly chiton with a flat belt knotted around the waist, long Oriental trousers and a long himation or other drapery over the shoulders.[74] Although a dress is not always proof of ethnic origin, the very few instances of votaries in Persian dress make it likely that they are representa-

[65] See Hermary, *Catalogue Louvre*, for example, the male heads nos. 229, 234 and 532 (see *Fig. 4* in the present paper) from the sanctuary at Golgoi, and nos. 239, 241, 244 and 529 from Ayios Photios.

[66] Hermary, *Catalogue Louvre*, no. 532; cf. ibid., nos. 529 and 533. See also *idem*, 'Témoignage des documents figurés sur la société chypriote d'époque classique', in *Early society in Cyprus*, ed. by E. Peltenburg, Edinburgh 1989, 180–196; cf. F.G. Maier, 'Priest kings in Cyprus', in *Early society*...(supra), 376–391, discussing whether sacral kingship was peculiar to Paphos or whether it applied to other Late Archaic and Classical Cypriote monarchies as well.

[67] Hermary, *Catalogue Louvre*, nos. 597, 603 and 604.

[68] Hermary, *Catalogue Louvre*, no. 791; L. Palma di Cesnola, *A descriptive atlas of the Cesnola Collection of Cypriote antiquities in the Metropolitan Museum of Art* I:1, Boston 1885, pls. XII, no. 14 (upper part of male harper) and XIII, no. 15 (upper part of male flute player).

[69] Hermary, *Catalogue Louvre*, nos. 534, 537–541 and 543–546.

[70] Hermary, *Catalogue Louvre*, nos. 647–648, 650, 652, 654, 656, 657 and 662. Probably similar are the headless nos. 666–669 and 672.

[71] Cf. Hermary, *Catalogue Louvre*, nos. 747, 749–759, the heads nos. 688–690, 697 and 698 (complete) and the heads wearing *sakkos* nos. 702–706, 709–712, 716–717, 719, 725 and 730–731.

[72] Cf. the colossal torso from Idalion (*Fig. 1* in the present paper) and a head in the Louvre, see Hermary, *Catalogue Louvre*, no. 245, p. 126 (h. 33 cm), who also notes the resemblance.

[73] See Hermary, *Catalogue Louvre*, 269, no. 547, dated between the late 5th and early 4th centuries. Cf. the sturdy boy or man in Oriental costume (h. 63 cm) of the Hellenistic period, see H. Ergüleç, *Large-sized Cypriot sculpture in the Museums of Istanbul* (SIMA, 20:4), Göteborg 1972, 27f., C.44.

[74] Cf. Antigoni Zournatzi, 'A limestone figure wearing κάνδυς from Cyprus', *RDAC* 1989, 127–134, pls. XXX–XXXI, dating from the mid-5th century and unfortunately without provenance; see also Cesnola, *Atlas* I:2, Boston 1885, no. 562, pl. LXXXV, limestone statuette found in the ruins of the Apollo Hylates temple at Kourion (h. 1 foot 1 1/4 inches) showing a male figure wearing a Phrygian cap, a knee-length, long-sleeved chiton, girt at the waist, and a mantle; fruit (?) in the left hand; cf. also a standing youth, similar to the preceding, from Lefkonico, see *BSA* 41, 1940–1945, pl. 20, no. 548.

Fig. 6. Male statuette from Golgoi; Persian? Limestone, h. 31 cm. Possibly late 5th century B.C. Musée du Louvre, AM 3375. Photo: Courtesy of the Louvre, Département des antiquités orientales.

tions of authentic persons. With Greek dresses, on the other hand, one can never be certain whether they are worn by Greeks or by persons adopting the Greek culture because of its higher status.[75]

An important group among the votive statuary at Golgoi is formed by the children. These can be divided into typical temple-boys,[76] some of which probably wore an Oriental ("Phrygian") type of cap or peaked hood and earrings,[77] other children (or temple-boys) wearing Macedonian-type *kausia*,[78] taenia or diadem.[79] Taenia and diadem seem to be phenomena of the third century and chiefly limited to Golgoi. The latter fashion is inspired by Greek prototypes, but what is its social message here?

Kition

The situation at Kition on the south coast is both similar to and different from the sites at Idalion and Golgoi. Similar, because there are several *temene* and cults of Astarte (Aphrodite) and Melqart (Apollo). Different, because the architecture is impressive, while the votive stone statuary is more modest in size and the big, partly hand-modelled terracottas are missing. The newly excavated, large, Phoenician temple in Area II, probably dedicated to Astarte from at least the mid-9th century,[80] is a sophisticated ashlar-masonry structure, measuring 35 x 22 metres, and closely linked with four other sacred buildings.[81]

On the "acropolis" (the *Bamboula* hill) are two further temples once associated with Herakles-Melqart[82] and Astarte.[83]

Both historically, from the numismatic evidence and scattered epigraphic testimony, it is evident that Kition was the most important Phoenician city on Cyprus. One of the longest Phoenician inscriptions also comes from Kition, perhaps associated with the Astarte temple on the Acropolis, and it gives us some important insights into the temple administration. Although the double inscription from Kition (*CIS* I, 86A-B) dates from the first quarter of the 4th century,[84] it may give us some indirect

[75] Cf., for example, the use of Greek names among Phoenicians in Cyprus, even Phoenician (most likely) kings of Lapethos writing their Greek names with Phoenician legends on the city's coins; see Masson & Sznycer, *Recherches*, 97–100, for references. Cf. also the comments on this practice by Einar Gjerstad, 'The Phoenician colonization and expansion in Cyprus', *RDAC* 1979, 247.

[76] See, for example, Hermary, *Catalogue Louvre*, nos. 108, 111–114, 117, 119–120; cf. the loose heads, nos. 122–137, 139–172 and probably others which are more uncertain.

[77] Cf. the head-dresses of some loose heads; see Hermary, *Catalogue Louvre*, nos. 457–459, 461 and 463.

[78] Only heads; see Hermary, *Catalogue Louvre*, nos. 476–485 and 488–491.

[79] Only heads; see Hermary, *Catalogue Louvre*, nos. 492–514 and 516–526.

[80] See A. Dupont-Sommer, 'Les Phéniciens à Chypre', *RDAC* 1974, 91; and *Kition* III, 149–160, with earlier references.

[81] See *Kition* III, 4f., for a plan of Area II.

[82] On the typological evidence of the limestone statuettes in the deposit associated with the sanctuary, see *SCE* III, 26ff. (catalogue of finds) and pls. V–XXXVI.

[83] For the locations of the Herakles-Melqart and Astarte temples, see K. Nicolaou, *The historical topography of Kition* (SIMA, 43), Göteborg 1976, fig. 25, nos. 1 and 2, and a brief review of the sites with references, pp. 102–108.

[84] Date suggested, for example, by Masson & Sznycer, *Recherches*, 25, and Guzzo Amadasi in *Kition* III, 103, and most generally accepted; cf. also M. Delcor, 'Le personnel du temple

clues regarding the composition and functions of the cult personnel also during somewhat earlier periods.

The so-called temple tariff consists of two inscriptions, painted in black, on both sides of a limestone tablet.[85] It has been discussed repeatedly from the linguistic point of view, and questions of both translation and interpretation have been debated without solving some fundamental enigmas.[86] The 29 lines are unevenly divided on the two sides of the inscription and deal with the total of the monthly expenses (of the temple). The month in question is Etanim, and the inscription lists groups of functionaries with specific duties. The following translation is by John C.L. Gibson.[87]

Side A.

Line 1. "Expenses for the month of Etanim".

Line 2. "(Paid) on the day of the new-moon in the month of Etanim", and whatever was spent on that obscure occasion is lost.

Line 3. "To the **leader**(**s**) of the new-moon festival, 2 QP'". We ignore the value of that amount or what it represents.

Line 4: "To the 4 **masons**[88] who repaired the temple of Astarte at Kition, 2 QR". Also this kind or value is unknown.

Line 5: "To the 20 **janitors** and **men** who (were stationed) at the door of the sanctuary[."

Line 6: "To the **singers** from the city who were in attendance on the Holy Queen this day, ...["

Line 7: "To the 2 **pages**, 2 QP'".

Line 8: "To the 2 **sacrificers**, 1 QR".

Line 9: "To the 2 **bakers** who baked the basket of cakes for the [Holy] Queen (= Astarte)"

Line 10: "along with ......, 3 QR".

Line 11: "To the 3 **pages**, 3 QP'".

Line 12: "To the **barbers** working at the service, 2 QP'".

Line 13: "To the 20 **craftsmen** who made the pillars[89] of stone in the temple of MKL ["

Line 14: "To Abdeshmun, **chief of the scribes**, on duty this day, 3 QR and .. QP'".

Line 15: "[To the 'dogs'] and to the 'lion's whelps',[90] 3 QR and 3 P'".

Line 16: "[ ] on duty this day 2 QR and ..QP'".

Line 17: ......

Side B.

Line 1: "... audit".

Line 2: -"(Paid) on the day of the new-moon in the month of P'LT".

Line 3: -"To the **leader**(**s**) of the new-moon festival, 2 QP'".

Line 4: -"To the **master**(**s**) **of the days**[91] at the procession round the deity ["

Line 5: -"To the temple **personnel** who were (responsible) for the pillars of MKL and ...["

Line 6: -"To 'BD' BST, the Carthaginian, [".

Line 7: -"To the man who removed their .... QP'".

Line 8: -"To the **shepherds** who (live) in D-PLKD, 2 QR; (to those) who (live) in Ki[tion"

Line 9: -"To the (**temple**) **girls**[92] and to the 22 **girls** (employed) at the sacrifice ["

Line 10:-"To the '**dogs**' and to the 'lion's whelps', 3 QR and 3P'".

Line 11: -"To the 3 pages, 3 QP'".

Line 12: -"[ ], 2 QP'".

There is no doubt that this is a list of expenses paid out by the temple. QP, QR and P certainly refer to some kind of money or other hard currency, the value of which is unfortunately hidden from us. Although this document is thus far unique, it seems reasonable to assume that the practice of paying out wages or fixed salaries, for services rendered or work finished, on a monthly basis to a series of persons with special tasks attached to the regular temple activities or more occasional duties at festivities, was not a practice limited to this particular temple at Kition. Guardians, temple "personnel" and prostitutes[93] appear to have been part of the more permanent staff in sanctuaries. Others were probably called in more occasionally, for example sacrificers, musicians and archi-

d'Astarté à Kition d'après une tablette phénicienne (*CIS* 86A et B)', *Ugarit-Forschungen* 11, 1979, 147. However, B. Peckham, 'Notes on a fifth-century Phoenician inscription from Kition, Cyprus (*CIS* 86)', *Orientalia* N.S. 37, 1968, p. 317, and J.C.L. Gibson (infra n. 87), 123, favour a date in the mid-5th century.

[85] In the British Museum, inv. no. 125.080.

[86] See Masson & Sznycer, *Recherches*, 26–68; cf. *Kition* III, 103–106, as well as references cited supra n. 84.

[87] *Textbook of Syrian Semitic inscriptions*, 3. *Phoenician inscriptions*, Oxford 1982, 125–131; cf. also Masson & Sznycer *Recherches*, 26ff.

[88] Or the "architects", see *Kition* III, 105.

[89] Or "the bases", see Masson & Sznycer, *Recherches*, 27.

[90] Or "little ones" or similar, cf. the interpretation of Masson & Sznycer, *Recherches*, 27 (at the symposium this French translation was used and "minets" were explained by someone as "pussy-cats").

[91] Cf. Masson & Sznycer, "Pour le maître de l'eau", *Recherches*, 27.

[92] Cf. Masson & Sznycer, *Recherches*, 27, "pour les prostituées (sacrées) et les 22 prostituées (sacrées) dans le sacrifice, [".

[93] On the numerous references related to this topic, see W. Fauth, 'Sakrale Prostitution im vorderen Orient und im Mittelmeerraum', *JAC* 31, 1988, 24–39. Whether it was really a "sacred" prostitution is, however, dubious. For references challenging such an interpretation of the evidence, particularly in Mesopotamia and the Near East, see my forthcoming *Templeboys. A study of Cypriote votive sculpture* (SIMA), Ch. V.

tects. Similar staffs must have existed also at sanctuaries where the written evidence is still silent (for example at Idalion and Golgoi).

But, more important, from where did the money (or the means) come into the temple? How did it accumulate enough means to pay its staff?

One obvious source of income in an ancient Semitic environment would have been the prostitution associated with sanctuaries of the Phoenician Astarte-Aphrodite.[94] Although there are many unsolved difficulties regarding the temple prostitution, such as organisation, fees, the exact functions of the male prostitutes (the *klbm*), the destiny of children borne by prostitutes etc., it is clear that it filled a need in harbour towns frequented by sailors and travelling merchants often away from home for years. The riches collected by certain temples are well known.[95]

Curiously, according to the Kition list (side B, line 9) the prostitutes also received a payment or reward (we do not know what or how much), together with other servants and members of the temple personnel. This implies that whatever the prostitutes received from their clients went directly to a common temple treasury, from which the means were taken to pay the various categories of temple servants.

A further enigma is presented by the mention of "little ones" twice (side A, line 15, and side B, line 10) directly after "the dogs" (*klbm*). If the dogs are really to be understood as male prostitutes, how are we to explain the "little ones"? One thought that immediately comes to mind is whether this is a reference to the votive sculptures of young (sometimes baby) boys, the so-called *temple-boys*. It is true that very few have been found at Kition, and these were related to the Herakles-Melqart temple, but this may be due to archaeological circumstances. On the other hand, temple-boys are very frequent in the Aphrodite-Astarte *temene* and the Apollo-Reshef temple of Idalion (see *Fig. 7*). Many of them carry small fortunes around their necks in the shape of signet-rings with mounted scarabs (gold, silver and precious stones) strung on a necklace, as well as other valuables. Are these objects gifts to the sanctuary or do they only give the boys a high status? Similarly, how are we to interpret the even richer jewellery with which many of the female votaries or temple attendants are adorned, especially at Idalion, Arsos and Salamis? They often remind us more of ambulant saleswomen carrying their load of pendant-rings or other jewellery. Are these pieces of gold and silver gifts from visitors to the temple collected by a female servant? And what were the hoards of coins found in the Apollo temple at Idalion, perhaps in the rooms of the priests? Were they payments to servants or gifts from votaries?

Fig. 7. Temple-boy from the sanctuary of Apollo at Idalion. Limestone, h. 41 cm. Late 4th century B.C. London, British Museum, C 164. Photo: Courtesy of the Trustees of the British Museum.

There are also some evident omissions in the Kition text: no mention of priests or sculptors. Or are they included among "sacrificers" or "temple personnel"?

The sculptors and craftsmen active in the workshops producing stone and terracotta sculptures were very industrious over a long period of time. A separate study scrutinizing local workshops and the diffusion of their products between sites, especially the interplay between the sanctuaries of Idalion, Golgoi and Kition, is still de-

94 See Cr. Grottanelli, 'Santuari e divinità delle colonie d'Occidente', in *La religione fenicia. Matrici orientali e sviluppi occidentali*. Atti del colloquio in Roma, 6 marzo 1979, Rome 1981, 109–133, and particularly 119ff.

95 See S. Ribichini, 'Temple et sacerdoce dans l'économie de Carthage', in *IIe colloque international sur l'histoire et l'archéologie de l'Afrique du Nord, Grenoble, 5–9 avril 1983*, (=*Bulletin archéologique*, N.S. 19, 1983), Paris 1985, 29–37, esp. 31.

sired. Stylistic similarities between large-sized statues found at different sites suggest itinerant artists travelling from one sanctuary to another. An intriguing question is then how these craftsmen were organised and to what extent the workshops were dependent on the temple authorities?

From the above, it emerges with some certainty that Cypriote sanctuaries were frequented by persons from all sorts of social strata, from simple votaries to aristocrats and even royalty. We know most of the Phoenician high society, although the evidence is scanty. We can also conclude that Orientalizing (Egyptian or Asiatic) dress was fairly widespread during the 7th and early 6th centuries, but that towards the late Archaic period Greek dress was generally assumed. The examples of representations of persons clad in Persian costume are extremely few all through the Classical period and, although most of our Phoenician inscriptions are late Classical, the Phoenicians from that era do not betray themselves by their dress fashion but adopt the Greek *koine* of the Eastern Mediterranean.[96] Not surprisingly, our most explicit epigraphic evidence from Cyprus comes from Phoenician Kition, but it is possible that some of the information from the double inscription reflects a practice at least partly copied by the mixed societies at Idalion and Golgoi.

Cecilia Beer
Dept. of Classical Archaeology
and Ancient History
Stockholm University
S-106 91 STOCKHOLM

[96] Cf. the marble statues from Sidon (Phoenicia) of the early 4th century in purely Attic style, although partly somewhat awkward.

Discussion

Tullia LINDERS: Have you any suggestions of how they could make an ethnic differentiation among the offerings you have shown us? Are there any among them you would call definitely Phoenician, for instance, or definitely Greek or Eteo-Cypriote?

CB: The only group that I personally find fairly convincing as being a Phoenician one are the so-called Idalion ladies. Because, as I said, at least on some of them there are these insignia on the head, and also the dress makes them look a little foreign. But without these insignia it could just be a fashion or anything; we cannot be sure.

TL: Are those ladies with very elaborate jewellery included in that group? You compared the jewellery depicted on the statues with actual jewellery which has been found, I suppose, in excavations. What about them: is that distinctive in a way, and could it point to an ethnic rule?

CB: Well, those pendant rings are typically Phoenician, especially the ones that are curved like that. Typical of the 7th-6th century Phoenician jewellery. And they are not Greek.

Michael VICKERS: I would like to make an observation about the dogs. I'm not suggesting there is any connection at all between your inscription of the 4th century and the bronze tablets in Gubbio, which are of about the same period, but one of them goes into great detail on ways to sacrifice dogs.

CB: Concerning the cult and/or *sacrifice* of dogs (the animals), there is also intriguing evidence from both Cyprus and Phoenicia; at Tamassos concentrations of dog bones were found near the two offering spots to Aphrodite as well as in *bothroi* (Archaic and Classical period).[1]

A different kind of evidence for the special importance of dogs comes from Tell Ashkelon where the largest dog cemetery ever found was excavated. Over 700 dog burials (Persian period) had been recorded in 1990.[2]

[1] For the accumulation of animal bones, see H.-G. Buchholz, 'Tamassos, Zypern, 1977 bis 1986, vierter Bericht', *AA* 1987, 181, fig. 9, especially the black dots in the sector αα–εε/0–8 which indicate the finds in the two altar areas of Aphrodite. The final analysis of this material has not yet appeared.

[2] See S.R. Wolff, 'Archaeology in Israel', *AJA* 95, 1991, 519f.; and L.E. Stager, 'Why were hundreds of dogs buried at Ashkelon?', *BibArchRev* 17:3, 1991, 27–42.

Sara B. Aleshire

The Economics of Dedication at the Athenian Asklepieion

The cult of Asklepios at the Athenian Asklepieion, located on the South Slope of the Akropolis, was, from the time of its founding in 420 B.C. through the rest of antiquity, one of the most active cults in Athens. We are fortunate in having preserved from this cult a large body of evidence both about individual dedicants and about the types of dedications they made. This information comes primarily from two sources: nine more or less intact inventories taken by the Athenian boule and demos of the contents of the Asklepieion[1] and a large number of surviving dedications on stone.

The inventories of the Athenian Asklepieion preserve either complete or in part the records of 1377 dedications, including 30 dedications from a new fragment of *IG* II^2 1534 to be published in *Horos* 8 (1990). This is the largest single group of such dedicatory records preserved from any sanctuary at Athens. For the third century B.C., it is the only such group. Unfortunately, the corollary of this last fact is that, while no comparative evidence survives in the form of contemporary records from other sanctuaries, the evidence from the Asklepieion is heavily biased towards the third century: the dedications from the third-century inventories comprise 78.5 per cent of those known from the inventories. Further, although the first twenty-nine lines of Inventory III seem to record all dedications from the years 341/0-339/8 B.C., the dedications listed in this inventory differ both in quantity and in nature from those listed in the two large inventories, IV and V, from the third century. It is, therefore, difficult to supplement the picture drawn from the two large inventories with information from the inventories of the fourth and second centuries, and, in any case, the nine documents of this type all derive from a period of only slightly more than two centuries. Thus, evidence from the inventories is likely to be, in its details, valid only for a period near the middle of the third century and must be supplemented, with care, by information derived from surviving dedications on stone.

The dedications on stone from the Asklepieion also form the largest single class among surviving dedications. Further, inscriptions of this type form the largest single class among surviving inscriptions from the Asklepieion; as *Chart I* indicates, 69 per cent of those inscriptions are dedications. The dedications, however, also show chronological bias: 54.2 per cent of all these inscriptions come from either the fourth century B.C. or the second century A.D. In addition, any analysis based on this evidence must take into account the vagueness of epigraphical dates, especially severe with inscriptions of this type. Nevertheless, here the greater range of time from which such dedications are preserved, from the early fourth century B.C. to the middle of the third century A.D., may mean that the picture drawn from them is more generally valid.

For these reasons, therefore, I have chosen to confine my focus to the third century B.C. This analysis will, however, be supplemented by an analysis of the dedications from the fourth- and second-century inventories and of those dedications which survive on stone, an analysis which is primarily anecdotal rather than statistical; that consideration suggests that the major outlines of the third-century picture hold true, with only gradual changes, for most of the history of the Asklepieion.

The information about the practice of dedication at ancient Greek sanctuaries offered by the inventories and dedications from the Athenian Asklepieion has unfortunately been almost entirely neglected by scholars. Much work clearly remains to be done, both in terms of statistical analysis of the data and in more general interpretation. I wish here, however, not to attempt a full-scale economic analysis of this data but to consider only two related points about the economies of dedication at the sanctuary: Who were the dedicants, i.e. what can be said

Abbreviations:

Asklepieion = S.B. Aleshire, *The Athenian Asklepieion*, Amsterdam 1989.

Girard = P. Girard, *L'Asclépieion d'Athènes d'après de récentes découverts* (BEFAR, 23), Paris 1881, 83.

[1] In this paper, I cite the inventories from the Asklepieion by the numbers assigned to them in *Asklepieion*, 112.

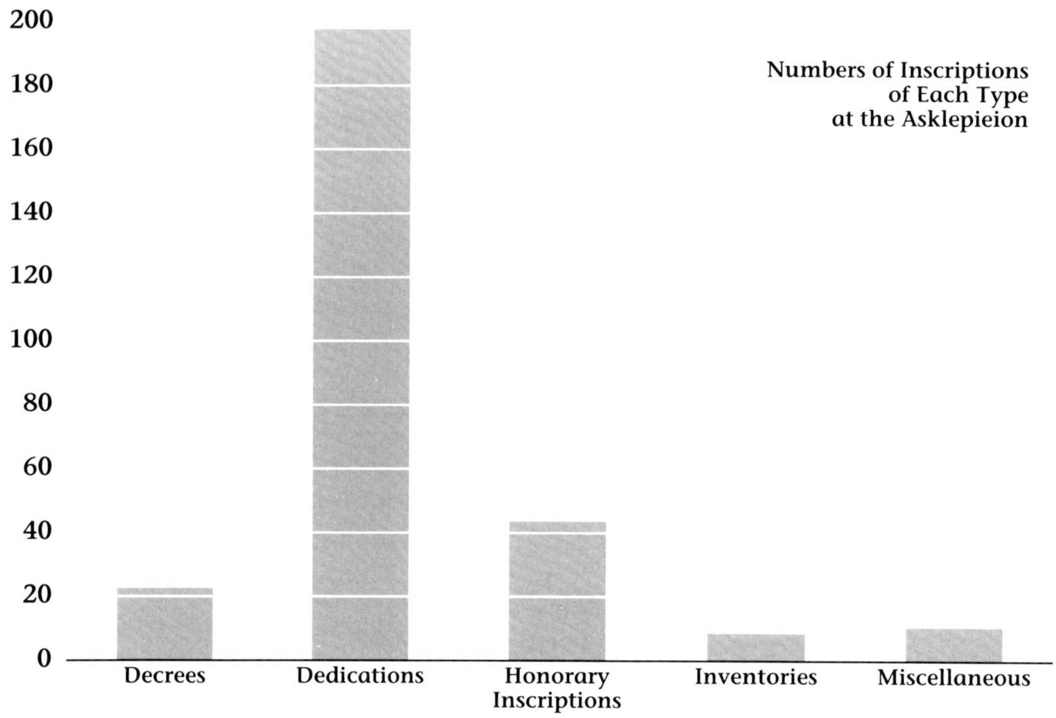

Chart I

of their economic status, both those whose dedications are recorded in the inventories and those whose dedications on stone survive? And what can be said of the dedicatory process, i.e., from the time when the dedicant decided to make a dedication until the time when the priest and the commissioners ordered it melted and re-cast, how was a dedication acquired, placed in the temple, preserved, and finally selected for liquidation and re-cast into a larger and grander dedication?

The work of earlier scholars on these two topics has been somewhat haphazard. The economic and social status of the dedicants has received cursory consideration in a few works not directly concerned with this question, but P. Girard's interpretation of most as courtesans or other slaves has gone largely unchallenged. In fact, the notion that a large proportion of the dedicants at the Asklepieion—and, specifically, many of those known from the inventories—were persons of such low social and economic rank has, over the years, assumed the status of orthodoxy. This interpretation, although now not always explicit, underlies the recent work of D.M. Schaps[2] and C.J. Castner.[3] In its fully articulated form,[4] this notion holds that all dedicants who are listed in the inventories with neither patronymic nor demotic fall into one of these two categories and that those listed with patronymic only were metics. Turning to the second of our two questions, two almost inaccessible works from the late nineteenth century,[5] together with an anecdotal work of the same period,[6] two works of a general nature—the classic study by Rouse[7] and the recent study by van Straten[8]—together with my own brief consideration,[9] comprise the entire body of literature directly concerned with the dedications which are recorded in these inventories. Therefore, the time has come to give both topics fresh consideration.

The interpretation that most dedicants were metics or

[2] D.M. Schaps, *The economic rights of women in Ancient Greece*, Edinburg1979, 71-73.

[3] C.J. Castner, *GRBS* 23, 1982, 51-58.

[4] Girard, 83.

[5] C.F. Pezold, *De membris humanis diis gentium dedicatis*, and J.J. Frey, *De more diis simulacra membrorum consecrandi*. Rouse was not able to obtain either at the turn of the century.

[6] A.C. Merriam, *Galliard's Medical Journal* 40, 1885, 355-375.

[7] W.H.D. Rouse, *Greek votive offerings*, Cambridge 1902, esp. 187-239, 397-399.

[8] F.T. van Straten, 'Gifts for the gods', in *Faith, hope and worship*, ed. H.S. Versnel (Studies in Greek and Roman religion, 2), Leiden 1981.

[9] *Asklepieion*, 37-51.

slaves is open both to criticism on methodological grounds and to challenge from analysis of those dedicants and dedications listed in the inventories. Most of the dedicants are listed by name only; if we follow the orthodox interpretation literally, virtually all of those who made dedications at the Asklepieion were foreigners or slaves of one sort or another. Of a total of 1377 dedications recorded in the inventories, 29 may be considered official dedications, made by priests in their capacity as priests or by the Athenian demos or one of its formal constituent groups. For another 433 dedications the name of the dedicant is so poorly preserved that we cannot determine whether it was recorded with patronymic and/or demotic or not. Further, 137 dedications are either described in the inventories themselves as ἀνεπίγραφα[10] or listed with no indication of dedicant's name, a type of notation which, as I have argued elsewhere,[11] seems to carry the same indication about the dedication itself. Here it may be helpful briefly to pause and note that the proportion of such dedications differ quite widely from inventory to inventory, varying from a low of 8 per cent in Inventory V to a high of 40 per cent in Inventory III; for the inventories taken together, the proportion of ἀνεπίγραφα is 13 per cent. These data suggest that the dedications and the records which lie behind the compiled *paradoseis* of Inventory III are not strictly equivalent to those behind the *kathairesis* of Inventory V.

For those dedications which were in some way inscribed, as *Chart II* makes clear, of 944 dedications where the dedicant's name is sufficiently well preserved to make it clear whether a patronymic or demotic was recorded, 716, or 76 per cent, have neither. When we exclude priestly and other official dedications as well and consider personal dedications only, the proportion is similar. Of the one thousand three hundred forty-seven personal dedications in all inventories, 942 have records which are sufficiently well preserved to determine whether a patronymic or demotic was inscribed in the inventory. *Chart III* indicates that, of these, 76 per cent were recorded by name of dedicant alone. Finally, if we restrict our analysis to the two large third century inventories, it is clear that Inventory IV differs significantly from Inventory V. In Inventory IV 136, or 72 per cent of the dedicants were recorded by name only, while in Inventory V the percentage is 86.4 per cent. A similar paucity of patronymics and demotics exists also with regard to dedicants recorded in the inventories of the epistatai of Artemis Brauronia, which have been skillfully and carefully analyzed by T. Linders[12] and P. Brulé.[13] It is difficult to believe that such a high proportion of the participants in the cult at the Asklepieion were persons of lowly status or that all those listed by name only were slaves or metics. It is similarly difficult to believe that any cult at Athens except those specifically restricted to metics would draw so high a proportion of its participants from those from without Athenian citizenship.

Similarly, the number of dedications listed in the inventories as ἀνεπίγραφα has been seen as indicating that the dedicants were of a lower class and were illiterate.[14] This category is the second largest among all dedications, with 152, or 16 per cent described as uninscribed. Of personal dedications 137, or 15 per cent are ἀνεπίγραφα. In Inventory IV 16 per cent and in Inventory V 8 per cent of the dedications were uninscribed. The proportion of such dedications is not higher at lower weights, and some of the heaviest dedications were not inscribed with a dedicant's name, as can be seen from *Chart IV*. Here I would also point to the kanoun at IV.121b, the heaviest single dedication in the inventories (although here the lack of the dedicant's name is probably to be ascribed to the fact that, as part of the official cult equipment, the basket was not the dedication of an individual dedicant). I would also cite the gold typos weighing 10 dr. 4 ob. at V.85c and the uninscribed dedication of 20 tetradrachms at V.173b. The lost dedication listed without dedicants and weighing 328 dr. at IV.120a is almost certainly another example of this type.

Turning to dedications for which the dedicant's name was recorded, there is significant variation in the tendency of men to be listed with patronymic and/or demotic and women to be listed with patronymic or husband's name and demotic. In Inventories IV and V, 37 men are listed by demotic; one couple is listed twice by the man's demotic (V.111, 119). In these same two inventories, one woman is listed by husband's name and demotic (IV.86) and one by patronymic and demotic (IV.70); one man is listed twice by patronymic and demotic (IV.62). One woman is listed by patronymic or husband's name and ethnic (V.36a). Similarly, six women are listed by patronymic only, but only three men are listed in this way. But if we eliminate those dedications the preservation of whose records precludes determination of whether a patronymic or demotic was

[10] Cf. *Asklepieion*, 157, 232-233, for further discussion of the meaning of this word.

[11] *Asklepieion*, 232-233.

[12] T. Linders, *Studies in the treasure records of Artemis Brauronia found in Athens* (Skrifter utgivna av Svenska Institutet i Athen, 4°, 19), Stockholm 1972.

[13] P. Brulé, *La fille d'Athènes*, Paris 1987, 225-240, 245-249.

[14] Girard, 84.

Chart II

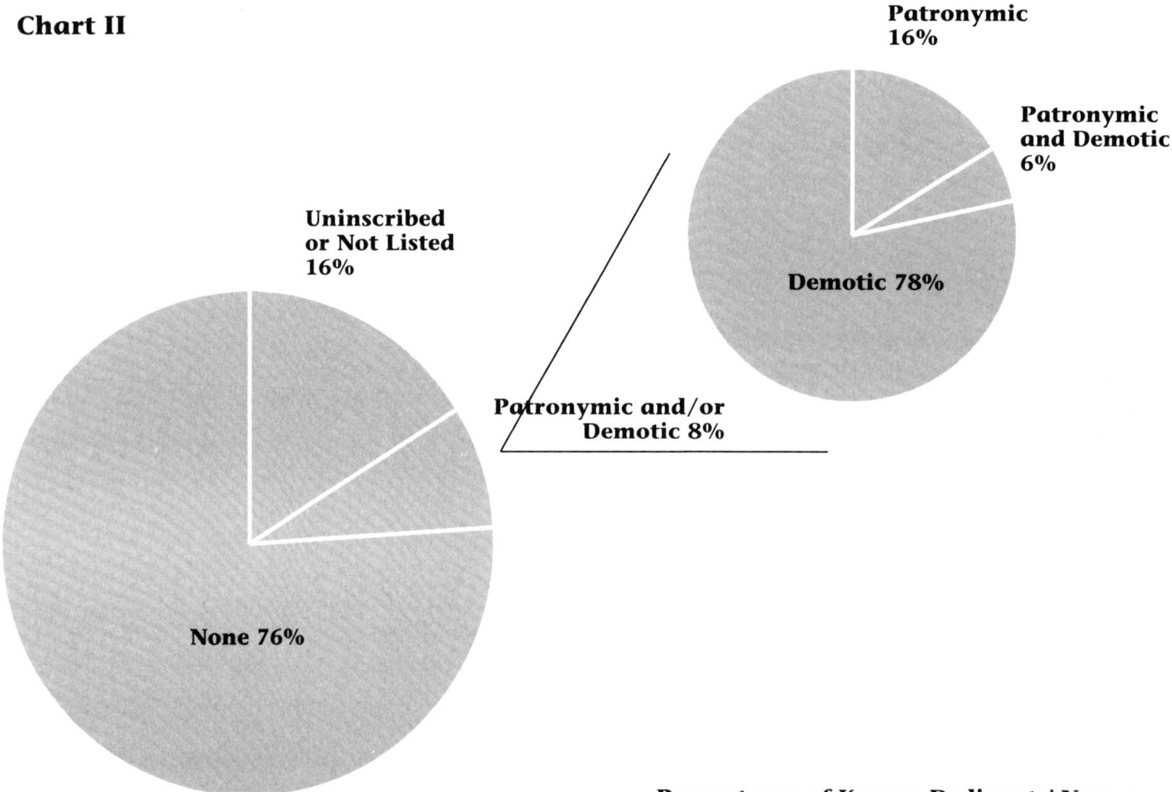

Percentages of Known Dedicants' Names with Patronymics and/or Demotics

Chart III

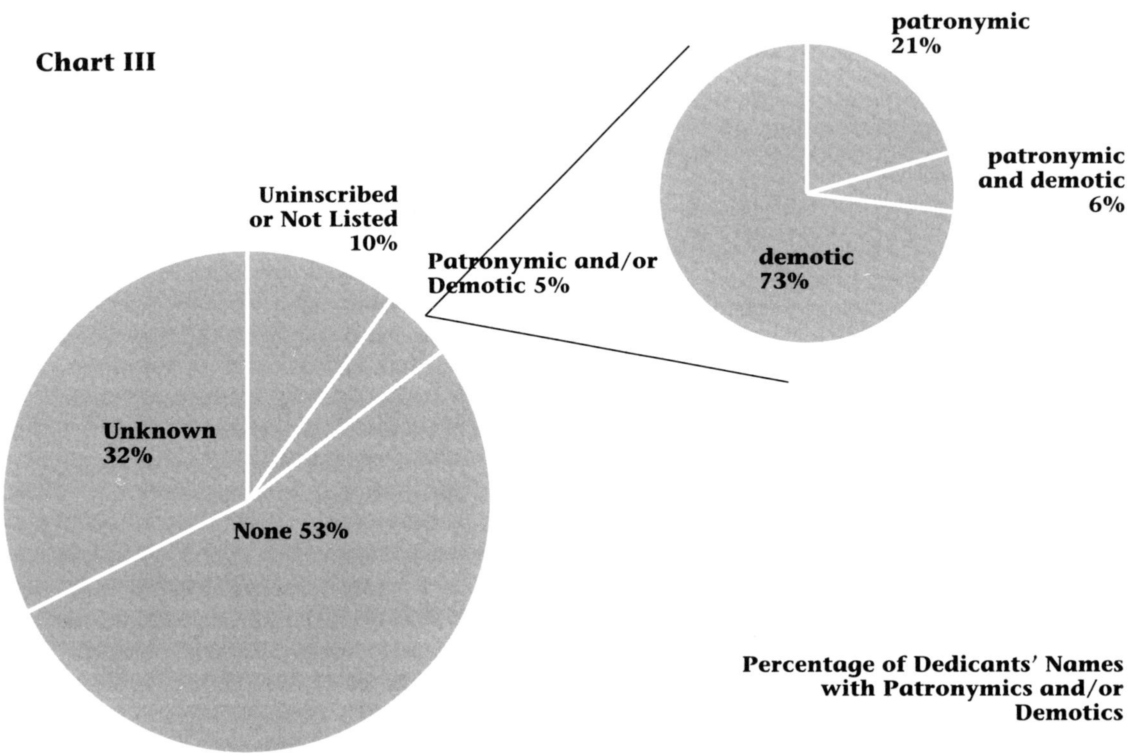

Percentage of Dedicants' Names with Patronymics and/or Demotics

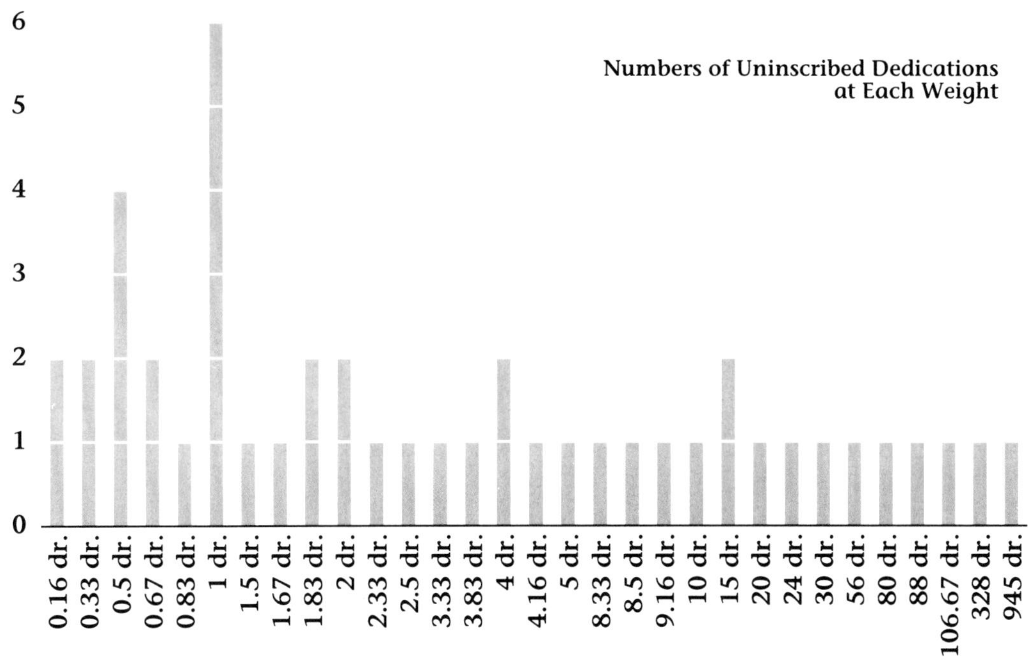

Chart IV

inscribed and those which are listed as ἀνεπίγραφα and take only those dedications where the name is well preserved, 7.4 per cent are listed by demotic, 1.5 per cent by patronymic, and a mere .5 per cent with both, while 90.6 per cent were listed with name only. As *Chart III* illustrates, of those dedications with patronymic and/or demotic, 78 per cent have only the demotic, while 16 per cent have only the patronymic, and only 6 per cent both. If we restrict our analysis to those dedications made by individuals in a personal capacity and exclude those made by priests in their official capacity, the most convincing explanation for this variation is that the names recorded in the inventories derive directly from those recorded on the dedications themselves, as is in fact implied by the procedure of ἐξετασμός itself, which underlies both the hybrid exetasmos of Inventory IV and the καθαίρεσις of Inventory V.[15] In this light also, the most convincing explanation for the dedications recorded as ἀνεπίγραφα is that they were literally "uninscribed" because the dedicants lacked either the means or the inclination to record their names.

This interpretation and that suggested above—that a significant proportion of those dedicants recorded with neither patronymic nor demotic were Athenian citizens—is reinforced by study of rare names recorded in the inventories. The Ὅπλων who made a dedication in the preisthood of Boiskos Phlyeus (V.169) is probably the Ὅπλων Φαληρεύς who was later archon and Asklepieion commissioner;[16] his dedication seems not to have recorded his demotic. Similarly, Μειδίον Γλαυκίππου Κολλυτέως γυνή was recorded once with her full name (IV.87); in view of the rarity of her name, it is likely that the Μειδίον who made another dedication placed nearby in the temple (IV.104) is the same woman. Likewise, although the Μίκα who is twice associated with Κάλλιππος Φαληρεύς as dedicant (V.111, 119) has a name which appears frequently at Athens, their repeated zeal as joint dedicants as well as his individual dedications (V.108, 121), suggest strongly that the Μίκα recorded as an enthusiastic (or desperate) individual dedicant in the same period (V.74, 83, 80, 89, 125, 151) is the same woman. There has, however, been one dedicant whose status as hetaira has, on the basis of her name, had a certain plausibility. Castner's[17] argument that certain dedicants in Inventory IV are to be identified as Epicurean hetairai is based largely on the rarity of the name Μαμμάριον; I have discussed elsewhere[18] the improbability that these identifications are

[15] For discussion of the procedure and vocabulary of different classes of inventories, see *Asklepieion*, 103-111.

[16] For discussion of Hoplon's career and the date of his archonship, see S.B. Aleshire, *Hesperia* 57, 1988, 253-255.

[17] Castner (supra n. 3), 51-58.

[18] *Asklepieion*, 67.

Chart V

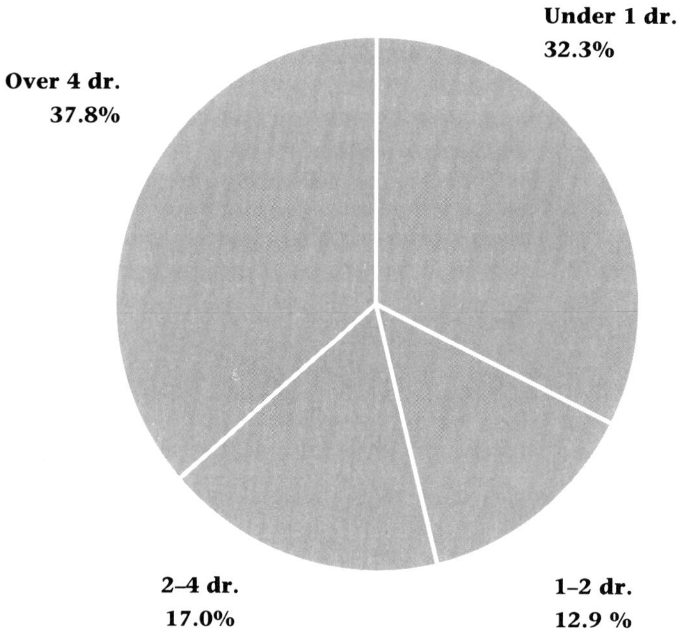

Proportion of Dedications in Each Weight Category

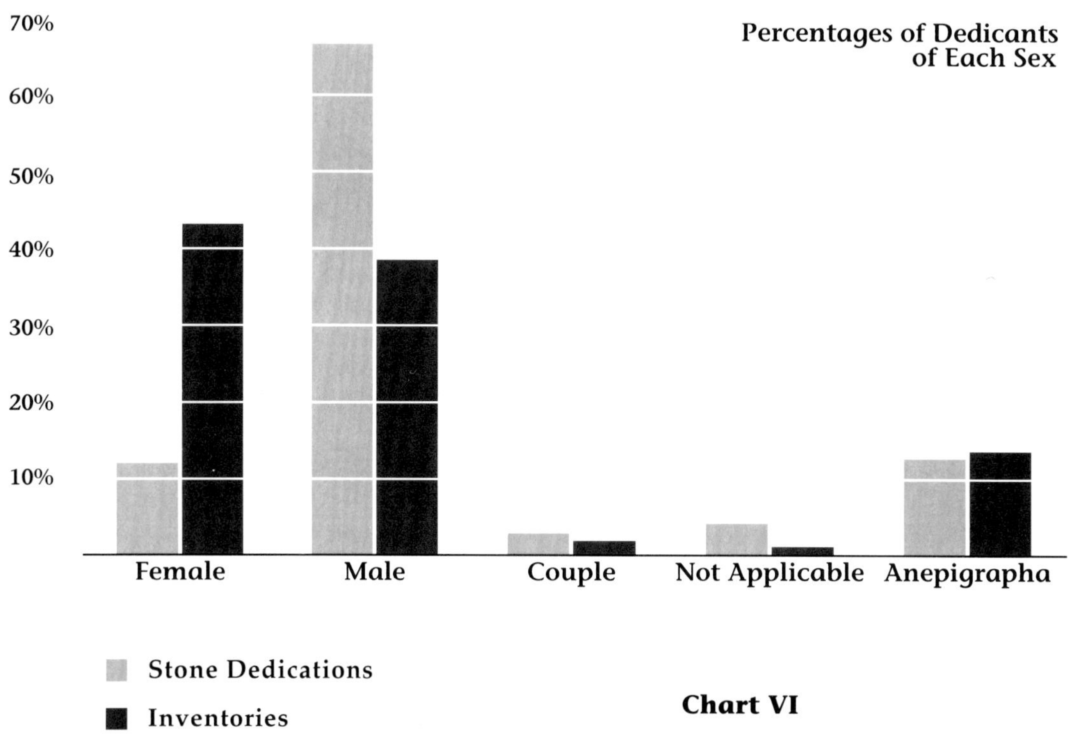

Chart VI

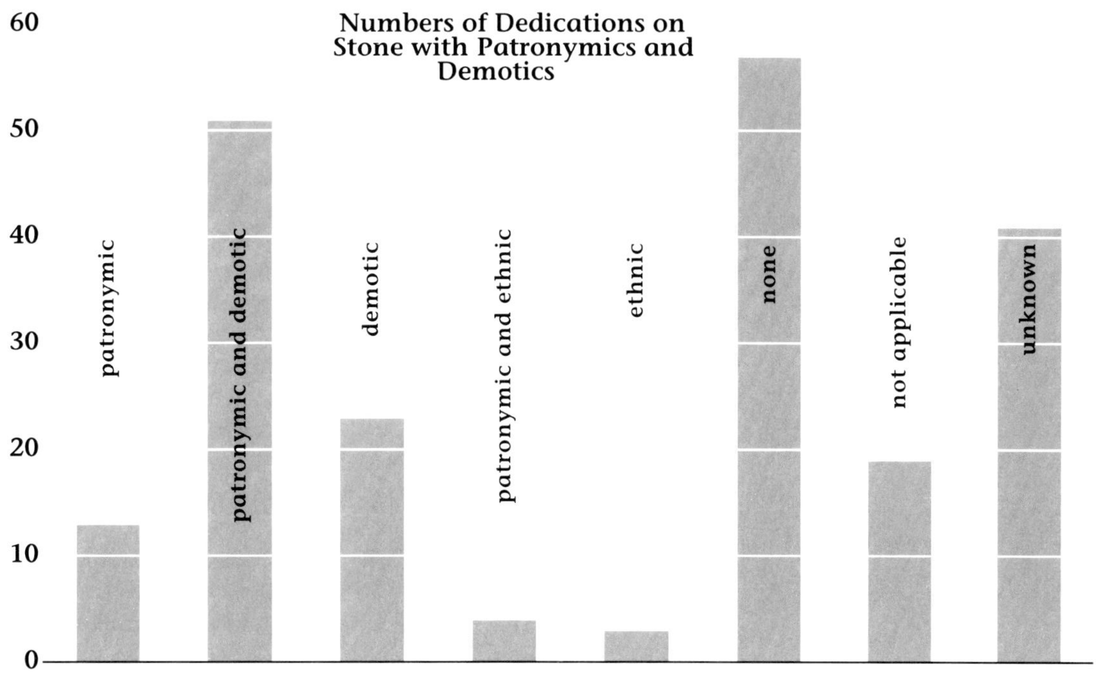

Chart VII

valid, and note here only that the argument from the rarity of the name has now been further undermined by the discovery at Athens of a funerary pithos bearing the same name (*SEG* XXXVII,185).[19]

Finally, the small size of many of the dedications in the inventories has also been held to lend support to the notion of impoverished or enslaved dedicants. As can be seen from *Chart V*, almost one third (32.3%) of all dedications for which the weight is preserved weigh less than 1 dr.; almost one half (45.2%) weigh less than 2 dr.; and almost two thirds (62.2%) weigh less than 4 dr. But it would seem to be sufficient to show that not all dedicants of these small offerings were metics or slaves to point to the eyes (V.127c) given by the priestess of Themis, who should have been the wife of a citizen, weighing only 1 obol, and to the two gifts for the god (V.115a, 144f) of about the same time, each weighing a mere two obols, both of whose dedicants were listed by name and demotic. At the other end of the scale, the phiale dedicated by [---]othea and Menon (V.93c), who were listed with neither patronymic nor demotic, is one of the heaviest dedications at 166 dr. Of course, not all citizens were rich or even well-to-do, nor all metics or slaves impoverished, but in many cases, the slight weight of a dedication may more accurately reflect the weights of dedications for sale at the silversmith's shop (a point to be argued in more detail below) than the economic status of the dedicant.

In the case of the surviving dedications on stone, the picture is somewhat different. Here the percentage of dedicants of each sex varies substantially from those known from the inventories. As has long been noted,[20] in the inventories women dedicants outnumber men by a slight margin, 43 per cent to 38 per cent. Among dedications on stone, as indicated by *Chart VI*, the situation is completely reversed, with men constituing 67 per cent of the dedicants and women only 12 per cent. Similarly, of 151 dedications (summarized in *Chart VII*) where the name of the dedicant is sufficiently well preserved to indicate whether the patronymic and demotic or both were

[19] This funerary vase has also been dated by T. Karagiorga-Stathakopoulou, *ArchDelt* 34 B1, 1979, 19, to the early third century B.C., but, on methodological grounds, the multiple epigraphic attestations of the name must weaken any link between the woman known from the inventory and/or the funerary pithos and that known from literary sources.

[20] See *Asklepieion*, 45-46, for further discussion of this situation.

inscribed, 57, or 37.7 per cent, show the name only; 51, or 33.7 per cent, recorded both patronymic and demotic, while 13, or 8.6 per cent recorded patronymic, and 23 or 18.5 per cent listed only demotics. This information suggests that dedications on stone were both more costly and more prestigious than the majority of the dedications in the inventories and, in fact, indicates what can be inferred from the known sums paid for the inscription of decrees: that stone offerings were more expensive than many dedications of precious metals. Further, this analysis points up the fact that stone dedications offered a more highly visible opportunity for conspicuous display and self-advertisment. Such offerings should be associated with the tradition of masculine conspicuous display connected with careers in public life so vividly illustrated by the dedications of *korai* on the Akropolis. In this context it is significant that the one dedication in the inventories which was made by a famous political figure, Aristophon of Azenia, is a phiale weighing 100 drachmas, which was apparently firmly affixed to the wall and could not be weighed, but which was itself conspicuously inscribed with the weight. Nevertheless, this analysis does not suggest that the dedicants of stone dedications were all—or even largely—citizens and well-to-do, while the dedicants whose dedications are recorded in the inventories were impoverished or enslaved. Rather, the discrepancy no doubt stems largely from the fact that the stone dedications were larger and more visible and thus offered a greater opportunity for the inscription of a complete name.

Thus the dedicants at the Asklepieion seem to have been a rather heterogeneous group. Those who made dedications both large and small might be recorded in the inventories with their full names if they had inscribed their dedications with a complete series of names, but if they had inscribed only a *nomen*, then that is what those conducting the inventory recorded. The small size of many of the dedications in the inventories is probably a more accurate indicator that the dedicants were not as well-to-do as those who made dedications on stone, but here again the size of the dedications does not seem to correlate directly with the economic or social status of the dedicants.

Turning to the second question I wish to consider in this paper, so far as I am aware, no one has considered the question of the "life history" of a typical dedication in precious metal at the Asklepieion in the third century B.C. Who made such votives? Using what techniques? How were they offered for sale? I have attempted to answer the question "Who bought them?" above. But how and where were they placed in the temple? How long did they remain there? And what was their final disposition?

In attempting to answer the questions, we must carefully define the types and weights of dedications which we are considering. The classifactory system used here is discussed in more detail in *The Athenian Asklepieion*,[21] but, in brief, it classifies dedications into the following categories: body parts, coins, cult equipment, jewelry, medical dedications, miscellaneous dedications, typoi, and vases. The number of dedications in each class in all inventories and in those from the third century can be seen from *Chart VIII*. Our analysis must be confined to personal dedications, not only because official and priestly dedications form a very small proportion of those recorded in the inventories (29, or 2.1 per cent of all dedications), but also because they generally have heavier weights than dedications by individuals and range in weight from 10 dr. to 945 dr. Further, these dedications appear usually to have been manufactured to the order of the boule or demos or of the individual priest,[22] since no two such dedications as recorded in the inventories are identical in weight. Among personal dedications, we must also exclude such types as jewelry and vases which may have been personal articles in the possession of the dedicant. It is important to note that, as *Chart VIII* indicates, these objects do not form a large proportion of the dedications recorded in the inventories.

Likewise, dedications of coins should be discounted, since they almost inevitably were made in weights of round figures: 1 dr., 2 dr., 4 dr. (1 tetradrachm), 5 dr., 10 dr., 20 dr (5 tetradrachms), and so on. See *Chart IX* for the numbers of such dedications. Here it may be noted that dedications of this type which do not represent round figures may represent the ancient equivalent of our "pocket change" or "nest egg" turned to dedicatory purpose. Dedications of coins provide one other significant piece of information. All those from the third century are of silver, with the only dedications of gold coins to Asklepios at Athens recorded in Inventory III and dating from the 330's B.C. The preponderance of silver coins among such dedications in Inventories IV and V reinforces what we may infer from those few third century hoards from Attica,[23] which have almost no gold. These two pieces of evidence indicate that in the

[21] *Asklepieion*, 37-48.

[22] For discussion of the manufacture of such dedications to order, see D. Harris, 'Nikokrates of Kolonos, metal-worker to the Parthenon treasurers', *Hesperia* 57, 1988, 337.

[23] Cf. M. Thompson, O. Mørkholm & C. Kraay, *An inventory of Greek coin hoards*, New York 1973, 19-24, nos. 125, 127, 128, 134-136, 142, 157.

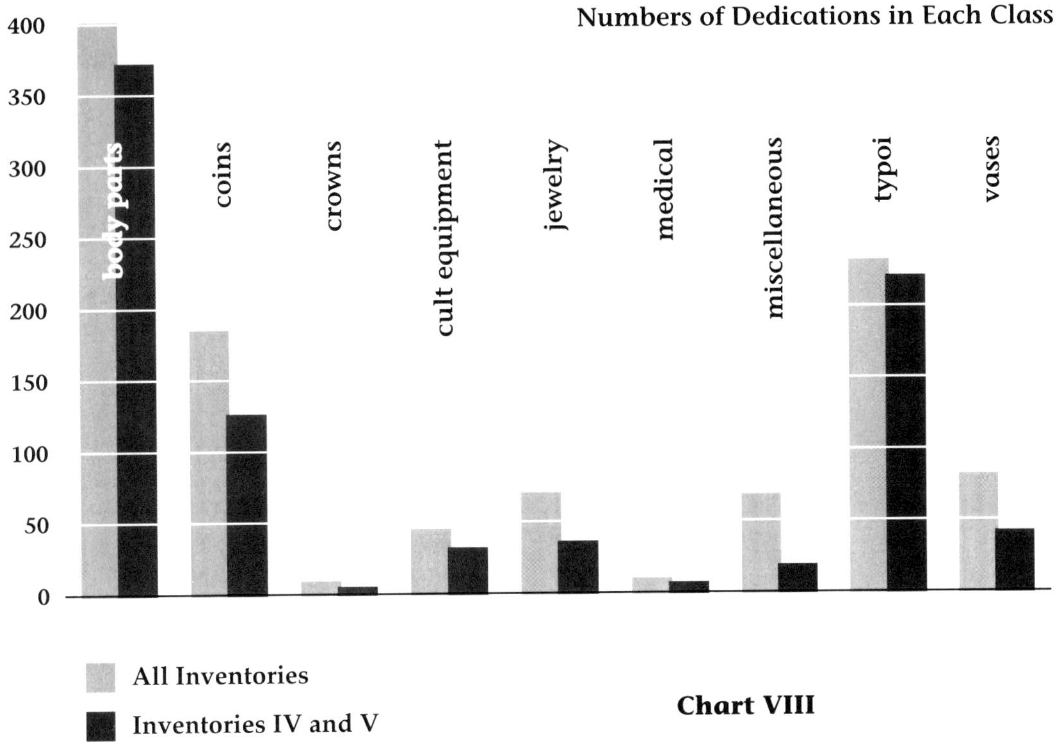

Chart VIII

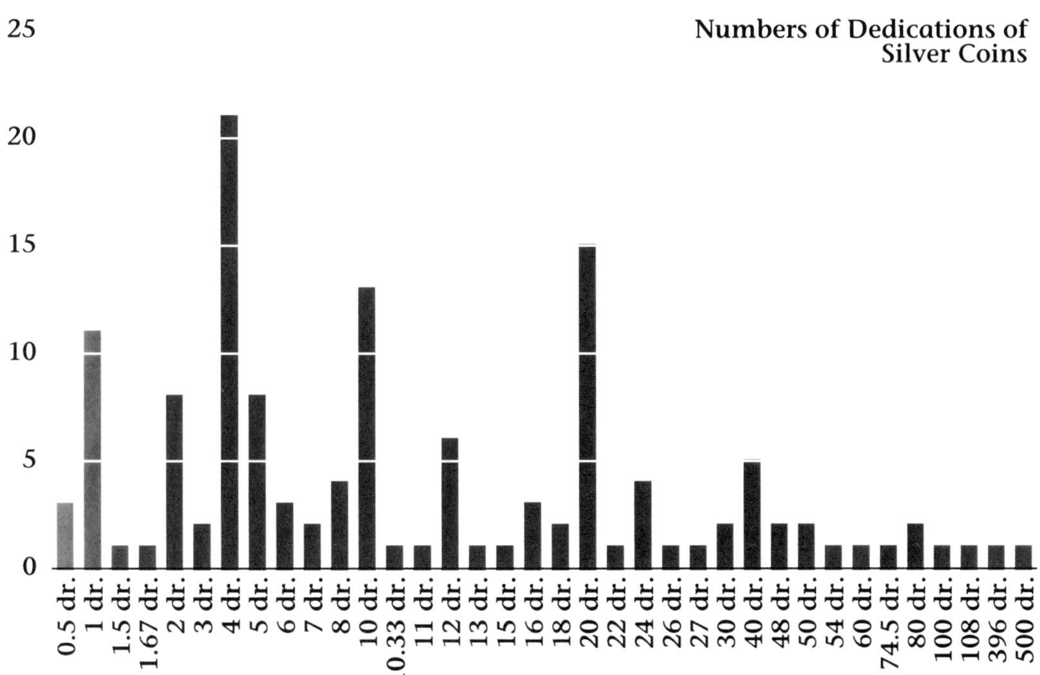

Chart IX

troubled and impoverished years near the middle of the century little gold coinage was circulating in Attica. This conclusion in turn lends emphasis to those relatively few gold dedications recorded in the third century inventories.

These restrictions mean that analysis of dedications with a view to answering the questions posed above must essentially be limited to dedications of anatomical ex votos and typoi. The anatomical ex votos are dedications which were designed specifically for dedication to a healing deity, and, given the exceptional popularity of the Asklepieion as the center of Athens' premier healing cult, many must have been designed specifically for dedication there. The typoi—at least those typoi which showed only the dedicant in an attitude of prayer—could have been dedicated to any deity, but they were clearly designed primarily for dedication rather than for secular uses. It is fortunate for our analytical purposes, as *Chart VIII* emphasizes, that both among all dedications and among dedications for which the inventories preserve a weight, these two classes are the most numerous.

Analysis of the numbers of dedications recorded at each individual weight shows a number of interesting discrepancies. *Chart X* shows the numbers of dedications in all classes in all inventories arranged by weight; the sharp peaks at many round drachma figures are very suggestive. *Chart XI*, which gives the numbers of anatomical ex votos and typoi for each weight, shows similar peaks. Here it is clear that significantly higher numbers of dedications are recorded at round drachma weights. If the dedicants had usually brought silver in the form of jewelry or coins to the silversmiths to be fabricated into dedications, we would expect to see a more nearly random distribution of numbers at each weight.[24] This is clearly not the case, a fact which becomes even more striking when our analysis is restricted to the large third century inventories, especially Inventory V (*Chart XII*). For dedications of less than about 8 dr. in weight, the large numbers of dedications weighing 1 dr., 2 dr., 4 dr., 5 dr., and 8 dr. suggest strongly that dedications of these weights were prefabricated by the silversmith and offered for sale ready-made. For dedications greater than 8 dr. in weight, the more nearly random distribution of numbers suggests that such relatively heavy dedications may have been made to order, but the total number of

[24] This statement may be thought to contradict that above (p. 92) that dedications of coins were almost inevitably made in weights of round figures. Such an interpretation would, however, leave nothing to be accounted for in the way of cost of fabrication.

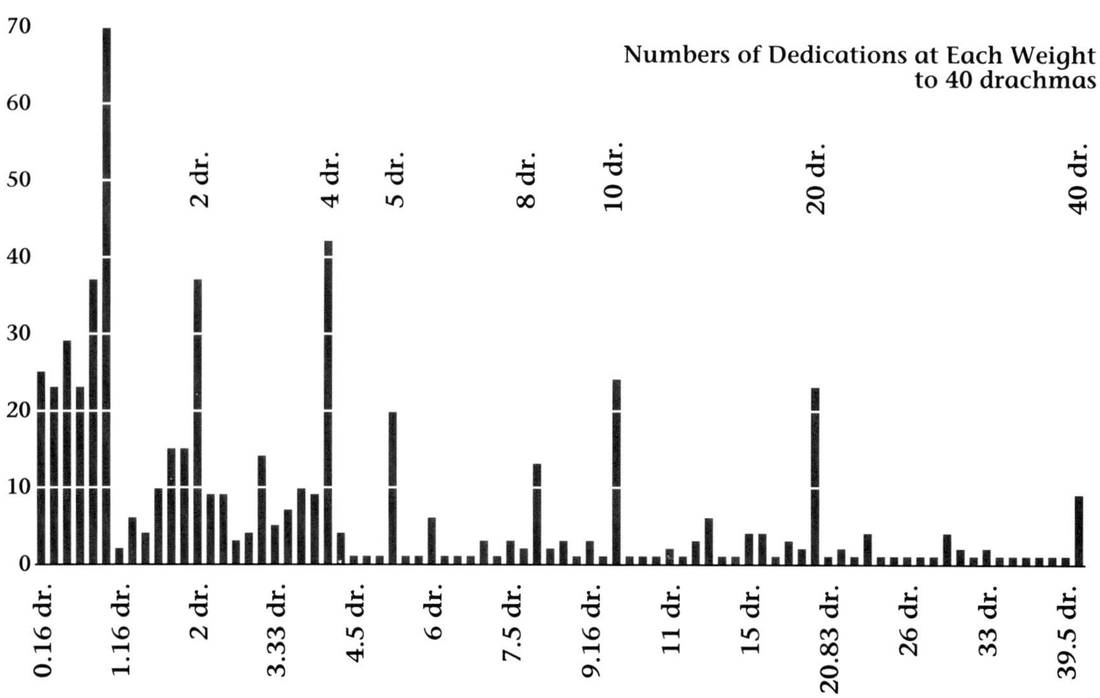

Chart X

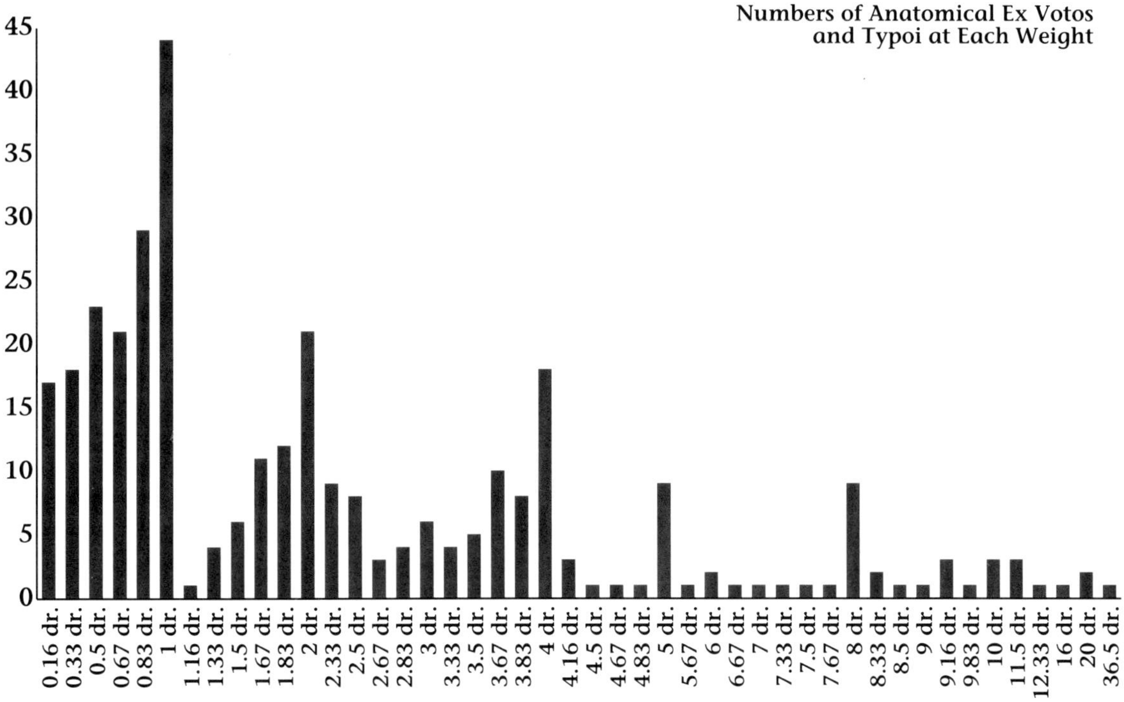

Chart XI

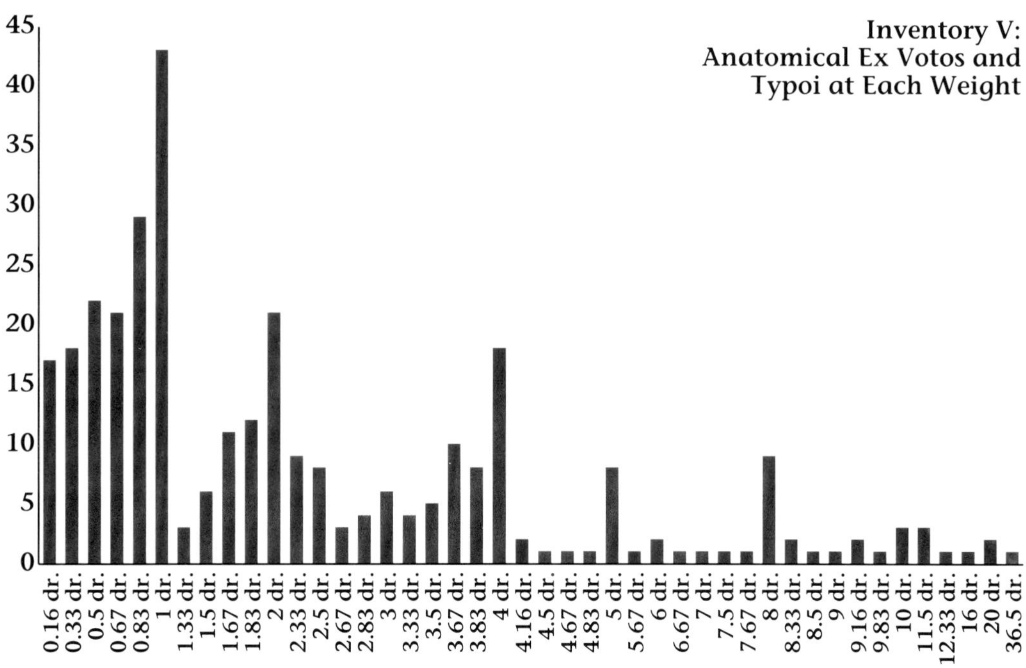

Chart XII

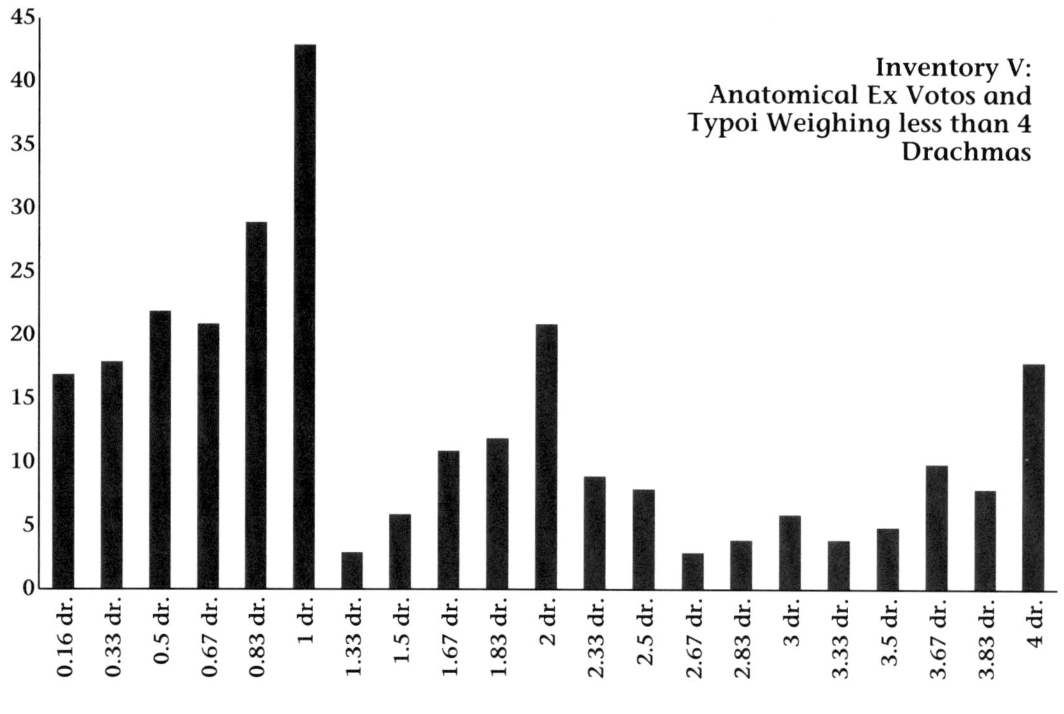

Chart XIII

dedications is so small that it may not be statistically significant. The major peaks in the chart suggest, therefore, that when a dedicant went to the silversmith to purchase a dedication showing a part of the body or the figure of a praying man or woman, that dedication would be there waiting to be purchased and would weigh some even number of drachmas. The purchaser would then pay the silversmith that number of drachmas plus an amount to cover the silversmith's overhead—his costs beyond the cost of the silver—and profit.

The minor peaks in the chart may help determine in general terms how much that amount was. Since the numbers at individual weights between 4 dr. and 8 dr. are too small to be statistically significant, we must restrict this analysis to those dedications weighing 4 dr. or less (*Chart XIII*). Here there are minor peaks at 4 ob., 5 ob., 1 dr. 4 ob., 1 dr. 5 ob., 3 dr. 4 ob., and 3 dr. 5 ob. These suggest that these dedications may also have been prefabricated and may have sold for prices expressed in even drachma figures. This interpretation in turn suggests that the silversmith's overhead and profit ranged between 16 per cent and 33 per cent and that a dedication weighing 1 dr. probably sold for 1 dr. 1 ob. or 1 dr. 2 ob. To borrow a term from David Lewis, this "making charge" is significantly higher than the 12 dr. (or 7 per cent) recorded for the fabrication of the oinochoe for the Hero Doctor in the late third century (*IG* II^2 839.85) and those calculated by Lewis for the fourth century.[25] Two possible explanations for this situation suggest themselves. Perhaps those fabrication costs that are calculated directly from the inventories reflect special rates given to agents of the Athenian demos or for work done directly for the gods, i.e., that the craftsman's labor constituted his portion of the dedication. Or, more likely, since the time required to fabricate a large votive is not proportionately greater than that for a small votive in geometrical proportion, the fabrication costs expressed as a percentage of the whole price are significantly lower for larger dedications. Here, too, especially in the case of the smaller votives, bargaining no doubt played as big a part as it does in the business of a modern Greek gold- or silversmith's shop and must have had a major role in determining the actual price. Those dedications with weights

[25] For discussion of the costs of fabrication, see D.M. Lewis, 'New evidence for the gold-silver ratio', in *Essays in Greek coinage presented to Stanley Robinson*, eds. C.M. Kraay & G.K. Jenkins, Oxford 1968, 108; *idem*, 'Temple inventories in Ancient Greece', in *Pots and pans*, ed. M. Vickers (Oxford Studies in Islamic Art, 3), Oxford 1986, 79.

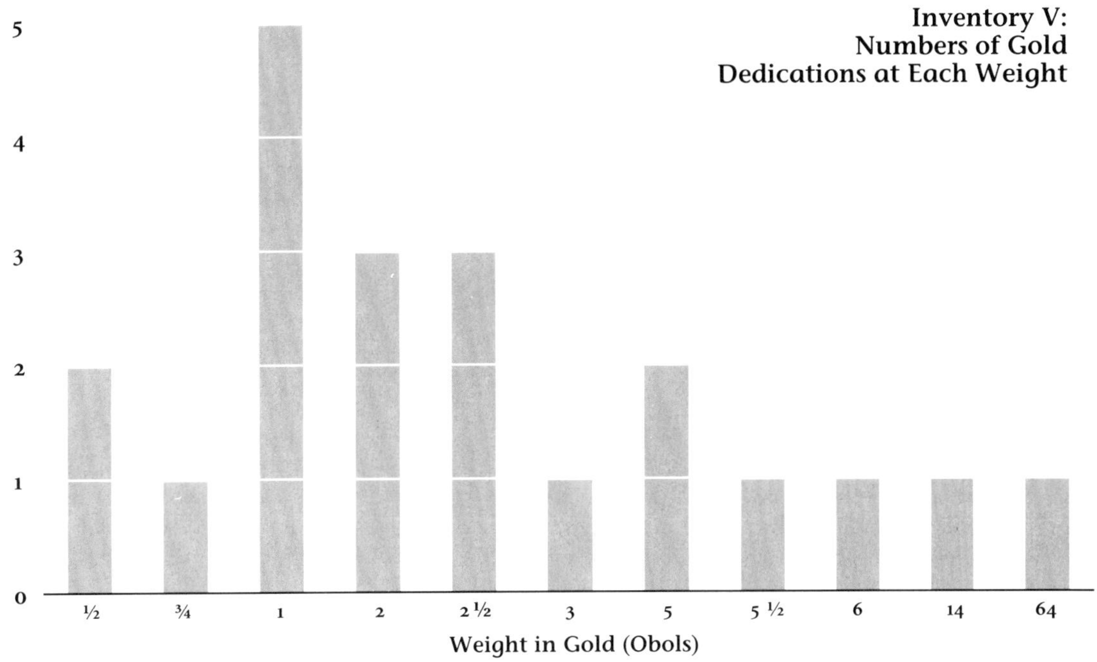

Chart XIV

other than those discussed above probably result from the dedicant's having brought in jewelry, coins, or other silver objects to the silversmith for fabrication into a custom-made dedication.

In this context, the gold anatomical ex votos and typoi in Inventory V pose some interesting questions. As *Chart XIV* shows, almost one fourth of these dedications (4 or 22.2 per cent) weigh 1 ob.; another 3, or 16.7 per cent, weigh either 2 ob. or $2^1/_2$ ob. Here the numbers are small and the statistical argument must not be pressed too hard, but these two peaks seem to be significant. Further, if we assume a gold-silver ratio at this period of 12:1,[26] these weights are equivalent respectively to 2 dr., 4 dr., and 5 dr. in silver and correspond to the peaks at those weights among the silver dedications in *Charts XI* and *XII*. Presumably these gold dedications would have sold for about 2 dr. 3 ob. and 5 dr. Similarly, the smaller peaks in this chart—those at $^1/_2$ obol and 5 obols—match those in the charts of silver dedications at 1 dr. and 10 dr. and suggest that gold dedications at these weights may have been prefabricated also.

Thus if we outline the "life history" of an anatomical ex voto or typos in precious metal at Athens in the third century B.C., we can say that it was manufactured by a silver- or goldsmith, perhaps often using the special technique described as κατάμακτος,[27] who used a quantity of gold or silver previously weighed to an even weight in drachmas. When finished the dedication was offered for sale, perhaps in a shop like those in Athens and other Mediterranean cities which sell those dedications called τάματα in Modern Greek. Here it was priced 16 to 33 per cent above the price implied by its weight in silver. When he had made his purchase, the dedicant usually attached it to a wooden or terracotta πινάκιον which might or might not be inscribed; if he or she inscribed his name, it would almost always be the simple nomen rather than a fuller name. The dedicant then took the dedication to the temple, where he or the priest saw to its placement on the walls, the rafters, or the cult statue; in some cases, the priest might control the placement of the dedication quite rigidly.[28]

After this point the dedication came under the control of the administrative machinery of the sanctuary, with its

[26] For the gold-silver ratio in the Hellenistic period, cf. M.I. Rostovtzeff, *Social and economic history of the Hellenistic world*, Oxford 1941, I, 165; III, 1353 n. 39.

[27] For discussion of the meaning of κατάμακτος, cf. *Asklepieion*, 232.

[28] For further discussion of priestly control over the placement of dedications in the temple, see S.B. Aleshire, *Asklepios at Athens* (Amsterdam, forthcoming).

elaborate administrative mechanisms designed to account for the continued existence of votives in one form or another. I do not have time to consider this administrative apparatus in any detail here, but content myself with a brief sketch of its workings, leaving for future discussion such specific questions as the following: Just who routinely and on special occasions kept track of the dedications? How did they do so? How often were inventories made? Were they usually inscribed? And on what medium and where were the records usually kept?

To return to our hypothetical offering dedicated by an individual, near the end of his year as priest or early in the following year, the priest might choose this dedication, especially if it were small, to be melted along with others and—supplemented by additional silver provided by the priest—re-cast into a larger and more impressive dedication labeled with the priest's name, his priestly title, and the notation ἐκ τῶν τύπων.[29] If the dedication escaped being chosen by the priest to be melted for a dedication ἐκ τῶν τύπων, the priest remained responsible for its continued presence in the temple during subsequent years.[30] Finally, after a shorter or longer time depending on circumstances, the Athenian boule and demos, probably at the urging of an enthusiastic and active priest, would decree a general καθαίρεσις of the votives in the temple.[31] After a complete canvass of the dedications in the temple, either on the basis of an ἐξετασμός or of a complete and accurate series of παραδόσεις from the priests of a given period, the commission for the καθαίρεσις would choose many votives to be melted and re-cast into larger and more conspicuous cult equipment. Even so, not all dedications would be chosen by the commissioners for liquidation, but many more would be melted than for a priestly dedication ἐκ τῶν τύπων. Thus, the silver from the small dedication whose cycle we have been following would come to form a part of a larger dedication, part of the official cult service of silver. What fate it would eventually come to at the hands of later ἱερόσυλοι or barbarians, we cannot know.

Sara B. Aleshire
Department of Classics
University of California
Berkeley, CA 94720
USA

[29] For discussion of the practice of melting and re-casting small dedications into priestly dedications ἐκ τῶν τύπων, see *Asklepieion*, 83.
[30] For discussion of the priest's responsibility for the continued presence in the temple of dedications of his priesthood, see *Asklepieion*, 83, 147.
[31] For discussion of the procedure of καθαίρεσις, see *Asklepieion*, 104f.

Discussion

Tullia LINDERS: You have presented a full and "meaty" lecture. It shows what can be done with numbers. Those charts, I think, were extremely interesting, and it is a good argument that the dedicants were not slaves or poor people, on the ground that only their first name was noted, but that they were quite normal Athenian citizens. The same applies to Brauron; the names of dedicating women at Brauron have also been interpreted as being slaves and prostitutes. But it cannot be doubted that they were quite normal wives and daughters of Athenian citizens. A detail I wanted to ask you about: you differentiate between parts of bodies and *typoi*; did not *typoi* very often represent parts of bodies?

SA: Occasionally a dedication on which there is a leg, or whatever, would be described as a *typos*. Just by itself a *typos* seems to me a relief showing a praying person and/or a figure of the deity.

Ingrid STRÖM: You were saying that people went to silversmiths or goldsmiths to buy vessels or anything of quite distinct weight and carried them to the temple. Don't you think it possible that the goldsmiths were actually situated inside the sanctuary and that the sanctuary controlled them?

SA: There is no sign of that at the Athenian Asklepieion, but I certainly wouldn't exclude it elsewhere. But there are physical reasons to think that it may not have been possible at the Athenian Asklepieion, which is an extremely cramped sanctuary. I would prefer to see the silver- and goldsmiths further down the slope on the path back up to the Asklepieion.

TL: As to the question whether the sanctuary controlled the silversmiths, I wonder who in the sanctuary would have done that, and how it would have been done? I could imagine that if the smith had his booth inside the sanctuary, he had to pay a tax. Could there have been any other control of it?

SA: Well, once the sanctuary got its hands on the dedication, it was very tightly controlled, but I simply don't have any evidence one way or the other at the Asklepieion, except for the fact that there is certainly no place to put a permanent installation inside the sanctuary.

TL: These dedications by the priests, *ek ton typon*, do you think that they were made every year?

SA: The smaller weren't made every year.

TL: What are the weights of the dedications *ek ton typon*?

SA: They are not among those really heavy dedications up above 300 drachmas, which is heavy for the Asklepieion.They vary fairly widely within what we might call the middle range of dedicatory weights.

Signe ISAGER: Is it known how the dedication took place? Would there always be a priest or some other person present besides the dedicant?

SA: There is a certain amount of evidence to indicate that individual priests controlled where the dedications were placed in the temple, that is, dedications that were made in their priesthood. And there is a bit of evidence to indicate that individual priests might use that method to keep all the dedications of their priesthood together so that at the end of the year, when the time came for them to account for all the dedications of their priesthood, they would all be there and could be tipped off.

SI: So there would never be a really anonymous gift even if there was no inscription?

SA: I don't know. That inventory has anonymous dedications in it, and so, some of the inventories say "uninscribed", dedicated in the priesthood of so and so. I suppose the priest might remember who, but I assume that his records would not have included that.

Jacques TRÉHEUX: Je me demande pourquoi les offrandes d'une drachme étaient plus anonymes que les autres, d'après vos tablaux. Je me suis dit que les dédicants qui faisaient des offrandes d'un poids si ordinaire, n'avaient peut-être pas voulu donner leurs noms. J'ai imaginé aussi, en voyant vos tablaux, qu'on pouvait en faire d'autres, par exemple, vous auriez pu faire le dénombrement des démotiques et replacer ce dénombrement sur une carte de l'Attique. On aurait su ainsi si ceux qui fréquentaient l'Asclépieion étaient des gens qui étaient plus proches du sanctuaire ou non. Je pense que cela aurait été aussi une enquête à faire.

Je vous pose une question en rapport avec votre livre. Il y a parmi les dédicants, une femme certainement qui s'appelle Mamarion, et elle apparaît plusieurs fois dans les inventaires. Est-ce que vous pensez que c'est une femme libre ou une esclave?

SA: Mamarion only makes one dedication at the Asklepieion. There is no reason to think that she is necessarily a slave. A woman by this name is known as one of Epikouros' *hetairai* working with him, and Castner has argued on the basis of the rarity of her name that the woman at the Asklepieion had to be the same woman.